Modernist Humanism and the Men of 1914

Modernist Humanism and the Men of 1914

Joyce, Lewis, Pound, and Eliot

Stephen Sicari

The University of South Carolina Press

© 2011 University of South Carolina

Published by the University of South Carolina Press
Columbia, South Carolina 29208

www.sc.edu/uscpress

Manufactured in the United States of America

20 19 18 17 16 15 14 13 12 11   10 9 8 7 6 5 4 3 2 1

Library of Congress Cataloging-in-Publication Data

Sicari, Stephen.
  Modernist humanism and the men of 1914 : Joyce, Lewis, Pound, and
Eliot / Stephen Sicari.
    p. cm.
  Includes bibliographical references and index.
  ISBN 978-1-57003-956-0 (cloth : alk. paper)
  1. English literature--20th century—History and criticism. 2. Modernism
(Literature)—Great Britain—History. 3. American literature—20th century—
History and criticism. 4. Modernism (Literature)—United States—History.
5. Humanism in literature. 6. Joyce, James, 1882–1941—Criticism and
interpretation. 7. Lewis, Wyndham, 1882–1957—Criticism and interpretation.
8. Pound, Ezra, 1885–1972—Criticism and interpretation. 9. Eliot, T. S. (Thomas
Stearns), 1888–1965—Criticism and interpretation. I. Title.
  PR478.M6.S53 2011
  820.9'112—dc22
                                                                    2010027593

Quotations from poems by Ezra Pound, from THE CANTOS OF EZRA POUND,
© 1934, 1937, 1940, 1948, 1950, 1956, 1959, 1962, 1963, 1965, 1966, 1968, 1970,
and 1971 by Ezra Pound. Reprinted by permission of New Directions Publishing
Corp. and Faber and Faber Ltd.

Quotations from poems by T. S. Eliot, from COLLECTED POEMS, 1909–1962,
by T. S. Eliot, copyright 1936 by Harcourt, Inc., and renewed 1964 by T. S. Eliot.
Reprinted by permission of Houghton Mifflin Harcourt Publishing Company and
Faber and Faber Ltd.

This book was printed on Glatfelter Natures, a recycled paper with 30 percent
postconsumer waste content.

For my wife and children:
"Amo ergo sum, and in just that proportion"

CONTENTS

Preface
"Mock mockers after that"—
A Twenty-First-Century Humanism ix

Introduction
Toward Modernist Humanism 1

1
Bloom and the Vulgar Body
The Christian Imagination and
Modernist Humanism 34

2
A Most Unlikely Humanist
Wyndham Lewis and
The Revenge for Love 91

3
Conflicting Humanisms
The Development of
The Cantos of Ezra Pound 124

4
"In the fullness of time"
Eliot's Christian Humanism 161

Conclusion
Modernist Humanism—
A Love Story 197

Notes 201
References 209
Index 217

PREFACE

"Mock mockers after that"—
A Twenty-First-Century Humanism

Must something called "humanism" in the twenty-first century appear conservative or retrograde or tied to hegemonic power? Or, to phrase it another way, must the belief that there is something permanent and universal outside language and cultural difference be seen as reactionary? That is the underlying question of this study, and my answer is "No."

I do not pretend that humanism and modernism are not in need of defense. My purpose is to show how certain writers in the modernist era—the ones we have long called "high modernists"—enacted experimental literary projects designed to renew a set of values and ideals called "humanism." Hence the first part of this book's title: *Modernist Humanism.* I shall be pursuing a definition of "modernism" intended to hold together both a critique of modern life and an attempt to advance a reconstituted humanism adequate to the realities of an inhuman century.

When Wyndham Lewis called himself and his fellows "the Men of 1914," he was calling attention to a pose he and selected peers were trying out: young, hard-boiled literary men who were going to blast away at convention and cliché and usher in a bold new experimental art. They need not have bothered. The Great War put an end to a lot more than clichés. But the four young men to whom Lewis referred did indeed adopt this pose and attempted to create a new modernist poetics. This story has often been told, and there have been many important and successful studies designed to broaden our notion of literary modernism to go beyond these four men.[1] But I want to retell their story with a twist. Starting out as iconoclasts, they developed literary projects designed to renew the values and ideals of a humanism with roots in a Christian humanism from the late Middle Ages and Renaissance.

Lewis used the phrase "the Men of 1914" in his memoir *Blasting and Bombardiering* (1937) to describe himself, James Joyce, Ezra Pound, and T. S. Eliot, "my particular companions" (252). In retrospect he claimed that this group did not succeed in their ambitions: "*We are the first men of a Future that has not materialized. We belong to a 'great age' that has not 'come off.' We moved too quickly for the world. We set too sharp a pace. And, more and more exhausted by War, Slump, and Revolution, the world has fallen back*" (256). These men of the avant-garde went too quickly for the world in which they lived, and it has fallen back into such decline that it must be addressed again. In this book I study their later responses to this culture, their more mature and considered responses, which I call "modernist humanism."

The command to "mock mockers after that," quoted in the subtitle of this preface, comes from the fourth stanza of the fifth section of *Nineteen Hundred and Nineteen*, a long poem in William Butler Yeats's *The Tower* (1928). The poem details the horrible violence of what may be the most violent year in Irish history; its place in *The Tower* volume—which attempts to depict the poet as both within and above the historical realities of the period, safely in his tower, where he can be a keen spectator of the violence—is to bring the dangers of the Irish civil war into the poem as the context for Yeats's depiction of his own creative acts. It might seem useless to be writing poems during civil war, or to engage in *Meditations in Time of Civil War* (to cite the title of the long poem preceding *Nineteen Hundred and Nineteen*); it might seem as if poetry is useless when action is needed, but Yeats worked to provide his meditative acts with a larger meaning and purpose in the political-historical context. In the fifth section of *Nineteen Hundred and Nineteen*, there are three stanzas before the phrase "mock mockers after that," and in each stanza he invites the reader to join him in the cynical act of mockery: in mocking the great (first stanza), the wise (second), and the good (third). In this way Yeats gave voice to the cynicism about ideals that seems almost an inevitable result of witnessing brutality. As intellectuals and artists, we are asked to join in the mockery of the ideals we have hoped for, which now seem futile, if not entirely empty. But the last stanza turns that mockery against itself, as we are called on to:

> Mock mockers after that
> That would not lift a hand maybe
> To help good, great or wise
> To bar that foul storm out, for we
> Traffic in mockery.

Yeats understood and perhaps even appreciated the radical skepticism that the twentieth century was prone to, whether it was the result of intellectual developments, technological achievements, or events such as the Irish civil war. But the artist's job is not to yield entirely to this tendency to debunk and reduce, though we are invited to indulge in it up to a point. As intellectuals, we have the duty to be skeptical about the ideals and beliefs that have been handed down to us and accepted perhaps with uncritical passivity, but that skepticism can never be the end in itself. When we mock the mockers, we turn that skepticism against itself and show it to be a limited tool, best seen as a means to a higher end.

As I did in my previous book *Joyce's Modernist Allegory,* I want to note my debt to Tobin Siebers and Charles Altieri for first alerting me to a way of critiquing poststructural methodology. In his *Cold War Criticism and the Politics of Skepticism* (1993), Siebers argues that by the early 1990s poststructural skepticism had become so powerful and so enshrined that ironically it had become as dogmatic and as uncritical as the values and ideals it sought to debunk. Siebers values the cleansing skepticism but sees it as severely limited: "We may wish to abandon belief for the best of all possible reasons—for example, to avoid the violence of belief—but skeptics cannot live outside the risky tautology of belief any more than ordinary mortals can. Skepticism can never be the philosophical basis of a politics, and when skeptics strip themselves of founding beliefs they deprive themselves of political direction. This explains in part why proponents of radical hermeneutics are sometimes tossed in the direction of reactionary politics: hermeneutic skepticism leaves criticism without the orienting beliefs necessary to direct its politics" (28–29). In this study I am not always interested in politics, though I do deal directly with Pound's political project, and with Lewis and Eliot, we may want to think about their descent to reactionary politics in the way Siebers sketches. But I am always interested in how skepticism needs something after its sweeping motions have been completed, some "orienting beliefs" that can direct a value system worthy of renewed interest and commitment, a value system we once called "humanism."

Siebers talks about the "skeptical project" in his account of poststructural theory, and my own position is that the modernist project includes this skeptical project but also sees the need to move beyond mere skepticism. Siebers claims that the "skeptical project dreams of mastery by opposing itself to 'false' groundings and constructions of thought, be they called 'the self,' 'truth,' 'authority,' 'value,' 'violence,' 'reality,' or simply 'belief.' It makes a virtue of thinking otherwise without thinking about the directions in which it may lead" (28). That is what a modernist humanism is concerned with. After cleansing the culture with a scathing skeptical methodology, it seeks to place something back at the center to orient a new cultural direction.

Likewise, Charles Altieri, in his introduction to *Canons and Consequences,* a collection of his essays from the 1980s, has also warned us about the philosophical implications of "the hermeneutics of suspicion." His critique centers on his conviction that these ways of reading against the text "trap us in impoverished languages for talking about values. Unwilling to overthrow deconstruction, these positions bind themselves to semantic models and attitudes toward human agency that cannot sustain an adequate theory of value or provide goals for political action" (2). As with Siebers, Altieri is concerned that the powerful methodologies designed to debunk and demystify lack the language or the technique necessary for establishing something positive, something that can center or ground a debate about values and meaning. They both want to position themselves as being "after theory," as having appreciated its enormous contribution as a rigorous methodology capable of demystification and cleansing but also aware of the void left by such radical skepticism.

Not much seems to have changed, then, between Yeats's call for us to "mock mockers" and what thinkers such as Siebers and Altieri are calling for, something to come after mockery, after skepticism, after postmodernism, and after theory. And not much has changed since the early 1990s in this regard, though more and more intellectuals do seem to agree that we are somehow after theory. My fundamental proposition for this study is that certain modernist writers, such as Yeats but more especially the Men of 1914, had already anticipated the skeptical methods of poststructuralism and used them as a tool to clear the culture of false and decaying ideals. Yet sweeping clear was only a first stage in a more positive effort to place at the center of the culture something permanent and something universal that could ground us in a renewed humanism. The Men of 1914 began as iconoclasts who made war on their culture, blasting away at all that they considered deadening and dangerous,[2] and developed into what I am calling "modernist humanists."

The second part of the title to this preface, "a twenty-first century humanism," is meant to play with the title of Marjorie Perloff's 2002 book, *21st-Century Modernism,* in which she makes the case that what we have been calling the postmodern was already part of modernism. Her interests are squarely on issues of technique as she argues that the avant-garde experimentation of the postmodern was already developed by modernist writers. My own analysis does consider the question of style and technique, but I also engage in analyses of themes and strategies. My position is that the experimentation for which the modernists are so justly famous does indeed anticipate the skeptical project of postmodernism, but that is only half the story. The other half is the more positive engagement with values and ideals on the other side of this skepticism. Literary modernism may be best situated to provide us with the basis for humanism in the twenty-first century because it may have been the last great expression of the higher ideals we have long associated with humanism.

I was thinking of this problem one day when I was reading Luke's Gospel. Jesus explains that, when an unclean spirit is expelled from a person, it roams through arid regions seeking rest, but it finds none. The unclean spirit returns to his former dwelling, finding it swept clean and put in order. He then gets seven other spirits to join him, and they all move in, "and the last condition of that person is worse than the first." It seems perhaps that not much has changed since Christ's time either. It is one thing to expel the demons of our culture through the application of a rigorous postmodern critique, but if there is nothing to place inside the culture that can serve as the foundation for identity and value, then the vacuum might indeed be filled up with new demons that make the aftermath of the postmodern critique more violent and more unjust than what was formerly in place. The postmodern has developed a host of powerful analytical tools to debunk, demystify, and deconstruct, but has it found a way to place something at the center to take the place of the old constructs, something that, if placed there with great care and watched over with great vigilance, might become a stable and permanent ground for a new humanism, one not complicit with imperialism or capitalism or fascism but newly constructed to function as an open and tolerant site for the exchange of differences and for elevating human potentiality?

For many writers in the modernist era, the problem of humanism is fundamental, associated with the category of the human itself. Some of the writers of the modernist period seemed to recognize the need to construct the fiction of the human once again in their texts, as if the category of the human were very much contested and its validity very much in doubt. I have attempted to trace how some of my favorite writers of the first half of the twentieth century were able to show the human as a problem and how they worked to fill the void left by their own withering critiques with a constructed entity that might indeed be able to ground our sense of value and virtue. I say that these are some of my favorite authors, and so they are, but a more legitimate reason to study them is that they all seem to have recognized, as forcefully if not as rigorously as those we call theorists of the postmodern, the ways in which the human was under attack by social trends and movements and also by those who wanted to think beyond the present and see new possibilities. For the Men of 1914, blasting and bombardiering prepared them to develop their scathing, "postmodern" critique, which soon seemed insufficient and only half the story. When they reached maturity perhaps, or when the demands of the times seemed to call for something more positive, they developed a humanism on the other side of their skeptical blasting. I believe that these authors can be placed at the center of our thinking of a new humanism, as they themselves faced the issues of our postmodern theorists without submitting to the cynicism and despair that accompanies the failure to believe. These Men of 1914 did not merely expel the demons, they tried to fill that void with something that could center the culture and stabilize meaning and value. What they established is what I call "modernist humanism."

This study is meant to defend both humanism and modernism from some of the recent charges against them, how in the name of the first some inhuman atrocities have been committed and how the second has become confused with modernity in general. Those more general social, political, technological, and economic conditions made of the twentieth century a period of great change, great opportunity, and also great horror and carnage. The modernists that I have selected to examine here have in common one thing: a desire to counter modernity through literary artifice and experimentation designed to break the individual and the culture free from the coercive grip of institutional power. As the Men of 1914, they began as literary radicals who, under pressure from various cultural events, came to discover the need for a renewed set of values. And in their opposition to modernity these modernists reinvented the human and humanity in their texts, presenting a self that is able to be the foundation of a new cultural order based on freedom and love. Modernism is a project, perhaps a perennial one, in which a radical skepticism is preliminary and necessary to a concentrated effort to discover a permanent basis for an understanding of humanity and humanism. The writers in this study, writing in the period we have come to call "modernism" in the arts, exemplify this project and can provide us with a map for what a twenty-first century humanism may look like, one grounded in the transcendental category of love.

For what I discovered, as if by accident and with pleasant surprise, is that these hard-boiled modernists—James Joyce, Wyndham Lewis, Ezra Pound, and T. S. Eliot—all came to the conclusion that love is the only legitimate basis for a renewed humanism. That could be another title for this study: "Modernist Humanism: A Love Story."

Modernist Humanism
and the Men of 1914

Introduction

Toward Modernist Humanism

It is the intention of this study to describe certain writers of the modernist era—the ones often called "the high modernists"—as working to preserve the human in an age regarded as strongly dehumanizing. The urgency of the modernist project may be best explained by a reading some emblematic stories by Jorge Luis Borges and Franz Kafka, writers not central to this study who nonetheless provide cogent and powerful depictions of the problem at hand. Attempting to set forth a distinction between modernity and modernism that will allow certain confusions of terminology to be identified and corrected, this introduction also sketches the history of humanism, locating the source of modernist humanism in the early modern humanists of the fifteenth and sixteenth centuries—not in the rationalist humanism of the Enlightenment—and describing the intellectual inheritance and background against which the modernists strove to enact their projects of recovery. James Joyce, Wyndham Lewis, Ezra Pound, and T. S. Eliot each contributed to a larger sense of a movement in modernism that may justly be called "modernist humanism."

Two Cheers for Alienation: Modernism and the Preservation of the Human

At the end of the Borges story "Tlön, Uqbar, Orbis Tertius," the narrator—evidently a scholarly man who is writing what looks more like a scholarly essay than short fiction—decides to ignore what is going on around him in the world and to retreat into the obscurity of his study, to "go on revising, in the quiet of the days in the hotel at Androgue, a tentative translation into Spanish, in the style of Quevedo, which I do not intend to see published, of Sir Thomas Browne's *Urn Burial*" (35). The situation of this translator is an exemplum of the humanist and the humanities in the first half of the twentieth century.

The narrator finds himself in a world being taken over by a secret society that has imposed a new reality. He is one of the first to discover signs of this society and its plot when quite accidentally he comes across a volume of the *Anglo-American Cyclopedia* that contains an entry on a hitherto unknown country called Uqbar. When he tries to look up Uqbar in another copy of the *Anglo-American Cyclopedia*, he finds that no other set contains that entry, which occupies the final four pages of volume 46 of the one set. This accident sparks his interest in Uqbar. One of the few "facts" he learns about it is that its literature refers only to imaginary places, one of which is called "Tlön." When he then discovers volume 11 of *A First Encyclopedia of Tlön*, he is further along on his discovery of the secret society Orbis Tertius, which has created these encyclopedias.

Most of the rest of this story is the narrator's account of what he learns from the eleventh volume of *A First Encyclopedia of Tlön*. Tlön turns out to be an imaginary planet created by writers in an imaginary country; yet it has all the trappings of reality. After all what is more reliable than an encyclopedia for presenting pure and undisputed facts? Borges's story has a postscript, however, which is dated seven years after the first part of the narrator's 1940 essay, the date of the story's composition. In this postscript the narrator describes what has occurred in the interval. All forty volumes of *A First Encyclopedia of Tlön* have been discovered, and the world has become fascinated by the illusion of this orderly and systematic alternate reality. "Almost immediately reality gave ground on more than one point. The truth is it hankered to give ground. Ten years ago, any symmetrical system whatsoever which gave the appearance of order—dialectical materialism, anti-Semitism, Nazism—was enough to fascinate men. Why not fall under the spell of Tlön and submit to the minute and vast evidence of an ordered planet?" (34). Orbis Tertius set in motion a fiction so well designed that it has taken over what we are wont to call reality: "Contact with Tlön and the ways of Tlön have disintegrated this world. . . . The world will be all Tlön" (34–35). A new "reality" has taken over.

Borges was careful to place this story in the context of the events of the 1930s, most particularly the development of European totalitarian states that advanced symmetrical systems purporting to explain the totality of human experience. Borges imagined a successful imposition of a new reality on the world, a new system of thinking and being that banishes the older version of reality until it is almost forgotten. For the last words of this story announce the narrator's retreat to his study and come immediately upon the pronouncement that "The world be all Tlön. I take no notice." This scholar intends to retreat into the world of texts and scholarship—the world of the humanities—as his way of ignoring the new system and keeping some contact with an older reality. The plight of the humanist is to turn backward to obscure texts and to maintain a tenuous relationship with them through the mechanism of scholarly activity. Borges's narrator is translating a relatively obscure text into classical Spanish, with limited hopes for a readership or an audience—and with severely limited hopes for communication with other human beings. But this narrator does not even intend to see the translation published; his act is purely for himself.

Should we lament this? It certainly seems reasonable to infer from this story that the humanities are impotent, useless, or marginal at best. Borges must certainly have wanted his readers to acknowledge that such might be the plight of the humanities in an age of ordered systems. The role of the individual in the developing totalitarian world is smaller; the status of individual human agency is at best limited and at worst useless. But there is also a more hopeful reading of this story: that the humanist scholar is working—at the margins of his culture to be sure and in ways that are perhaps futile if hope is to be measured in terms of active intervention in the world of public affairs—to keep available for other interested parties contact with texts that may be the source of value and virtue, of our feeling and acting and even being human. The benefits of this marginalized activity may be for only the lonely humanist himself, who is imagining a community of interested people sharing his concerns and enacting conversations with the past. Not only do the modernists Joyce, Lewis, Pound, and Eliot fit this model, but in a very real sense this book is like the essay in Borges's story, an account of past texts that perhaps few will read but that allows its author the illusion of a community within which to remain human in a posthuman age.

The recognition of the loss of the past as a result of new conditions defining and determining a radically new sense of reality is one of the hallmarks of modernist literature, and this recognition is tied to the realization of the danger of our losing a sense of what it is to be human. The writers studied in this book were anxious about this loss of the human to a new reality that threatened to replace the free individual with constructed subjectivity. Borges—or at the very least his narrator—believed that the texts from the past are worth keeping. Borges's narrators are often scholars, and his stories are often cast in the guise of scholarly essays. It is the humanist scholar who works at the margins of his culture, ignoring the brutal and degrading present and struggling to maintain the past through the texts it produced.

In another Borges story, "Pierre Menard, Author of *Don Quixote*," another humanist scholar advances a description of a modern writer's effort to write the great humanist classic *Don Quixote*. The twist is that Menard is not trying to translate the original, or to write a modern version of *Don Quixote* the way Joyce did for the *Odyssey*. Menard's goal is to write the very same book, word for word—and not by going back in time imaginatively and trying to see the world as Cervantes did. The oddness of the story is that Menard wants to remain a twentieth-century Frenchman and to write *Don Quixote* from his own experience. The narrator of this story enjoins the reader to marvel at the audacity of this effort and the great genius of its partial realization (for Menard writes "only" two full chapters of *Don Quixote* and a fraction of a third). Borges's conclusion is typically complex and demands careful attention to determine his attitude toward such classic texts and our reading of them. The narrator reports that Menard wrote to him these words: "'To think, analyze and invent . . . are not anomalous acts, but the normal respiration of the intelligence. To glorify the occasional fulfillment of this function, to treasure ancient thoughts of others, to remember with incredulous amazement that the *doctor universalis* thought, is to confess our languor or barbarism. Every man should be capable of all ideas, and I believe that in the future he will be'" (54). This is Borges's version of the humanist notion of the transcendence of literature; there are timeless texts, or at any rate there is a timeless realm in which we read great books. We read texts from the past not to understand the past (not to historicize) but to think those thoughts for ourselves in our concrete present. That we need to read the past to feel amazement and wonder is a sign of our own languor, a sign of our lack of confidence and energy to think and invent great things. Borges manages to have it both ways: we do not read the past nostalgically but actively; we do not read the past to lament our present but to think those thoughts in the present and perhaps (to intervene optimistically in his story) to be inspired to write these stories again, to think greatly today and from our own experience.

Such valorization of alienation falls right into the powerful postmodern critique of modernism that castigates the modernist texts as impotent and useless. Alan Sinfield has provided the grounds for serious objections to such posturing in "Reinventing Modernism." His essay takes issue with modernist artists and those scholars who invented modernism as a category for institutional study in the 1950s and 1960s, who turned the work of art into an alienated object, and who then saw the artist or scholar as part of an elite that feels alienated and out of the moment, which too quickly and too easily becomes a feeling of being above the moment. Sinfield's objection to modernism is that it celebrates alienation as timeless instead of castigating it as out of touch with material conditions of existence that need improvement. Sinfield wants an art that intervenes in social life, not one that seeks to turn away from it and hide.

Sinfield's objections to modernism provide a first glance at the postmodern critique of modernism that is one of the central features of this study. While Sinfield offers a powerful call for relevance and practical intervention, a more sympathetic interpretation of the modernists' movement away from the conditions of a degrading and dehumanizing social life is to point out their efforts to hold onto something called "the human." Such an effort is a way for literary texts to intervene, perhaps the only important way in which something like literature can do so. For literature cannot compete with journalism and politics in practical intervention, but it might just provide a philosophy or an embodied model of a renewed humanism that could direct the reforms we seek in politics. Borges's call to scholarly attention to great texts from the past—worthy acts of creativity that are relevant to our present condition—may be quite personal and devoid of any public significance, but such attention allows the individual scholar to remain tied to a tradition of human greatness that permits him, in the present and for himself, to think greatly and highly.

These two Borges stories depict the humanist scholar as the protagonist in the late 1930s, the decade in which most of the modernists discussed in this book developed their humanist projects. Borges was writing on the eve of World War II, and. like these stories, most of the other stories in *The Garden of Forking Paths* (1941) may be read as responses to the plight of the individual in a world threatened by totalitarian states, governments aiming at the subordination of the individual to the state and the transformation of the individual into the subject. But more than twenty years earlier, another great modernist writer made the human subject and human agency the theme of his great fiction. Just before World War I, Kafka was already worried—even more anxious perhaps than Borges—about the fate of the human being in the modern world of bureaucratic systems, of large institutions that have taken over society and that threaten the individual less sinisterly than fascism perhaps but just as effectively and, in the long run, more successfully. Indeed the institutions, human systems, and bureaucracies that characterize the modern period might well be seen to have their fulfillment in the efficiency of the final solution.[1] Kafka wrote two short stories that may serve as the basis for a brief meditation on the status of the human in the age of bureaucracy. What Kafka shared with Borges is a way of presenting alienation as something not wholly negative, indeed as the only positive solution to an overwhelming public problem. The way to teach Kafka may well be with the slogan "Two cheers for alienation"—not a full-throated celebration of an unhappy condition but a muted and hopeful recognition that only in alienation can the human being remain as such, a human being.[2]

Kafka's great short story "In the Penal Colony" expresses his nightmarish sense of the modern world as a complex bureaucratic machine constructed explicitly to condemn and punish. The island to which the Explorer has come is a penal colony with a torture machine that is invariably called the Apparatus. The new Commandant of the island would like to dismantle the machine but cannot, even though there are no longer any adherents of the machine—or the old Commandant who invented it—left on the island, except the Officer, who is charged with showing the Apparatus to the Explorer. The bureaucratic machine existing at any given moment has a human origin, but it has come to have a life of its own and operates beyond the control of its human maker or makers.[3] No matter how much we might want to dismantle the mechanisms of our society because they seem cruel and unfair, we seem helpless to do so and can at best make only small gestures of reform. One such reform in the story is that the condemned man now gets to eat sugar candy the day before his execution, which actually makes the punishment worse but at least makes the ladies of the island feel that they have expressed their compassion. The bureaucratic system, which does have a human origin (it is certainly not natural or divine), will continue to operate in its tortuous manner as we look on helplessly. The gap between the human world and the systems it has set in motion is huge and unbridgeable. Paul Sheehan has noted that humanism in the modernist era is made almost impossible by the workings of these "human systems" that come to have a life of their own and threaten the individual most because the individual is helpless to change or affect the very things he has set into motion (5, 20). Sheehan sees this as evidence that human agency has become so small as to be irrelevant, but let us consider what the human individual can accomplish not by intervention but by alienation.

That we all live out our lives in a sort of penal colony seems evident in this story, and that we are riddled with a guilt for which the bureaucracy ruthlessly and relentlessly punishes is its great theme, one more elaborately played out in Kafka's unfinished novel *The Trial*. In the short story, the Apparatus inscribes on the condemned person's body the virtue that his crime has violated. In the particular case the story depicts, the man has neglected to salute the office door of his superior; so the phrase "honor thy superiors" is being inscribed on his body. It is worth noting that the condemned man failed to salute a door, not the human being himself. That is, in the bureaucracy that rules our lives, we are functions not humans, subjects not individuals. The office must be respected, not the living human being who occupies it at any particular moment. That is why the characters in this story do not have names, which would make them seem more human, but only titles drawn from their bureaucratic roles. The Apparatus that inscribes our guilt represents the workings of our modern culture, which writes our guilt so deeply into us that our very bodies are marked by its workings. We are wounded, psychically and physically, by guilt that our system of life enforces.[4] It becomes intimately a part of us. There is no escape.

The main figure in this story is called the Explorer, evidently a famous man whose reputation is high and noble. He has been asked to witness the workings of the machine and report back to the new Commandant, who will use the Explorer's judgment to aid in his effort to dismantle it. The Officer meanwhile is hoping he can get the Explorer to see the virtue of the machine. When the Officer realizes that his efforts have failed, he decides that the time has come for him to change places with the condemned man and put himself in the machine. His sentence is "be just." But the machine cannot be just: with this phrase in place, the machine goes out of control and becomes a butchering device.

This is Kafka's parable of revolution: a change of government, a revolution in the social order, will merely exchange the positions people occupy, as the condemned man becomes the torturer and the torturer the condemned man. Revolutions cannot write justice; they become, for a while at any rate, a bloodier and more violent machine than the smooth operation of the bureaucracy has been. This seems a hopeless situation. The Explorer does not return to the new Commandant but instead leaves the island. He does not try to aid in the amelioration of suffering caused by such bureaucratic machines, and his last gesture is to make sure no one from the island comes with him, as he uses a heavy knotted rope to keep the condemned man and a soldier from joining him. He runs away and remains alone. One might be tempted to say that, as an "explorer," he has nowhere to return to and will wander the earth, alienated from any system that threatens his humanity. Only in this state of self-imposed exile, of willed alienation, can the Explorer maintain his humanity.

One moment from "The Metamorphosis" may serve as the emblem for this study. As his sister and mother try to think of ways to help Gregor once he has lost his human appearance, they decide to take all his furniture from his room, making it much more fitting for a bug's happiness than his "regular human bedroom." Gregor is pleased with this prospect until he hears his mother express some concern. Then he suddenly feels confused: "Did he really want his warm room, so comfortably fitted with old family furniture, to be turned into a naked den in which he would certainly be able to crawl unhampered in all directions but at the price of shedding simultaneously all recollection of his human background?" (102–3). This moment of confusion makes humanity something to be remembered, something that is in danger of not only being lost but also being forgotten. Nostalgia for a human past is not wistful and debilitating if it is the only way to remain in contact with our humanity.[5] Perhaps the only experience of our humanity left for us is the experience of its loss, the nostalgic emotion that something good has been lost from the world. It is, therefore, backward looking and anachronistic. We feel that something we once possessed—our humanity—has been taken away from us.

Texts produced in the past, which we call the basis of the humanities, are the "furniture" that reminds us of our human background, of what we were once and can be again. This is one of the cardinal positions of many modernist authors, who wanted to remain in contact with a tradition of great texts as they tried to use them to steer a course through the present and toward a future that would not be dehumanized and dehumanizing. The space for individual human agency became smaller and smaller in the bureaucratic nightmare of Kafka and in the totalitarian world of Borges. Both writers made the recovery of the human an urgent project that fought against the mainstream of their modernizing cultures. The need to preserve the human in the midst of this modernizing culture is the great goal of modernist humanism.

The nightmarish events of the twentieth century have had a negative impact on the reputation of modernism in particular and of humanism in general, as if the literary texts that preceded the nightmares of Auschwitz and Hiroshima were, because precedent, in some way complicit with those ends. It has become almost a critical commonplace to view modernist texts with suspicion, as if their literary efforts somehow led to the death camps. We have become so cynical about modernism and have praised postmodernism so uncritically that I am afraid a new dogmatism is preventing us from a genuine appreciation of what the modernist projects were attempting. Some of the great modernist texts may in fact be read as complex attempts to reinvent humanism for the twentieth century, and I refuse to assign them blame or complicity in the negative developments of the era. In fact one might say that developments such as totalitarianism, the death camps, Hiroshima, and the cold war show the need to review the great modernist texts again and to hear their warnings about the threatened demise of the human and of humanism.

Modernism and Modernity

It is crucial to make a firm and clear distinction between modernism in the arts and modernity in the general social life of the West. The Men of 1914 responded to the degrading effects of the modernizing world. Modernism is an artistic response to the negative effects of modernity.

It is also essential to draw a distinction between two versions of humanism. One is based on the Enlightenment philosophy of rational mastery over the material world, a humanism that may indeed be linked to modernity. Another more playful, more skeptical humanism is based on our relation to the supernatural, which was developed in the early modern period and which the modernists in this study retrieved and renewed. We can call the former an Enlightenment humanism and the latter a theistic humanism. Modernist humanism is a theistic humanism.

In an essay with the suggestive title "The Postmodernity of Modernism," Sanford Schwartz has tried to redress the error made when modernism in the arts is confused with modernity in social life, noting how many influential theorists of the postmodern—Theodor W. Adorno, Jean Baudrillard, Gilles Deleuze, Michel Foucault, and Jean-François Lyotard—"identify modernity with systemic and coercive rationality, and . . . they seem to support the equation of the postmodern with resistance to (or at least recognition of) the pervasive rationalization of modern life" (12). Furthermore "Lyotard associates modernity with the project of Enlightenment rationality, which in his view achieved its ultimate and grotesque realization in the death camps at Auschwitz." What troubles Schwartz is that these theorists or their followers "are prone to conflate the modernity/postmodernity problematic of contemporary theory with that of modernism/postmodernism in the arts. Never mind that modernism was once regarded as a reaction against modernity" (12). In fact some recent historical accounts of modernism have emphasized its opposition to rationality and logic. For example Vincent Sherry in *The Great War and the Language of Modernism* describes the influence of World War I on the modernists' loss of faith in rational language and logic. Such studies have been inspired by the call to correct the confusion between modernity and modernism, attempting to revise our understanding of modernism as antimodern. Modernism in the arts does not blithely follow the Enlightenment project as the postmodern theorists often want to assume. Instead modernism seeks to counter that project through experiments and technical innovations. Modernism in literature has more in common with the postmodern critique of modernity than it does with modernity itself.

Schwartz has also described the postmodern tendency to decenter the Cartesian subject as something already under way in modernist literature, and he points to the influence of Friedrich Nietzsche, William James, and others on modernist efforts to disrupt the subject. Schwartz rehearses Helmut Lethen's argument that the "prevailing division between modern and postmodern is simply 'modernism cut in half,' and what we call the postmodern is nothing other than the forgotten side of modernism" (16). It is important to "remember" the fullness of modernism in literature, that it already anticipated much of what we now call a postmodern critique in its attitudes toward society and culture and that it provided a powerful literary movement attempting to debunk some prevailing modern concepts and structures while at the same time trying to establish an alternative view of the individual and its place in a general social life.

David Harvey has also made a distinction between modernity and modernism that is both convincing and helpful. He relies on Jürgen Habermas to provide the description of "the project of modernity" that "came into focus during the eighteenth century. That project amounted to an extraordinary effort on the part of Enlightenment thinkers 'to develop objective science, universal morality and law, and autonomous art according to their inner logic'" (Harvey, 12). Harvey goes on to explain that this is a great and important project because "the development of rational forms of social organization and rational modes of thought promised liberation from the irrationalities of myth, religion, superstition, release from the arbitrary use of power and well as from the dark side of our own human natures" (12). But this project can be said to have ended poorly in the first half of the twentieth century: "The twentieth century—with its death camps and death squads, its militarism and two world wars, its threat of nuclear annihilation and its experience of Hiroshima and Nagasaki—has certainly shattered this optimism. Worse still, the suspicion lurks that the Enlightenment project was doomed to turn against itself and transform the quest for human emancipation into a system of universal oppression" (13). Harvey cites Max Horkheimer and Theodor W. Adorno as the pursuers of this connection between the Enlightenment project and the horrors of modernity: "they argued that the logic that hides behind Enlightenment rationality is a logic of domination and oppression" (13).

This understanding of "modernity" and the Enlightenment project based on the rational cogito prepares for Harvey's understanding of "modernism" as a reaction against developments in technology and the human sciences that were seen as threatening to the human. Harvey follows Habermas and wants to define "modernity" as a project rooted in rationality and science, but unlike Habermas he is willing to accede to the postmodern critique that this project precipitated and participated in the nightmarish events of the first half of the twentieth century. Ultimately Harvey wants to describe a "cultural modernism" that works against the Enlightenment project of modernity. This distinction between modernity and modernism is extremely important.

Stephen Toulmin has also tried to establish a concrete definition of modernity and to locate its origins with some clarity and precision. While he acknowledges Habermas's contention that modernity "began when, inspired by the French Revolution, Immanuel Kant showed how impartial, universal moral standards can be applied to judge intentions and policies in the political realm," Toulmin wants to trace Kant's universalism back to its origins in René Descartes' ideal of rationality: "'Modernity' is the historical phase that begins with Galileo's and Descartes' commitment to new, rational methods of inquiry" (8–9). For Toulmin the contribution of these two thinkers lies in their efforts to pose problems and seek solutions in timeless and universal terms. According to Toulmin, this is the great revolution that began modernity, the ability for thinkers in various fields to be able to decontextualize a problem and seek to resolve it in an abstract world that knows no change. Toulmin sketches a series of transformations that the emergence of modernity occasions: from the oral to the written, from the particular to the universal, from the local to the general, from the timely to the timeless. For Toulmin this is a shift from humanists to rationalists (30–36).

This concise and lucid account of the beginnings of modernity is not unique to Toulmin; his contribution to our thinking about these problems lies in his claim that modernity may have had "two distinct origins, rather than one single origin, the first (literary or humanistic phase) being a century before the second" (23). The first origin is with the Renaissance humanists, who "displayed an urbane open-mindedness and skeptical tolerance," while the second,

Enlightenment origin sought certainty in abstract, universal theory (24, 25). So different are these two origins that Toulmin considers the second phase, the one he has called modernity, a counter renaissance, seeking the dogmatic certainty that the humanists had refused in their playful and self-deprecating, self-doubting, and often open-ended projects. Modernity is a commitment to science and logic and rationality that, above all else, wants certain answers to be universally and permanently true.

Toulmin in fact wants to know why this commitment to abstract theory and reasoning occurred at just this time, in the 1630s. His answer has much to do with the turmoil in Europe during the first half of the seventeenth century, which is most easily seen in the horrible violence of the Thirty Years' War. In an effort to escape the political, military, and religious violence of the time, intellectuals sought to flee from the local and the concrete into the general and universal. Modernity may then be seen as an intellectual and political movement that places great faith in abstract reasoning and rational thinking, and it may indeed have had its early impulse from the need for certainty in an uncertain age. The humanists of the early modern period did not feel this radical need for total certainty or rational mastery, and they were able to write texts characterized by benevolent tolerance and playful skepticism. So we have two distinct kinds of humanism: there is the humanism of the early modern period, with figures such as Desiderius Erasmus, Thomas More, and François Rabelais; and then there is a humanism that is more closely tied to the Enlightenment ideals of rationality and universal certainty. In a book with similar aims to the present study, Paul Sheehan has defined humanism in terms that have much more to do with the Enlightenment that with the early modern humanists: "Philosophically, humanism is that discourse of the modern subject derived from the Cartesian tradition of reason, logic, cognition, reflexivity; and its Kantian affiliates of responsibility, duty, respect, self-sovereignty, agency" (6). Certainly humanism does not reject or deny all these, but placing humanism after Descartes and not before has led to a simplifying of humanism. A clear distinction must be drawn between an Enlightenment humanism that leads to dogmatism and rigidity and the early modern humanism of Rabelais and company, which delights in playful skepticism. The modernist humanists studied in this book are the heirs of the latter and not the former. In fact the modernist humanism of the Men of 1914 can be regarded as a reconstituted Christian modernism in the spirit of the early modern humanists.

Early Modern Humanism as a Response to Crisis

Toulmin wants us to consider an earlier origin for modernity in the early modern humanists of the late fourteenth and early fifteenth centuries, positing that those thinkers were responding to sudden and eruptive changes in European culture with an open-minded and tolerant skepticism that the later modernity, the one associated with Descartes and Galileo, sought to counter. A brief description of the work of these first humanists provides a basis for my project of describing a modernist humanism, for the modernists have much more in common with these writers than with those Toulmin describes as coming out of the Cartesian counter renaissance.

Toulmin's understanding of these first humanists is accurate and sensible as far as it goes, and his focus on Michel de Montaigne makes perfect sense for Toulmin's argument that they were devoted to the skeptical debunking of received dogmas and rigid positions. But Toulmin has missed some important features of the early modern humanists that allow a broader understanding of this vexed term and provide the foundation for my study of modernist humanism. For while writers such as Erasmus, More, and Rabelais did indeed work to debunk entrenched authorities and to loosen up rigidities in thinking, they also sought to lay a foundation for thought and belief by appealing to ancient texts and trying to define humanity in terms that elevate and ennoble. This twin purpose—sweeping away stale and coercive rigidities and opening up a space for a renewed understanding of human dignity—characterizes both early modern humanism and the modernist humanism of the present study.

The first humanism was in large part a response to sudden and dramatic events that called into question various aspects of what can be called authority. Within a period of fewer than fifty years, there were a series of culture-shaking events in Europe: the invention of moveable type, the discovery of the New World, the Protestant Reformation, and the Copernican revolution. There was also the more gradual development of the new mercantile system that became capitalism. Most of these events not only changed the shape of the culture, but they undermined traditional authorities. The size of the globe and what it contains changed suddenly with the discovery of the New World; the Reformation posed a strong and sudden challenge to the enormous authority of the church; the Copernican revolution violated "common sense" and led to a radical skepticism concerning what we can trust even in our sensory perceptions.

In particular the printing press drastically and suddenly changed the authority that words could carry as they circulate throughout the culture. Before the printing press, written words that circulated throughout the culture already had authority, in that some institution (usually the church but also the emerging institution of the university) made possible their being copied and disseminated. That is the church or the university had already placed its authority behind the writing that it wanted disseminated. If something existed in multiple copies throughout Europe—in monasteries and libraries and wealthy men's homes—it already had authority (even if it had no known author). Within a generation or so of the advent of the printing press, the conditions of authority had shifted. Now anything could be printed. In fact authority now had to be earned in the marketplace. Rabelais was the first major European author to be aware of the implications of the printing press, as *Gargantua and Pantagruel* demonstrates with its irreverent attitude toward words as mere things to be piled up and enjoyed. His lists, for example, are nothing other than a series of items, piled up indiscriminately to no end other than the delight of thinking of as many ludicrous things as one could and putting them under some silly heading (such as what was Gargantua's favorite arse wipe). Words became things in Rabelais.[6] No longer was it assumed that words must refer clearly to something outside language called truth, or that at least they must be measured against something outside language called truth; now words have become things in themselves. The authority of the written word was undermined and subjected to a mocking critique.

Rabelais played with the concept of authority quite explicitly. At the birth of Gargantua, his father, Grandgousier, assigns him colors, white and blue, and assigns a meaning to them that goes contrary to expected meaning. Rabelais addresses the reader as if the reader is outraged by this breach in signification:

> Who is exciting you now? Who is pricking you? Who is telling you that white stands for faith and blue for steadfastness? A mouldy book, you say, that is sold by pedlars and ballad-mongers, entitled *The Blason of Colours*. Who made it? Whoever he is he has been prudent in one respect, that he has not put his name to it. For the rest, I do not know which surprises me more, his presumption or his stupidity: his presumption in daring, without reason, cause, or probability, to prescribe by his private authority what things shall be denoted by what colours; which is the custom of tyrants who would have their will take the place of reason, not of the wise and learned, who satisfy their readers with display of evidence; or his stupidity in supposing that without other proofs and valid arguments the world would regulate its practices by his foolish impostures. (57–58)

This is an early recognition that a radical break in authority had occurred. No longer could a book be presumed to have authority merely by its status as book; now authority had to be earned by reasoning, proofs, and valid arguments. The tyranny of older authority had been broken, for good or for ill, and replaced by a new world of printed books vying with one another for positions of cultural esteem and authority.

Rabelais took his place as one of the early modern humanists, those who were working in the late fifteenth and early sixteenth centuries to make valid responses to the radically new conditions for authority and meaning brought about by sudden and unexpected cultural events. In *The Praise of Folly*, the great humanist writer Erasmus invented as his spokesman the goddess Folly, whose targets include human reason and the pride we take in our mastery over our lives. There is in Erasmus a playful debunking of the place of reason in our lives:

> And we'll notice first how providentially nature, the mother and creator of the human race, has arranged that men shall never be without a good seasoning of folly. For if, as the stoics define the matter, wisdom consists of being ruled by reason, while folly is being moved by the emotions, Jupiter, to prevent our life from being gloomy and sad, mixed into our composition far more feeling than reason. How much more? Well, I would say about ten pounds of feeling to a half-ounce of reason. Besides, he cramped the reason into one narrow corner of the head, but distributed the feelings through all the rest of the body. Then he set up two furious tyrants to war on solitary reason, anger, which occupies the fortress of the breast, and therefore the very fountain of life, which is the heart; and lust, which maintains its mighty empire further down, around the area of the groin. What reason can do against these twin powers, the common life of man makes sufficiently clear; she does all she can, scolds herself hoarse, and repeats all the platitudes of proper behavior. But the passions just tell their so-called ruler to go hang, and bluster on more offensively than ever until reason submits out of sheer exhaustion and throws up her hands. (17–19)

Written in the first decade of the sixteenth century, these lines demonstrate the humanist concern with feelings and the body as essential in defining our humanity while relegating a small role to reason. While it is always unclear exactly how much authority one can give to any of Folly's pronouncements (and that uncertainty is part of the desired effect, promoting healthy doubt and debate and discouraging dogmatic positions and claims to certainty), it may be fairly inferred that Erasmus felt compelled to write an encomium of the nonrational aspects of our lives, as if the embrace of the rational by medieval theology had been a misplaced confidence that recent and contemporaneous events had given the lie to. Reason probably was not as small for Erasmus as Folly claims, but such excess is strategically necessary to bring the nonrational into some prominence in our lives. Feeling is much more important to our lives and well-being than reason, which by itself makes us gloomy and sad. Wise men are sad men, and fools are happy: "I restore the selfsame man to the best and happiest period of his life [his childhood]. So that if men would refrain completely from any sort of commerce with wisdom, but spend their time entirely in my company, they would never grow old, but instead would live happily in the enjoyment of perpetual youth" (15). As silly as this may seem, it is consistent with Christ's command that we should become like children if we wish to enter the kingdom of heaven (Matthew 18:3). If we can forget evils and hope for good, that is because of Folly (31), and we are told that in the golden age "simple men flourished, without the armour-plate of the sciences, under the leadership of nature and natural instincts alone" (33). Folly provides the basis for friendships and marriage, allowing us to tolerate each other's faults that reason would despise. Erasmus made reason look coercive and narrowly judgmental while folly is what gives us the better things of human being.

Folly's main philosophical enemy is the philosophy of the Stoics, who "banish all emotions from the wise man's life, as so many diseases. Yet these emotions not only serve as guides for those who press toward the gates of wisdom, they also act as spurs and incitements to the practice of every virtue, and stimulate men to the performance of good deeds. No doubt that double-dyed stoic Seneca strongly rejects this idea, denying that the wise man is entitled to any emotion whatever; but in doing so he doesn't leave him a shred of humanity" (29). Plato's story of the cave is also reevaluated, with the conclusion that those who seek the truth with the pure mind and its reason are doomed to be unhappy and that those who stay in the cave will fare more happily. Wisdom and goodness, as well as our well-being, are founded not on reason but on emotion, which, we may presume, the reason can direct and develop.

Erasmus's text comes to center on a long list of respected professions, which Folly debunks as arrogant and misguided because they are without such a foundation. *The Praise of Folly* concludes with a meditation on Christianity as a religion of fools who believe in nonrational miracles and who behave in ways that to a rational man seem like nonsense but are really the highest and fullest development of our humanity. Folly's scathing irony does not hesitate to mock the church, its theologians and hierarchy, and even the pope himself as corrupt and debased. But she spares the core of Christian hope from her negative irony, allowing some good thing to stand immune from the debunking she is willing to perform at any sign of pretension or arrogance. Our hope in a heavenly afterlife is the epitome of folly, and it is not debunked as pretension but as the source of our greatest aspiration.

The work of another early modern humanist, Thomas More's *Utopia*, is complex in its ambiguity and open-endedness. It attempts to provide an alternative view to the emergence of a new way of living that seemed to be threatening traditional human values. *Utopia* enacts a scathing critique of an emerging mercantile system that proved detrimental to the humane values of the past. More's spokesman, Raphael Hythloday, tells of a fantastic place recently discovered by

Vespucci that follows very different rules—most of which seem superior—from those of the Old World he addresses. Like Erasmus in *The Praise of Folly*, More enacted a skeptical debunking of accepted institutions and beliefs.

More's spokesman sees private property as the chief source of evil in the world: "as long as you have private property, and as long as cash money is the measure of all things, it is really impossible for a nation to be governed justly or happily" (28). This is at the heart of part 1 of *Utopia*, and Hythloday takes care to connect his critique of European customs from his Utopian point of view to Christ's critique of the same:

> What if I told them [Europeans at a king's court] of the kind of thing that Plato advocates in his *Republic*, or which the Utopians actually practice in theirs? However superior those institutions might be (and as a matter of fact they are), yet here they would seem inappropriate because private property is the rule here, and there all things are held in common.
>
> People who have made up their minds to rush headlong down the opposite road are never pleased with the man who calls them back and tells them they are on the wrong course. But apart from that, what did I say that could not and should not be said anywhere and everywhere? If we dismiss as out of the question and absurd everything which the perverse customs of men have made to seem unusual, we shall have to set aside most of the commandments of Christ, even in a community of Christians. Yet he forbade us to dissemble them, and even ordered that what he had whispered to his disciples should be preached openly from the housetops. Most of his teachings differ more radically from the common customs of mankind than my discourse did. (26–27)

Hythloday's Utopian views are not the same as Christ's, nor are they More's way of bringing a Christian perspective into conflict with European views, but—in a more complex and subtle manner—Hythloday's Utopian critique of Europe is meant to remind us of a more familiar critique of worldly values, that of Christ, whose teachings are more radically different from European ways than Hythloday's but whose critique, because of its very familiarity, has become muted and has lost its ability to challenge and provoke. Hythloday's critique of European ways was meant to restore to Europe the fundamental challenges to custom and practice that Christ provided in his teachings, and the complex manner of presentation is needed in order to make the teachings of Christ seem as new and vital and extreme as they were originally.

That Hythloday is not completely to be trusted as a spokesman for More himself is evident in many small ways. Some of the Utopian practices that

Hythloday advocates cannot be reconciled with a view of the world that we would assume More could hold, especially the use of slaves for the lowest work, the use of violence to drive off natives who do not conform to Utopian practices, the almost absolute lack of privacy required to live safely in Utopia, and the need for permission to travel within Utopia. The most glaring evidence that Hythloday is not More is that one of Hythloday's interlocutors is a man named Thomas More, and this eponymous character registers his lack of credence in Hythloday's authority at the end. The chief narrator of most of *Utopia* is not someone we can trust implicitly, though we expect that much, maybe most, of his discourse is instructive and to be accepted positively. This is very similar to Erasmus's use of Folly as his spokeswoman, and for the same purpose of leading the reader into the privileged role of making decisions about what parts of the critique to apply and what parts of the critique to reject. This is perhaps one of the central features of the early modern humanists, as it is later of the modernist humanists: the use of indirection and suggestion to make the reader play a more central and empowered role in the process of the text. It seems as though we the readers are meant to be reminded of Christ's even more radical and more scathing critique of money and worldly values as we read Hythloday's and as though we are meant to employ—on our own, but actually led to do so by the author—Christ's teachings as the standard by which we judge Utopia and its values and practices.

Some of Hythloday's comments on religion and religiosity are especially relevant to this study. Utopia's religion is based on reason and rationality and not on revelation, but even as such it comes quite near to some of the fundamental beliefs of Christianity:

> They define virtue as living according to nature; and God, they say, created us to that end. When a man obeys the dictates of reason in choosing one thing and avoiding another, he is following nature. Now the first rule of reason is to love and venerate the Divine Majesty to whom men owe their existence and every happiness of which they are capable. The second rule of nature is to lead a life as free of anxiety and as full of joy as possible, and to help all one's fellow men toward that end. . . . Nothing is more humane (and humanity is the virtue most proper to human beings) than to relieve the misery of others, assuage their griefs, and by removing all sadness from their life, to restore them to enjoyment, that is, pleasure. (51)

A religion founded on reason and nature brings us near to Christian principles in its dictates to love God and to serve our fellow human beings, and it is worth noting in passing that Hythloday defines "humanity" as a virtue proper to human being that calls for benevolent service. What is foregrounded here, and not in Christ's teaching, is an emphasis on pleasure and joy, whereas Christ enjoins his disciples to accept suffering and to bear it for noble purposes. We see that reason comes close to Christ's teaching in its emphasis on love and service but misses what is nonrational about Christianity, the cross and its promise of Resurrection.

When Hythloday introduces Christ and "his teachings, his life, his miracles" to the Utopians, he is pleased to see "how they were impressed." What impressed the most was "the fact that Christ had encouraged his disciples to practice community of goods, and that among the truest groups of Christians, the practice still prevails" (73). The influence of Christ on Utopia may be seen in the fact that King Utopus has refused to lay down any laws for his people in matters regarding religious beliefs and practices: "The only exception he made was a positive and strict law against any person who should sink so far below the dignity of human nature as to think that the soul perishes with the body, or that the universe is ruled by mere chance, rather than by divine providence" (74–75). Not to believe in the immortality of the soul and in a God who has a plan for humanity is to sink below the dignity of human nature: "Thus Utopians believe that after this life vices are to be punished and virtue rewarded; and they consider that anyone who opposes this proposition is hardly a man, since he has degraded the sublimity of his own soul to the base level of a beast's wretched body" (75). What elevates humanity to its proper sublimity are these beliefs, which are, of course, central to Christianity. These early modern humanists are most properly Christian humanists in their sense that the dignity of human nature lies in our ability to believe in a higher destiny for ourselves beyond the material conditions of our lives, which we share with the beasts.

Like Erasmus and More, Rabelais also spared the Gospels and the hope in a heavenly home from his otherwise unsparing mockery. The Abbey of Thélème is in fact his vision of a Christian afterlife, in which all sorts of sinners are prevented from entering and only noble men and noble ladies, along with good preachers of the Gospel, are allowed entrance. The reason why there are no rules other than "Do as you wish" over its gates is that only good men and women, those who adhere to the Gospel stories and their values, will be present. They need no other rules but to act based on love and mercy. While Rabelais, Erasmus, and More enacted scathing and mocking critiques that debunk most of our pretensions and most of our institutions, they found one thing from the past to be immune from their mockery, and that is the Gospel stories and their hope in the Resurrection. That is folly. That is nonrational and opposed to any logical inference based on evidence gleaned from our senses, and it is our highest hope. The debunking of the early modern humanists did not leave their culture entirely devoid of a set of values, but rather enacted a skeptical debunking that swept most values away as partial and deceitful but spared what is sure and permanent as the anchor of a culture to be reformed and reshaped after the cataclysmic intellectual upheavals of the age. The figure of Christ, the figure of the Incarnation, is left as the one thing not debunked or reduced by mockery to mere pretension. In fact their "discovery" that the figure of the Incarnation stands firm in the midst of cultural upheaval helps to explain the efforts of modernists such as Joyce and Eliot, who were more willing to embrace their Christian heritage as a source for their imaginative efforts, and also help us understand why the modernists were so likely to see Dante as their most important precursor, one who made the Incarnation the organizing feature of his great Christian epic.[7]

What is also worth special emphasis is that these early modern humanists did not praise reason but instead praised folly, the nonrational aspects of human being, as the essence of our humanity. One hundred years before Descartes' cogito, one hundred and fifty years before Isaac Newton and John Locke, two hundred and fifty years before Kant and the French Revolution, the early modern humanists were skeptical about reason and presented a self not based on a cogito but on nonrational feeling. As one of the modernist humanists, Pound learned through much suffering, "Amo ergo sum, and in just that proportion" (Canto LXXX, 513).

Modernist Humanism

One of the most important critiques of modernism in literature from the postmodern perspective is that modernism, in Alan Sinfield's words, "imagined the poetic text as autonomous" and that modernism assumed that "the literary text embodies a profound truth about the supposed human condition" (188–89). Sinfield has been careful to distinguish the actual texts of the modernist period from the construction of the academic subject called "modernism." He alleges that the latter, influenced by New Criticism and formalism, has presented a version of these texts that do not attend to their specificity and subtlety. In my reading of the canonical modernist texts, I hope to counter such misreadings by attending to their specificity as they respond to concrete historical circumstances. My formalist readings are aimed at understanding certain high modernist responses to the social and historical circumstances of the period.

What Sinfield charged the academics defining modernism with doing is a criticism often leveled against the texts themselves: that the great texts of modernism seek to transcend the temporal and the concrete and express universal truths in an abstract manner. Sinfield himself has at times confused the literary texts with their treatment in the early days of modernism as a subject for scholarly inquiry, and he blames both the artists and their critics for not treating history properly, for seeing it only as "a nightmare from which one is trying to awake" (195). It is ironic that Sinfield mistakenly attributed this quotation to Eliot rather than to Joyce, for Eliot is a more convenient target for the postmodern critic than Joyce. Worse than the mistaken attribution, however, is Sinfield's missing Joyce's point in "Nestor": that history cannot be ignored blithely. Stephen's next comment makes this point clear: "What if that nightmare give you a back kick." "Nestor" is about history and the need for the artist to confront it, and later in *Ulysses* Stephen has to correct George Russell's Platonism for the same reason. The modernists are being charged with the tendency that Toulmin attributed to Descartes and Galileo, decontextualizing a problem and seeking for solutions in an abstract, timeless sphere. History is the great problem that the major modernists' imaginative texts seek to confront and resolve, and never do they seek to do so by fleeing to the timeless and leaving the concrete world of material existence behind. As with the early modern humanists, the modernist humanists in this study "discovered" the principle of the Incarnation as the solution to the vexing problem of time and history.

My first and fourth chapters develop fully how the mystery of the Incarnation directly and explicitly informs the texts of Joyce and Eliot, but this mystery of Christian faith is also relevant to the general concerns of this study.[8] In the Incarnation, God takes on a human form in the person of Jesus Christ, who is fully God and fully human. In the Incarnation is a figure who participates fully in both the divine world of timeless truths and in the temporal world of change and relativity. In the third of his *Four Quartets,* T. S. Eliot called Incarnation "the point of intersection of the timeless with time," "the still point in the changing world" available to human being where one can see the changing world from the perspective of the eternal. The modernists in this study did not seek to flee from the concrete and temporal into the timeless and the abstract, but rather they sought to find the point of intersection, that fixed point that allows a stable perspective from which to make valid judgments about the world of constant change. Joyce and Eliot were explicit in using Christian teachings and mystery in their imaginative texts, while Lewis and Pound transformed this religious doctrine into nonreligious (but not quite secular) terms.

Those who want to defend humanism from the postmodern critique like to point out that the postmodern skepticism has been unable to build anything new after it swept out the constructs that were masquerading as truths. Michael Tratner has noted this in passing, when he calls poststructuralism a critical tool that does not construct alternatives; in fact he seems anxious that the decentering of the self in the modernist texts leaves open a void to be filled with a mob self (4). Vincent Sherry worries that the modernists' antipathy to logic leaves them open to fears and anxieties that are not rational, most notably anti-Semitism (65–68). Both Tratner and Sherry have noted that modernist texts contain the postmodern critical tools of debunking and decentering and also register an anxiety that the sweeping clear of antiquated concepts and fraudulent claims to value leave the modernist open to negative forces. I hope to show that certain modernists anticipated this problem and seek to fill the void with a carefully constructed understanding of humanism as the foundation of a healthy culture.

No critic makes a more explicit and urgent point of this aspect of the postmodern critique than Richard Etlin in his *In Defense of Humanism*. Indeed Etlin's work is quite instructive in its one-sided "defense" of humanism against the postmodern and against poststructuralism. His argument is informed by an impatience regarding postmodern skepticism: "Poststructuralism is characterized by a radical skepticism about the nature of meaning and value. . . . It is argued that there are simply no absolutes." For Etlin this is bad enough, but things get worse: "Never in modern times since when Hegel in the early nineteenth century placed his own intellectual discipline of philosophy on a par with religion and divinity have intellectuals exhibited such hubris in attributing to themselves the power to arbitrate all meaning by insisting on the relativity of all thought and value (73–75). One may sympathize with Etlin's lament here, but his defense of humanism seems too soft and too glib, as if merely pointing out this relativity as a problem is its own solution or as when he claims early in his study, "Art can be a vehicle of a transcendent experience, which touches on the mystery and the sacred nature of life" (9). This may indeed be true, and I will argue for such a conclusion, but saying does not make it so. It requires close readings of the great texts to show concretely and precisely how art may accomplish such high ends.

Etlin's work suffers from two distinct but related errors. First his humanism is of the kind that derives from the Cartesian quest for certainty and the Kantian belief in universal moral values; it is the kind that derives from the Enlightenment and tends toward its own dogmatic assertions of truth and value. The humanism that derives from the early modern period is skeptical and debunking in its first movement and allows only the human self based on Incarnation to stand immune from its mockery and folly. Second, if we substitute "modernism" for "humanism" in Etlin's critique, it exhibits what Helmut Lethen has identified as the tendency to split modernism in half, and it ignores the fact that modernism already contains the postmodern critique. Etlin wants to ignore postmodern critique because of its radical skepticism, whereas I would like to assign it a more appropriate place within a modernist humanism, as a powerful cleansing tool sweeping away the fraudulent and the rigidly conventional. With that demystification accomplished, a space is cleared for the modernist humanist to establish a sure foundation upon which something healthy can be built. The early modern humanists did this for their culture, and, I argue, the modernist humanists did the same for theirs.

Faced with radically new conditions and information about the world in which they live, Rabelais, More, and Erasmus enacted scathing critiques of what these new conditions and new facts had thrown into doubt. They show a newfound ability to critique, with jesting and mockery, established institutions and practices; yet these three writers—along with many other writers and pedagogues of the time—anxiously looked to ancient texts as guideposts and landmarks by which to steer into the new cultural territory that their mockery opened up. The Greek and Roman cultures, along with the Christian Bible with the story of Incarnation as its pivotal plot, became the basis for their defining of the human being and our potential. The dignity of the human person, our potential for nobility and honor, are taken over from the classical texts and conflated with Christian theology to become the basis of their understanding of the human being. Arthur Kinney has described what he calls a "humanist poetics" as having a dual purpose: humanist in its concern for human dignity and humanist in its development of a poetics inherited from the classics (44). His fundamental attitude toward Continental humanism was that it was attempting to find a poetics capable of cherishing the old and the new, of finding ancient models to be used as a stable ground against which or within which new signs and new meanings could be located (36–38). Feeling as if they were living under radically new conditions for meaning and signification, they retrieved ancient texts and set them up as stable and permanent in value and meaning so as to be able to engage with the radically new and open-ended events of their day. If this sounds similar to the way we describe certain modernists who were in love with the past, such as Pound and Eliot, or the way I described the plots of the stories from Borges and Kafka, it might be because these two periods—the early sixteenth century and the early twentieth century—shared the same fundamental problems concerning meaning and identity.

The events of the nineteenth and early twentieth century were similarly dislocating, especially in the advances in technology that created a new material existence for humanity and in the development of certain "human sciences" that aspired to explain human nature in scientific terms. The place of the individual in these systems became urgently felt, and Kafka's texts are the great expression of the nightmare for the individual caused by these developing bureaucracies of meaning. These bureaucratic systems attack the autonomy and authority of the individual, a belief in the sovereign self and its freedom to think and to act independently of cultural impositions. These bureaucracies of meaning attack the very concept of transcendence and the possibility of a transcendent self, which I take to be the foundation of humanism and, by extension, the humanities. From structural linguistics—which Ferdinand de Saussure invented at the turn of the twentieth century—we learn about systems of meaning we can apply to bureaucracies: there is no transcendental signified to halt the play of meaning but only the endless deferral of signification through a detour of signs. There is no individual in a world of bureaucracies, only a variety of constructed roles (or "constituted subjectivities") circulating endlessly through a prison house of deferral, never halting because there is no transcendent self to ground the roles or subjectivities. As Joseph K. learns in *The Trial*, one can search for the truth in any number of institutions—the law, the church, the arts—only to be continually frustrated and rebuffed. The individual learns that no institution can explain him to himself, that no system of meaning has the answer to the questions he urgently poses. He is sent from one to another, as if the truth is constantly deferred and as if his movement will be endless deferral until death.

The threat of these systems to the individual is a threat to humanism as well, for the transcendent human self, a self that is anterior to and above any cultural or social context or set of conditions, is the basis of any humanism. But these systems present a more troubling obstacle to an Enlightenment humanism than to the kind that originated with the early modern humanists. The "old stable ego" that D. H. Lawrence disdained and rejected is the self of Descartes' cogito and Kant's moral imperatives, and not the prerational self of the early modern humanists, who delighted in folly and nonsense more than in logic and rational argument. The humanists I describe, both the early modern and the modernist variety, did not seek the self in logic and rationality but in feeling, the domain that Erasmus described as under the sway of Folly's playfulness. And the difference between the two is broad, for the self of the early modern humanists does not fall into dogmatic rigidity and demand adherence to absolute views about most of the values of its culture as Enlightenment humanism does; instead this humanism allows for, and actively encourages, skeptical debunking and mockery of established centers of authority. It finds in Incarnation a principle that supports the dignity of human being in a nonrational but nonetheless deeply felt hope for higher meaning and destiny, while at the same time it allows the changing world to change and develop and, in this continual change, to place most other values in continual conflict. There was no need for the early modern humanists or their modernist counterparts to insist on rigid adherence to traditional values, but rather in both groups there was a delight in iconoclastic debunking of cherished truths and an excitement in clearing the ground of newly exposed frauds. In the perspectives of both historical groups of humanists there ought to be little sign of reactionary righteousness about the dangers of relativity, for most cultural values are relative and subject to change. The self that remains in these humanisms—or in this kind of humanism, for the two groups shared a single humanist vision and orientation—is grounded in a permanent sense of its own higher dignity and destiny, but it refuses to fall into the mistake of blindly worshipping the past or its institutions. It is both debunking and preserving, debunking the institutions that try to construct the self in fabrications that are not genuine or true and preserving the prerational self that can hope and believe and love.

Again Toulmin's fundamental contribution to my thinking is his sense of the dating of modernity and of finding two distinct origins for it, one in Cartesian certainty that leads to Kantian universality and the other in the skeptical and playful critiques of the early moderns. He has sketched a history for the development of modernity, beginning in the 1630s with Descartes and Galileo and developing in the 1680s with Newton and Locke and in the 1780s with Kant and the American and French revolutions. Up to this point, the rational and stable ego of Descartes had a happy development and reached its epitome with Kant's projecting of the self as the source of absolute moral judgments. To continue this dating of modernity into the nineteenth and twentieth centuries, in the 1850s—in the aftermath of the 1848 revolutions—there were Karl Marx and Charles Darwin, who placed the self in the powerful defining contexts of political history for Marx and of natural history for Darwin; toward the end of the nineteenth century there was the work of Nietzsche, who undermined all traditional values, and the texts of Emile Durkheim, who founded the new "science" of sociology in which the individual self is less interesting than the behaviors of groups and institutions; in 1900 came the first of Sigmund Freud's published findings in the newly invented discipline of psychoanalysis, in which the self is largely unconscious of its own motivations and of most of its operations. Then came 1922—with the publication of *Ulysses* and *The Waste Land,* as well as Virginia Woolf's *Jacob's Room* among other notable works—a year of great literary experiment that is also known for the full emergence of Freudian theory into Anglo-American culture and the inauguration of modern anthropology, which again loses the individual self in a web of practices and customs that construct the individual's identity and meaning.

These more recent post-Kantian intellectual developments led to a less happy status for the rational cogito. In this obviously reductive sketch of major intellectual events, I want to emphasize the precipitous decline in fortune of the rational cogito, from the freedom of Kantian moral authority to a steadily narrowing sense of the individual's capacity for free thought and action. What happens in this intellectual development is a loss of the sense of human agency in a world of large systems and bureaucracies. In fact one can regard the self-proclaimed antihumanism of Louis Althusser as the logical end of this process of weakening of the human self and narrowing of human agency. But there is an ironic double movement for the rational cogito, one that becomes evident when we read a claim such as Paul Sheehan's: "Humanism possesses unwavering confidence, which licenses it to enact schemas of mastery" (20). The humanism that Sheehan describes is not the modernist humanism I describe in this study. The confidence he speaks of is perhaps that of the scientist who, as the heir of the Enlightenment, feels he has reached a position outside culture from which he can begin to engineer a future for the rest of humanity, most of which is reduced to herdlike status to be governed by the transcendent engineer. I would agree that this kind of humanism must be discredited and rooted out, but high modernist texts offer us an alternative humanism that aims at restoring confidence in the nonrational self of the ordinary individual. The intellectual events of the nineteenth and early twentieth centuries have shattered this confidence of the self and reduced it to almost hapless impotence, as my readings of Kafka and Borges suggest. To restore confidence in the self and its genuine agency is the goal of modernist humanism.

There are two main developments that put the "human" into question in the early twentieth century: the rapid rise of a technology that transforms culture into unrecognizably new forms of terror and luxury and the rise of human sciences—especially psychology, sociology, and anthropology—that attempt to explain human beings systematically and scientifically.

Foucault described the newness of the human sciences in *The Order of Things,* asking us to wonder how suddenly man became an object of his own knowledge and also if man is about to be erased as a category for our critical investigation. He pointed to psychoanalysis and ethnology as the two most developed of these sciences, and it is these two sciences that most affect the character of the modernist period. Michael North has noted that both of these sciences were becoming successfully institutionalized during the 1920s, pointing out that the year 1922 was not only the year of great innovation in literature with the publication of *The Waste Land* and *Ulysses* but also the annus mirabilis for anthropology, with the publication of groundbreaking studies by Bronislaw Malinowski and A. R. Radcliffe-Brown. The anthropological method placed the human self in a complex web of social practices and meanings that he or she is helpless to understand or control. In fact those who do become conscious of their own practices and identity—as constructed by the web of social signification—shatter the illusion that they are natural and real. Having attained self-consciousness, the anthropologist is the one who sees most clearly that there is no natural or transcendent self. The dual perspective of the anthropologist is that he is the one who sees most clearly the constructed nature of the self and that, in this very act of seeing, he has risen above that into the emptiness of an abstract universalism. Also during the 1920s, Freud's work became increasingly popularized and was at the same time the subject of violent critique, as writers who sought to secure human agency felt that psychoanalysis was offering an explanation of our behavior as determined by events outside our control and by forces that are not subject to rational thought. As North has demonstrated, these two human sciences became important to the popular and intellectual cultures of the 1920s, and both threatened the older, Enlightenment-based views of human agency and independence. To use language inspired by Althusser, these sciences threatened to replace the free individual with the constructed subject.

"Modernist humanism" is the phrase I want to inaugurate as I discuss some of the classic texts of modernism as working on behalf of the individual to find a way to establish a foundation for a new humanism, one that can provide scathing critiques of the developments that were threatening the status of the individual and, at the same time, to locate a ground on which a humanist culture might be restored and maintained in an age that was becoming dominated by intellectual and political systems that diminished the individual and reduced his prestige and potential for agency. The literary texts of a modernist humanism combine the skepticism of the postmodern critique with innovations in technique and style designed to reinvent the human and humanism. They seek to do for the modernist period what the early modern humanists did for theirs.

The goal of the analyses in this study is to respond to such institutional threats and to demonstrate how the literature of modernism can be read as a great and sustained effort to reject these systems and restore the individual to his rightful place as a sovereign self capable of free thought and agency. My understanding of the objection to humanism from the contemporary perspective of postmodern critique is that this concept of the individual as sovereign subject capable of escaping from the influences of a corrupt and decadent culture is under attack. Those who call for, announce, or merely describe the end of the human and humanism most often do so in light of postmodern analyses that make this concept (in their eyes) untenable. One of the most forceful expressions of this critique is offered in William Spanos's *The End of Education*. Spanos wants to replace the terms "poststructural" and "postmodern" with the term "posthuman," arguing that postmodern analyses have so thoroughly dismantled the concept of the sovereign self that we are entering a new era where—in describing a kind of education to be pursued by universities—we are no longer tied to concepts of the human and its attendant categories of the self and the individual.

The work of Charles Taylor is helpful in formulating a proper attitude toward the issues of selfhood and humanism. In his monumental *Sources of the Self*, Taylor sought to describe "the making of the modern identity," and one of his cardinal propositions is that there is a need for a fundamental self that can be the basis for a humanism, for a theory of human rights, a self outside culture and cultural difference that can be the ground for agency and autonomy (12–17). He sketches the history of the self from Plato through the twentieth century, emphasizing the more problematic fate of the self after Descartes. Descartes and the Enlightenment in general developed a mechanistic view of the world, including the body, and posited a complete chasm between the mind and the material world, which the mind must seek to control through its rational powers (144–45). The world has become disenchanted, emptied of feeling and passion, and made into a machine to be run regularly: "Rational control is a matter of mind dominating a disenchanted world of matter" (152). This is the theory of the self that becomes arrogant and dangerous; this is the "sovereign subject" that Spanos laments and that postmodern critics want to dismantle and move beyond, but it is not the only conception of the self possible for the modern world. A late chapter in Taylor's book sketches his sense of literary history from the Romantics to the modernists, which coincides with my general purposes, as the poets seek to oppose this self and construct a self based on feeling (459–65). Taylor claims that the Romantics turned to nature to combat the hold of mechanistic and utilitarian categories on our lives, while the modernists—he mentions Pound and Eliot frequently—turned to the retrieval of the experience of interiority.

Taylor shares my sense that the modernist period was an urgent moment in our history, as the technological successes of the material and scientific worldview led to a naturalism that wanted the world to be neutral, to be void of feeling or life. This worldview is disenchanted and disembodied. But naturalism, for Taylor, contains another related danger: it insists on doing away with all moral frameworks, wanting instead a value-free view of the world. Taylor argues that without a moral framework, there can be no sense of identity that can be the basis for autonomy and agency. The situation is grave. No longer is a moral framework given, as it might have been a given for Dante; the problem is not that there are competing moral frameworks (though that is the case); worse, naturalism wants the elimination of all moral frameworks, and that is tantamount to an elimination of the self as a functioning category. In the modern age, the moral framework became the object of a quest (17), and the modernists worked actively to retrieve a moral framework that can become the basis of a moral self.

Like the early modern humanists, the modernist humanists worked to retrieve something from the past that can function as a moral framework, but they also employed the rigorous skepticism of the postmodern critique to clear the ground for this retrieval. My analyses of the literature of this period should not appear retrograde or reactionary, as if I ignore this critique and pretend that it never occurred; nor do I wish to say that the critique itself is entirely wrongheaded and misguided, leading to the demise of Western culture. In fact I want to call my own defense of modernist humanism a postmodern critique as I use its tools and projects to rid the term "humanism" of much that is mere fluff and bluster and return the term to something more concretely based and culturally useful. I want to place a modernist humanism *after* a postmodern critique.

Following the arguments of Helmut Lethen and Sanford Schwartz, I do not think that such a placement is at all anachronistic. Fundamental to my readings of modernist writers in this study is my sense that each of them, to varying degrees, intuited the postmodern critique of culture and included a debunking attitude as central to their concerns. As always for me, Joyce is paramount in this, as *Ulysses* begins with the creation of one of the most engaging mockers in all literature, Buck Mulligan, the opening sensibility that the rest of the novel seeks to answer and overcome. In fact the appropriate literary company for Buck might well be the fools and the "praisers of folly" among the early modern humanists, those figures of derision whose job is to open up new spaces for exploration by debunking traditional authority through an often scathing mockery. In my *Joyce's Modernist Allegory:* Ulysses *and the History of the Novel*, I advanced a reading of Joyce's great novel that observed the author's trying out various stances and perspectives, only to find each possible description and narrative technique inadequate to his purpose, which was to elevate Bloom to the status of epic hero and beyond. *Ulysses* is a text that sweeps away all traditional narrative styles and techniques, including them and admiring them but also inevitably showing them up as partial or inadequate or downright fraudulent. The text debunks the history of the novel as it tries to find a way to present a heroic figure in Leopold Bloom. Joyce's "modernism" is quite postmodern in technique and attitude, but ultimately Joyce managed to establish a style capable of pointing to Bloom as a figure of Christ. Joyce cleared the ground with his scathing postmodern critique for the retrieval of a theistic humanism from our literary history. Postmodern in technique and attitude, it is a modernist humanism in aim and goal.

I begin this study with a chapter on Joyce to develop my understanding of what I consider the central modernist text. And the principle of purposeful mockery and debunking as precedent to more earnest and sober establishment of a center or ground for value is something I take from my earlier book and import to this as central to the modernist project of retrieving and reinventing humanism. Pressing back against Althusser's formulation of ideology and its near absolute control over the construction of the subject as the dominant critique of humanism, I have attempted to establish this modernist humanism. Althusser's critique of the individual and his insistence on ideology as nontranscendible is the most rigorous and most extreme formulation of the postmodern antipathy to the sovereign subject. Althusser sought to reject the humanist individual and replace it with the constituted subject, and I intend to allow his critique to explain one aspect of modernist humanism and then turn against his critique as I show how the modernists attempt to fill in this void.

While Althusser is useful for his extreme version of the postmodern critique of the self and his antihumanism, it is Charles Taylor whose history of the self in the modern era guides my larger argument. Along with Toulmin, Taylor provided a reading of the Enlightenment as a rationalist humanism that demands mastery over a disenchanted world, based on a self that is disembodied and detached. The modernists I describe seek to retrieve a moral framework from a humanist past capable of grounding modern culture in a self that does not demand rational mastery over a disenchanted world but in a self that feels love, a self that actively loves. Taylor has offered a neat schematic map of cultural history that I have borrowed and adapted to my purposes (see especially 495–99). The early modern period advanced a theistic humanism, grounding moral values in a sense of the supernatural; the radical Enlightenment developed a rationalist or naturalist humanism, a disenchanted humanism lacking a sense of the supernatural and therefore losing a sense of the absolute or universal ground for moral judgments; and the Romantic and modernist periods responded to this radical Enlightenment by trying to retrieve the supernatural framework. Joyce, Lewis, Pound, and Eliot all sought to retrieve what Taylor calls a theistic humanism, where a nonhuman (that is, a supernatural) source provides and grounds human values (see especially 506–9).

Each of the chapters in this study makes a distinct contribution to an understanding of "modernist humanism." It is my hope that in the aggregate they form a coherent set of statements that helps us approach the literature of the period with new eyes and with a new appreciation for its place in literary history, as renewing the principles of early modern humanism for the twentieth century.

The first chapter features an analysis of Joyce's *Ulysses,* which occupies a place of privilege in this study for reasons beyond that of mere chronology. The fact that *Ulysses* was begun in 1914 and published in 1922 is significant in itself. The other modernists discussed in this study were all around as early as 1914, but it took well into the 1930s and beyond for them to develop their modernist humanism. Joyce seems to have intuited the need for a renewed humanism earlier than his fellows and on his own, as it were, and he provided them with a valuable example as they were beginning their own literary projects in the late 1910s and early 1920s. It is worth recalling that, from 1917 onward, the other Men of 1914 were reading each episode of *Ulysses* as Joyce was sending them to Pound to place in the *Little Review*. While I am not sure if Joyce needed the historical circumstances surrounding the Great War to spur him to develop his modernist humanism, it does not seem mere coincidence that the others underwent major shifts in their literary projects during the 1930s. My claim is that the extraordinary events of the 1920s and 1930s led the others to their similar projects. In fact an underlying premise of this study is that the extraordinary historical pressures of the period led these high modernist writers to develop modernist humanism. An obvious corollary is that their texts can be read as responses to these extraordinary pressures.

Ulysses is not only the first, but also perhaps the most successful, example of a modernist humanism. Much of the energy of *Ulysses* is devoted to debunking conventions and demystifying pretensions, and Joyce deploys the "postmodern" critique so successfully that many critics see its radical debunking as the novel's essence, but the ultimate aim of *Ulysses* is to fill the space that sweeping skepticism has opened up with something permanent and universal, the feeling of love. Chapter 1 examines how in *Ulysses* Joyce found a way to describe the human body as the necessary site for transcendence and possible redemption. Often the examination of a literary artist's attention to the body serves as an antidote toward unearned claims of transcendence and elevation of spirit, but for Joyce the body is understood in a way that Christian writers, from Saint Augustine forward, have advanced, as the aspect of the human condition that Christian theology embraces and dignifies. The Christian attitude toward the body is strongly and explicitly opposed to the Platonic conception of the body and its sensory apparatus as corrupt and deceptive, an attitude emphasized once again by Descartes and his disembodied flight to the abstract and timeless. Joyce used the mystery of the Incarnation as pivotal doctrine for his purpose of elevating Leopold Bloom toward the height of epic and allegorical status, rising as a Christian ideal of love against the downward tug of gravity on his body. In Joyce (and later with Eliot), we can find an explicitly Christian humanism in the modernist era very like that of the early modern humanists.

In the mid-1930s, after establishing himself as perhaps the most iconoclastic figure in English letters and the least likely to be thought of as humanist (Taylor in fact calls him an antihumanist), Wyndham Lewis wrote something that most critics recognize as new and different for him. The second chapter of this book summarizes certain salient features of Althusser's critique of humanism and selfhood and then examines one of the most politically charged novels of modernism—Lewis's *Revenge for Love*—in that light. This novel appears to follow Althusser's critique quite closely as section after section seeks to demystify the status of the individual in light of a powerful political consciousness that proposes to understand the workings of ideology not only in the public sphere but in the private life as well. *The Revenge for Love* is justly known for its exposure of the many "false bottoms" that pretend to ground our identity and our ideals, bringing to light how what we assumed is natural is only constructed and therefore not "true" or "genuine." But underneath it all, at the end of this novel there is something "at the bottom." It may surprise the reader to discover in Lewis a secret humanist in his ultimate depiction of love as a transcendent human category.

One of the most compelling critiques of modernism is its affinity for and perhaps complicity with reactionary politics of the era. In the third chapter, I study Pound's *Cantos* from a new and unexpected perspective, viewing it as an effort to create a new humanist pedagogy similar to the ones inaugurated in the fifteenth and sixteenth centuries in Europe. Seeing *The Cantos* as a textbook is not a new idea, but to compare it to the "new learning" of the humanists (which is how Pound described his life's work in *Guide to Kulchur*) allows us to approach Pound again as someone who can teach us about knowledge and the process of freeing knowledge from the strangleholds of systematic thought. In an age that was beginning to feel overwhelmed with the sheer quantity of news and information available, Pound sought to find a new way to allow information to circulate and create meaningful knowledge. Of all the modernists in this study, Pound is by far the one whose project, in its first trajectory at any rate, resembles most the Enlightenment project of reason and knowledge, as if the right education can correct errors in politics and economics and begin a process of reform that will create a just world. I first examine the cantos written in the 1930s, when Pound became most interested in creating an American context for his understanding of Benito Mussolini, and I describe Pound's endorsement of Mussolini as the failure of his Enlightenment project of education and reform. But this is only part of the story. Pound was able to sweep away fraudulent claims of U.S. and world history, but he did not have anything sound and healthy to place in the empty space he created. Instead he succumbed to hero worship and a megalomania of his own that led him to see himself as someone who could counsel statesmen. In Pisa, suffering from the failure of his political dream and an incarceration that might end in death, Pound underwent a profound change that also transformed his project. As indicated in the line "Amo ergo sum, and in just that proportion," he learned that the self must be based not on reason but on love. I argue that from Pisa onward Pound developed a profoundly different understanding of the self and of history than he had advanced in the 1930s and through the war years. Pound began as an Enlightenment humanist and ended as a modernist humanist.

I believe that Pound's suffering in Pisa—which was the result of both personal and political disaster—led him to remake his project. A similar split occurred with Eliot. His fullest expression of a modernist humanism is found in the last three of the *Four Quartets,* the ones written after World War II began and five years after the first quartet (originally meant to be a stand-alone poem, his last poem in fact). My fourth and final chapter develops the language of a "modernist humanism" in an examination of the prose of T. S. Eliot, who worked assiduously in the late 1920s and early 1930s (the period of his conversion to Anglicanism) to expose the kind of humanism I have identified as Enlightenment humanism as something well-intentioned but ultimately inadequate. Eliot was most explicit in rejecting the humanism advanced by his teacher Irving Babbitt as lacking something essential, the grounding of an understanding of the human in relation to the supernatural. Eliot acknowledged Dante as the master who showed the proper way to understand the relation of the natural to the human (where Babbitt's humanism stops) and then of the human to the supernatural (which is where Dante continued the thinking about the human). This problem of the human as both within nature and above it relates to the problem of time and the temporal order. If we are bound to the temporal only, then all our judgments are partial and relative, but if we seek some timeless realm safely above the temporal order, then we exhibit a fatal arrogance. It is in the Christian mystery of Incarnation that Eliot could resolve this problem of the human and the divine, the time bound and the timeless. Eliot is important to this study because he is the writer who most explicitly placed his humanism in a Christian context and so most nearly resembles the early modern (or Christian) humanists. To use Taylor's terminology, Eliot rejected the rationalist humanism of the Enlightenment and retrieved a theistic humanism, one rendered adequate for the modern world: a modernist humanism.

The chapters of this book cohere around an effort on the part of the writers in question to find something permanent in human existence that can serve as the basis for a humanism that is not coercive and reactionary but rather playful and uplifting. I do not wish to negate the differences among these writers; the fact that they are in some ways so very different is what makes their shared effort to renew humanism so remarkable. It is as if the times demanded an experimental literature aimed at the successful laying of a foundation for a renewal of humanism capable of elevating and uplifting our sense of the human. It is not a coincidence that the writers studied here are those long-canonized high modernists who have often been celebrated and more recently been subjected to more negative critiques. It is an error in judgment to apply the poststructural or postmodern critique against the modernists without recognizing that modernism itself was poised against the very aspects of modernity that the postmodern critique wants to castigate. Harvey has noted that it is an irony in literary and cultural history that the very modernists once thought to be working against modernity and the Enlightenment project "were taken over and canonized by the establishment" (36), the very establishment they had worked to subvert and replace. We need to correct this error in judgment and place the high modernists back in their proper place. These are the writers who managed to anticipate the very critiques that have been turned on them, and a more just evaluation of these writers is needed. I want to locate my definition of modernist humanism squarely in the literary texts of this period and to use them as the basis for a humanistic theory capable of restoring not only these texts but also literary culture in general to a place of privilege in our culture's efforts to define our potential.

1

Bloom and the Vulgar Body
The Christian Imagination and Modernist Humanism

In *Ulysses* James Joyce achieved the first and perhaps also the highest form of modernist humanism. Written between 1914 and 1921, that is during and immediately after the Great War, the novel deploys both the most sweeping and devastating critique of Joyce's literary and cultural heritage and at the same time the most satisfying renewal of a humanism that can be traced back to the early Middle Ages and on through the Renaissance. Unlike the other modernists in this study, Joyce was not directly responding to historical circumstance, though he might in some way have been moved to an urgency by the conditions of this volatile era. Rather he seems to have been deeply involved in a profound meditation on an issue that had been plaguing him already and had surfaced in *A Portrait of the Artist as a Young Man* (1916). It is my contention that Joyce had been preparing for a Christian response to the Platonism of his culture.

This might not seem like an urgent issue, but Joyce made it one. The urgency lay in his need to find a way to escape successfully from a paralytic culture that seemed to doom most individuals to confinement within its labyrinth (which is how it plays out in *A Portrait of the Artist*) or in his need to find a way to elevate human being to heroic or even allegorical status (the issue in *Ulysses*). The problem for both novels is gravity, that incessant downward pull on anything that tries to move upward. It is a question of how to be Daedalus and not Icarus, how to become a Christ-like hero immune to the deflating mockery of a cynical culture. The problem of *Ulysses* may be mockery, but the solution to this problem cannot be the Platonic one. For Joyce that solution fails miserably because the Platonic denial of the body and the material world makes it susceptible to the powerful debunking of a cynical culture epitomized by Buck Mulligan. So Joyce was responding to the Platonic and Cartesian view of humanity and humanism by emphasizing the role of the body in human existence.

Joyce seems to have been aware that Enlightenment humanism may lead to two opposing positions that both suffer from serious error. Heading in one direction, the Enlightenment can lead to a powerful focus on the body and the material world as the horizon of all values, denying any nonhuman or supernatural grounding for understanding humanity. This is what we call naturalism, and it is represented in *Ulysses* most powerfully in the character of Buck Mulligan and in the initial style of the novel. But as the mind/body split begun by Plato is exacerbated in the Cartesian thesis, the Enlightenment can lead to a conviction that the mind can become independent of the body, that a human being may fly above the body and the material world and achieve transcendence. This idea dates back to Plato and is most fully represented in the "Scylla and Charybdis" episode by the figure of George Russell. These are the extremes that Joyce's retrieval and renewal of a Christian humanism seeks to avoid.

In *Ulysses* Joyce wrote a complex book about the simple theme of love, and he took on as his primary challenge in presenting this ideal perhaps the most permanent aspect of human being that threatens our claims to any ideal: our material nature, our physical bodies. As Richard Ellmann wrote in his introduction to Hans Gabler's edition of *Ulysses,* Gabler identified more clearly and definitively than in preceding editions that the mysterious "word known to all men" is "love," and "Joyce's theme in *Ulysses* is simple. He invoked the most elaborate means to present it" (ix). This chapter focuses on the "elaborate means" employed to present the ideal of love as embodied in the figure of Leopold Bloom. We may take "embodied" almost literally.

Joyce is part of a tradition of writers who have focused on the body as a problem to be addressed and understood. The points developed in this chapter derive primarily from imaginative texts written by Christian writers in the West, beginning with Saint Augustine and Dante, continuing through Rabelais and Jonathan Swift, and focusing finally on Joyce as the modernist fulfillment of a distinctively Christian paradigm of writers who have felt the urgency of depicting the body as the necessary site of God's redemptive action. This Christian tradition of imaginative writing is squarely opposed to the Platonic and the later Cartesian views that separate the mind from the body and therefore lay the foundation for a humanism that is above the body, outside time and outside history. A Christian humanism and in Joyce's case a modernist humanism are opposed to a rationalist humanism stemming ultimately from Plato and receiving its latest and most urgent formulation after Descartes.

The Christian faith is founded squarely on the twin mysteries of the Incarnation and the Resurrection, both of which focus on the human body as indispensable in God's plan of salvation: the Incarnation, in which the Word is made flesh, in which an aspect of the divinity takes on human form; and the Resurrection, in which this God-made-flesh rises from the dead in a resurrected body, which he presents in various manifestations as a still human body to his incredulous disciples. Defiantly opposed to Platonic notions of the truth as purely ethereal and wholly intellectual, the Christian faith values the body and sees it as perfectible, respects the body and its claims as an integral and essential part of the redemptive plan. In fact one of the main effects of making Bloom a Jew is to rescue Christianity from the ill effects of Platonism and to return it to its Judaic foundation in which the body and its life in history are fully respected.

This "Christian tradition of the body" is relevant to a modernist humanism because it provided its most important imaginative writer with a tradition of important literary texts that did indeed focus on the human body, not as an obstacle to be overcome but as a nontranscendible aspect of the human condition that is capable of being understood in ways that are not ironic or debunking. The modernist humanism I describe is not shy of addressing the body and its concerns but instead delights in its depiction and works steadily and well in ennobling humanity in this effort. Too often attention to the body and the material conditions of human existence have led to a debunking of our aspirations for higher things, as if the reminder of our bodily nature is enough to debunk spirit and ideals. In this Christian tradition, the body can be described most fully in all its aspects and still not be an obstacle to the ideal. Joyce's *Ulysses* is the culmination of this tradition of Christian writing, and Joyce is squarely at the center of a "modernist humanism." Joyce worked to retrieve a kind of humanism that avoids the pitfalls of the rationalist humanism leading to naturalism and the Platonic/Cartesian humanism that denies the body in an altogether too easy transcendence and is thus an easy target for that naturalism. Joyce had access to a tradition dating back to the Gospels, and in *Ulysses* he made this ancient tradition the foundation for his retrieval and renewal of a Christian humanism in the modern era.

Countering Plato: Augustine, Dante, and the Incarnation

Like so many of our intellectual problems, this one begins with Plato. With a glance at Plato's attack on the body and its senses in the *Phaedo,* one can see how the Western tradition of metaphysics was launched as strongly opposed to the body and its sensory apparatus. In this dialogue Plato made what appears a fairly simple and very sweeping distinction between the soul and the body—and the body comes off quite badly. Plato clearly asserted that the body is an enemy in our pursuit of truth and that the philosopher's entire life is a "rehearsal for death" (what Grube translates as "practise for dying and death," 64a) in that the seeker after truth spends his life trying to move as far away from the body as possible and attempting to intuit the truth with pure intellect. The true philosopher must disdain all the "so-called pleasures" of the body, which is explicitly called "an obstacle" in the pursuit of truth (65b). It is a movement inside, away from the senses and into the pure mind, which alone can perceive truth and ideal forms. "If we are ever to have pure knowledge, we must escape from the body and observe matters in themselves with the soul by itself" (66e). The body and its senses deceive and mislead. We must avoid the "contamination of the body's folly" and its "infection" in our pursuit of Ideal Forms. "As long as we have a body and our soul is fused with such an evil we shall never adequately attain what we desire, which we affirm to be the truth" (66b). The body is an evil to be overcome by the philosopher in the pursuit of truth.

This has always struck me as an odd place to begin the pursuit of wisdom, with the body and the senses dismissed as obstacles in the path of the philosopher who seeks what we must call disembodied truth. It is important to note that the ideal realm is wholly associated with the soul, and the body is clearly its antagonist.

Saint Augustine squarely and clearly opposed this aspect of Platonic philosophy in his *Confessions,* making the key to his conversion the Christian doctrine of the Incarnation. Augustine early on recognized that the use of rhetoric for mere power of persuasion was potentially fraudulent and therefore immoral, and also early on he decided that he would devote his life to the pursuit of truth, trying to reach upward to God by rising above earthly concerns and seeking some sort of heavenly truth. He credited Cicero for developing this love of truth, and he spent many fruitless hours searching for the right path, the right method, for reaching this truth. But the error of Platonism plagued the Roman world[1] in its adherence to the metaphysics of the Greeks, leading Augustine to the belief that truth was disembodied and abstract. His attempts to fly upward to the disembodied, ethereal truth keep failing because of the flesh, which weighed him down and brought him back to earth; the weight of the body dragged him back down to its needs and desires. The body is a problem, as the Platonists insist, but it is not to be escaped or degraded or denied. Its needs must be respected, its desires understood.

And this is where the Incarnation comes in. In his effort to lift himself upward (and Augustine used the language of rising and falling constantly), he was reading those philosophers whom he called the "Platonists." He read in them the same kinds of values and moral statements as he heard from Christian preachers and as he read in Christian texts. "But I did not read in them that *the Word was made flesh and came to dwell among us*" (7.9). What he did not read in the Platonists was anything like the mystery of the Incarnation. Every attempt he made to rise was unsuccessful because of the weight of the body and its sinfulness: "Your beauty drew me to you, but soon I was dragged away from you by my own weight and in dismay I plunged again into the things of this world. The weight I carried was the habit of the flesh" (7.17). He could not sustain his upward rise to God "until I embraced the *mediator between God and men, Jesus Christ, who is a man, like them,* also rules *as God over all things, blessed for ever.* He *was calling to me and saying I am the way; I am the truth and life.* He it was who united with our flesh that food which I was too weak to take; *for the Word was made flesh* so that your Wisdom, by which you created all things, might be milk to suckle us in infancy" (7.18). In the Incarnation, Christ becomes the mediator between God and men, partaking in both natures and showing men the way to become higher and move upward. It is the Incarnation that enables us to know God and not the withdrawal from the body into the pure intellect as the Platonists advocate. Christ in the Incarnation allows human being to reach upward toward God without denying the body and our physical nature.

The Incarnation provides a way to understand the body that does not ask us to deny the body, nor does it require—in the opposite movement that we are more accustomed to in our more ironic age—that we deny the higher realms of the ideal and reduce all to the body. This mystery of Christian belief allows the body to remain the often vulgar thing it is while at the same time allowing it to aspire to higher things. For as God humbles himself to take on this mortal and often vulgar flesh (and this humility is also important), the Incarnation also ennobles the flesh as it becomes the container of the divine. The body and its needs are made legitimate, worthy, and valid by the Incarnation. When in the Resurrection Christ shows his risen body and insists that it is a fully human one with its needs for food,[2] the body is even made more worthy of our attention and in fact something not to be transcended but perfected. This allowed Augustine to understand the nature of the body and its desires, which were plaguing him and seemed as if they would never allow for his movement toward truth. One of Augustine's most searching meditations is on the nature of beauty and human desire. He asks why would a benevolent God create a world filled with beautiful things that we desire to enjoy or possess and then make the flesh too sluggish to ever enjoy them or take possession? The early books of *Confessions* document how desire for Augustine became overwhelmingly powerful and how it became an itch that increased its demands the more he scratched, leading him to pursue with great energy the things of the world. But the itch only became worse and the scratching created sores and festering wounds. By embracing the Incarnation, Augustine understood that the desires of the body are not be denied but mastered, not to be rejected or overcome but to be directed, by a newfound will, away from the things of the world and toward their Creator. Desire is not sin, nor is it virtue. It is an energy of human being that must be properly directed. The body is not so corrupt that it must be rejected. It is perfectible; it is redeemable.

One final lesson that Augustine gleans from the Incarnation is humility:

> None of this is contained in the Platonists' books. Their pages have not the mien of the true love of God. They make no mention of the tears

of confession or of the *sacrifice that you will never disdain, a broken spirit, a heart that is humbled and contrite,* nor do they speak of the salvation of your people, *the city adorned like a bride, the foretaste of your Spirit,* or the chalice of our redemption. In them no one sings *No rest has my soul but in God's hands; to him I look for deliverance. I have no other stronghold, no other deliverer but him; safe in his protection, I fear no deadly fall.* In them no one listens to the voice which says *Come to me all you that labour.* They disdain his teaching because *he is gentle and humble of heart. For you have hidden all this from the wise and revealed it to little children.* (7.21)

Augustine discovered that it is arrogance to believe that we can on our own move upward away from the darkness of the body and earthly things toward the light of the heavenly truth; it is arrogance to believe that we do not have to turn to Christ to begin the movement of our redemption; it is arrogance to believe that we do not have to be humble in order to receive wisdom and approach the truth. The Platonists want to ignore our bodies, which weigh us down and keep dragging us back to earth. The Platonic image of upward flight toward a disembodied truth is one of arrogance and presumption. Augustine learned that the humility of God, who humbled himself to take on flesh, is our model. We must accept the humility of being fleshly creatures as Christ accepted the indignities and vulgarities of the flesh. In this humility we can finally begin the move upward.

As many commentators have pointed out, Dante's *Comedia* is also informed by the mystery of the Incarnation, a point well established in Charles Singleton's exposition of allegory and John Freccero's ingenious readings of various episodes in the poem. What I want to contribute to this discussion of the role of Incarnation in the *Comedia* is an analysis of Dante's depiction of the body, especially his own body as he undergoes his spiritual itinerary, and his depiction of the problem of language as inherently fraudulent. These two issues unite in and are resolved by the Incarnation, the Word made flesh.

In the very first canto of *Inferno*, when Dante tries to climb to the top of the hill so he can once again see and be guided by the sun, his ascent is blocked almost immediately by the three beasts that represent human sinfulness. This is the first and most dramatic instance of Dante's quarrel with Plato. Dante follows Augustine in having our sinful nature bring us back down from any easy flight upward to the light. According to Freccero, "The Platonic conversion toward the light is doomed to failure because it neglects to take account of man's fallen condition" (9). What is needed is humility: "the descent in humility helps remove the barrier that philosophy leaves intact" (9). Even the voyage of Ulysses in canto 26 of *Inferno* is read as an arrogant attempt to go right up to the light of God: "the voyage was an allegory for the flight of the soul to transcendent truth.... Dante's descent into hell enables him to reach the shore which Ulysses was only able to make out at a distance, a contrast that evokes ... Augustine's distinction between philosophical presumption and Christian conversion" (15). Dante must humble himself in a descent to hell in order to be able to begin the more painful ascent up Mount Purgatory, pulled downward by gravity to the center of the earth where Satan is eternally fixed in ice. The mortal body that Dante bears drags him downward and makes him unable to enact the Platonic flight to the light of truth. *Inferno* ends as Dante "passes the point to which weights are drawn from every part" (34.110–11), the force of gravity pulling him down to Satan and as far away from God as possible.

But this movement downward made necessary by the body is also the beginning of a successful movement upward, as Dante and Virgil find a hidden track on the other side of Satan that brings them out to the other side of the globe and onto Mount Purgatory, which they are allowed, even encouraged, to climb. Blocked of an easy ascent up the hill to the light of the sun back in the first canto of *Inferno*, Dante now may participate in an arduous climb up Mount Purgatory. In *Purgatorio* Dante's body becomes a dominant focal point, as the penitent souls frequently marvel that someone in the flesh is climbing the mountain of purgation. In one of the first instances of this in *Purgatorio*, Dante uses language that encourages the reader to connect this scene to one of John's Resurrection stories. Seeing the penitent souls stunned by what appears before them, Virgil says, "Without your asking I declare to you that this is a human body you see, by which the sun's light is divided on the ground. Do not marvel, but believe" (3.94–97). Just as Jesus invited Thomas to believe in his resurrected body, so Virgil asks the wondering souls to have faith: it is our mortal bodies that will be cleansed and perfected, as we become like Christ in his Resurrection. Dante continues to meditate on this story from John's Gospel when one of the souls, Manfred, whom Dante apparently knew in life, asks Dante to recognize him through his wound: "'Look now!' he said, and showed me a wound high on his breast; then said, smiling, 'I am Manfred'" (3.110–12). It is by the wounds we suffer during earthly existence that we are known, as Christ is known by his wounds.[3] As both Singleton and Freccero emphasize, in the *Comedia* Dante is on a spiritual itinerary allowing him to recognize that the pattern of his life is approaching the pattern of Christ's, as the individual human life has the capacity to participate in the mystery of Incarnation. Dante is bringing a body up Mount Purgatory that can become like the resurrected Christ's.

Purgatorio is the only part of the *Comedia* in which time is still operative, as the souls must spend the amount of time in each terrace that is required for the purgation of that particular sin for that particular sinner. It is the only section of the *Comedia* in which change occurs; the penitent souls become purified as they suffer and gradually move upward toward their great goal. As such, *Purgatorio* is the section most concerned with depicting Dante's human body as it undergoes a process of change and overcomes the ill effects of history, the wounds that being in space and time have placed on him in his body. It is the only section of the *Comedia* that Dante considers truly an epic, which he implies when he invokes Calliope as its muse in its first lines. *Purgatorio* is an epic because it recounts Dante's overcoming of the conditions of history and his heroic, but wholly personal, achievement of reaching back to human origins in Eden. Dante brings a full bodily existence, scars and all, as he makes his upward climb to Edenic purity. In this way he is imitating Christ, who in the Resurrection still has a human body scarred from his being in history.

When Dante finally arrives at the base of the mountain and just before he begins the penitential program, an angel places seven *P*'s on his forehead, each *P* representing one of the seven deadly sins. This sinfulness is what weighs him down and makes the ascent hard. But the spiritual law governing the physics of this mountain are explained to Dante early on: "This mountain is such that it is always hard at the start below and the higher one goes it is less toilsome; therefore when it will seem to thee so pleasant that going up will be for thee as going downstream in a boat, then thou shalt be at the end of this path" (4.88–94). At the end of each terrace, one of the *P*'s is erased by an angel; Dante becomes lighter and the ascent easier, until there is no effort at all in his movement upward. It is sin, and ultimately not the body, that drags the human downward and makes the Platonic flight impossible. Once sin is purged, the body is made perfect, and Dante rises "naturally." For the Christian poet, the body is perfectible and not to be scorned and degraded as the Platonists insist. When one of the penitent souls just happens to finish his centuries-long purgation during Dante's journey, his successful attainment of purity is signaled by angelic voices singing "Gloria in excelsis Deo," just as angels did at the Nativity of the Christ; and Dante compares himself and Virgil to those "shepherds who first heard those words" (20.136, 140). The purified soul is perfected, becoming like the Christ as he entered space and time in human form. The body will not be rejected but perfected in the Christian imagination. In fact Virgil's last words to Dante indicate that human desire is perfectible and that Dante has accomplished this great feat: "Free, upright and whole is thy will and it were a fault not to act on its bidding; therefore over thyself I crown and mitre thee" (27.140–42). The body and its desires, which so frightened Augustine that he seems to advocate denial and asceticism, are perfectible in Dante's understanding, and Dante has felt his body become lighter and lighter as he purges sin after sin. He defies gravity, being more able to ascend as the ascent becomes more arduous, as he feels lighter and lighter. The purified and perfected body obeys different laws than it does in its fallen state. As Beatrice explains to Dante in canto 2 of *Paradiso*, "Thou shouldst no more wonder at thy ascent than at a stream falling from a mountain-height to the foot; it would be a wonder in thee if, freed from hindrance, thou hadst remained below, as on earth would be stillness in living flame" (2:136–41). Dante is ascending through the various spheres of heaven as Christ performed his Ascension, fully in a human body freed of the hindrance of sin. It is natural for him to be able to do so.

The purgatorial itinerary is as much for Dante's language as it is for his body and his desires. The body and the word both are purged, as Dante gets ready to become like Christ, the Word made flesh. This is the double focus of *Purgatorio*: as the body is purified and its desire perfected, Dante is learning how to write a higher poetry, better and purer than what he had accomplished so far. Since poetry is about desire, the perfecting of desire is intimately bound to the perfecting of its poetic language.

This pedagogical component of *Purgatorio* begins right away, with Cato's response to Virgil's narrative intended to curry Cato's favor, "There is no need for fair words." Fair words, ironically enough, have the potential to be hellish, as Ulysses shows us in canto 26 of *Inferno*. Virgil's rhetorical powers are to be trusted less in *Purgatorio* than they were in *Inferno*, just as his authority as a guide is diminished in *Purgatorio*, where he acts more as a companion than a guide. We watch Dante develop his own "purgatorial poetics" as he proceeds up the mountain, able to see more clearly and more fully as he ascends. He must learn how to write about the heightened sensual experience of purgatory. In hell the sun was silent and the light was mute. Here he must learn to see more than he is used to and to record it. In *Paradiso* he will write the poetry of light; he will allow the sun and more brilliant lights to speak.

Dante develops a theory of language in the *Comedia*. For him language is inherently fraudulent, and one of the main themes of the *Comedia* is Dante's effort to find a true language that we can trust. This problem of language as inherently fraudulent was also a major theme in Augustine's *Confessions*, which is centered on the notion of hearing God's voice with the ears of the heart. Augustine was a teacher of rhetoric and became increasingly suspicious about the tendency of language to mislead and deceive. In fact Augustine noted how the Platonists are too arrogant to listen to the voice of God in their hearts, and the plot of *Confessions* moves toward the garden scene in which he was finally able, after having embraced the Incarnation, to hear the voice of God in the singsong nonsense of children saying, "Take it and read, take it and read" (8.12). Having rejected rhetoric as a way to truth, he achieved the humility needed to discern how God chose to speak to him.

The problem of language is pervasive in the *Comedia*, beginning from the first moment Virgil is present, when he is described as someone whose voice seems weak from long silence. It is Dante's failure to have been listening to Virgil's voice—his failure to have been reading and attending to the words of Virgil—that is indicated by this seeming weakness of Virgil. When Dante expresses fear to go on the journey Virgil describes in canto 2 of *Inferno*, Virgil's response is to tell a long story that comes to focus on Beatrice's solicitude for Dante. This story from the poet's mouth inspires Dante: "Thou hast so disposed my heart with desire for the journey by thy words that I have returned to my first intent" (2.136–38). The poet's words encourage and inspire the pilgrim to make this dangerous and difficult voyage.

So the poet's language has this rhetorical power. It becomes problematic most vividly in *Inferno* when Dante encounters the great figure of Ulysses, who is damned as a fraudulent counselor. Dante begins canto 26 of *Inferno* by expressing the great care he is about to take in recording this encounter: he will curb his powers more than he is wont. Because of Ulysses' excess, Dante wants to make his readers aware of his own self-control and rhetorical discipline. For Ulysses narrates his ability to lead his men on a doomed and (for himself at least) damned voyage. He uses all his skills as a speaker to inspire his men to go on this dangerous voyage, and the resemblance of his speaking ability to Virgil's rhetorical power is the crucial point. Language can be used fraudulently just as easily as it can be used truthfully—maybe much more easily, as attention to all the sins of fraud in Dante's lower hell may make us aware. And the association of Ulysses' voyage with the Platonists' desire for transcendence makes us wonder about the fraudulence of such calls to the light. So Dante is anxious about his own language: is he like Ulysses, leading his reader on a dangerous journey that can end in doom, or is he like Virgil, called by heaven to lead the reader on the true way to the heavenly city?

We see this anxiety early in *Inferno*, in a canto that at first might not seem to be about the poet's own language. In canto 5 Dante enters the second circle of hell, the first where sinners are punished, and witnesses the punishment of the lustful as they whirl about helplessly in a hellish storm. Their lack of will is underscored by their punishment. When Dante calls two of them over to speak with him, they must respond "such force had my loving call." His call has a force they cannot resist. Francesca speaks about her sin, and it is not original on my part to note how bookish her speech is, how much like a courtly romance she sounds. She has learned to speak like the books she loved to read. By internalizing their language, she takes on its ethics as well, which all seem to suggest that "Love" is the agent in a lover's life and the individual has no ability to overcome its power. When Dante hears this he asks for the specifics of her sin, and she tells the story about how she and her brother-in-law were reading an Arthurian romance that led them (against their will, as the courtly ethos would have it) to commit adultery. She blames the book for her sin, and when Dante hears this he "falls like a dead body falls."

Why does Dante faint? Among the various reasons that make sense and add to our sense of the richness of this scene, the one that is most compelling to me is Dante's own possible complicity in her sin. For what is Dante in the year 1300 but a writer of love poetry that might indeed be part of the romantic world Francesca has so deeply made her own? If the writer of the book is to blame (in addition to the adulterers themselves, for obviously God has not absolved them from their guilt merely because of their culture), then Dante might be damned for some sort of fraudulent counsel himself. Dante took great pains in *Convivio* and *Vita Nuova* to reassess his poetry, not as erotic love poems but as philosophical poems about divine love and Beatrice. He is anxious about his writing here, and Ulysses teaches exactly what he had to fear.

Inferno presents a subtle and profound lesson in the possibilities of discovering a true language, one that can be trusted to lead to redemption. Deep in the lowest hell Dante hears the heartbreaking story of Ugolino and his sons. Part of the drama of the scene is to note if Dante loses the faculty of rational judgment as he absorbs the sorrowful details of Ugolino's last days. If Ugolino were not a treacherous man, he would not be placed in this part of hell, and to question the placement would be to question God's justice. And this Dante does not do. Ugolino must have been a traitor, and he did not repent to earn God's mercy.

This failure to repent is the most important part of Ugolino's narration, and Freccero has analyzed this scene most thoroughly. Ugolino misses the opportunity to repent when he fails to hear in his sons' voices the sacrifice of Christ. For they offer their flesh for him to eat, as Christ has given humankind his body in the Eucharist. Ugolino most likely does eat his sons' bodies after they die, and this descent into cannibalism is a grotesque inversion of Christ's offer. Ugolino could have heard in his children's voice the voice of Christ and turned to God as he awaits his death. But he turned to stone and failed to be moved to repentance.

The words of Christ are the food humankind is to eat. Christ is the Word made flesh, and in the Eucharist the bread-made-body is the material manifestation of the Word. The two themes, of the body and of language, begin to merge here in the mystery of the Incarnation, in Christ as Word made flesh. The child's voice asking his father to eat was the way God tried to reach Ugolino to bring about his conversion, and this is reminiscent of Augustine's hearing God's voice in the voices of children playing a childish game. What Ugolino missed we must learn to hear.

One of Ugolino's sons speaks another line reminiscent of Christ's last words when he asks Ugolino, "My father, why doest thou not help me?" This is meant to recall Christ's sacrifice on the cross, which culminates in his agonized cry to God his father, "Eli, Eli, lema sabachthani"—"My God, my God, why hast thou abandoned me?" Again these are the true words being spoken in lower hell, and Ugolino cannot hear them. This cry of Christ's is given grotesque expression back in canto 31 of *Inferno* when Nimrod babbles, "Raphel may amech zabi almi." Giuseppe Mazzotta hears in the rhythm of this garbled line a reminder of Christ's last words and sees in Nimrod fallen man's attempt to utter true language (176–77). Nimrod is at the origin of man's fall from a pure language not fraught with fraud, and in this giant's mouth this grotesque psalm points out how hard it is for fallen man to hear God's voice. But Ugolino had that chance and missed it. We must learn that the true language is the language of God in scriptures.

Which brings us back to *Purgatorio*, for as the meditation on language continues, there is the constant utterance of psalms in their Latin "original." These psalms, beginning with the psalm that Dante uses in his letter to Can Grande and that Singleton describes as the key to Dante's allegorical method of writing, are a base of "true words," words in an authorized book and in an authorized language. But of course Dante wrote in Italian and wrote a treatise to justify his use of the vulgar tongue. His *Comedia* contains some of his most poignant reflections on language, and there are some significant discussions of poetry in *Purgatorio*, where both the poet and his language undergoes purification.

These discussions of poetry ought first of all to be placed properly in their context, that is as part of the itinerary of Dante's spiritual journey and in the upper terraces of the purgative process, where the sins of the flesh are purged. For Statius joins Dante and Virgil as the pair leave the terrace where avarice and prodigality are purged; Bonagiunta and Dante discuss poets and poetry where gluttony is purged; and it is on the terrace of lust that Dante exchanges compliments with and acknowledges his poetic father in Guido Guinicelli, who then points out to Dante "il miglior fabbro" (the better craftsman), Arnaut Daniel, who is given the supreme compliment of speaking his lines in his native tongue.[4] Conversations about poetry are most frequent and most explicit in the terraces where desire is purged of its excesses, and we can intuit from that mere fact Dante's understanding that poetry is about pleasure and sensual delight, about our sensual responses to the beauties and pleasures of the world. Poets too are for the most part not hellish—those in Limbo are impressive figures who had the bad luck to be born before Christ and so write about noble and lofty themes that fall short of the divine; Bertran de Born is the only poet punished as a sinner in hell, and that is for breaking the bond between father and son and not for his poetry itself. Poetry is purgatorial in that it brings us upward, away from damnation and up the mountain of purgation. Poetry can bring us near Eden, near our original powers of sensual perception and perfection, but only Dante's poetry (apparently) can bring us beyond purgatory, into Eden itself, and beyond the earthly into the heavenly spheres.

In canto 24 of *Purgatorio* is an exchange between Dante and Bonagiunta in which Dante explains to his predecessor how he writes his love poetry: "I am one who, when Love breathes in me, takes note, and in that manner which he dictates within go on to set it forth." This apparently simple assertion of being inspired by Love jolts Bonagiunta into insight: "Now I see the knot that held back the Notary and Guittone and me short of the sweet new style that I hear; I see well how your pens follow close behind the dictator, which assuredly did not happen with ours, and he that sets himself to examine further sees nothing else between the one style and the other" (52–62). The "sweet new style" of Dante's merely follows the dictator, Love, while Bonagiunta implies that he and his colleagues were wont to stray from truthful and plain utterance into merely rhetorical flights. Such poetry may do much to raise us up against the pull of gravity toward God and toward Eden, but it will not be able to move us beyond prodigality, gluttony, and lust. Dante claims that his poetry is simpler and more direct, offering "plainer words" than his more fanciful poetic fathers did. Only a poetry devoted to Beatrice and what she represents, only a poetry that follows closely what Love breathes within the poet, can get us through the wall of flame to Eden. Only Dante will be allowed to wander freely in the earthly paradise and describe its joys and beauties. Only he will be able to witness the divine pageant that only Ezekiel and John of the Apocalypse have attempted before. His poetry has been purged of its devotion to earthly things and has been purified so that it, like Dante himself and his perfected body, are now "pure and ready to mount to the stars."

In a very real sense *Purgatorio,* and the entire *Comedia,* is a love poem. For the punishments of purgatory are designed to correct our innate and natural ability to love. The first three terraces correct love perverted; the middle terrace love deficient, the last three terraces love excessive. We are born to love, but living in space and time and within the material conditions of human existence has distorted this innate ability, and it must be purged of defects and made ready for the ascent to heaven.

Dante has overcome the downward pull of gravity on the body as he has purged his body and its desire of its excesses and defects, and he has also purified his poetry so that it moves upward, as did the troubadours' verse, but unlike theirs Dante's poetry is able to pierce the final terraces and write of heavenly things, beginning with Beatrice and the pageant she brings and continuing through *Paradiso* to the heavenly court of God. In *Purgatorio* both the body's desires and their poetry are purged of their excess and made capable of bringing us to higher things, to the final vision where Dante's "desire and will, like a wheel that spins with even motion, were revolved by the Love that moves the sun and the other stars" (*Paradiso*, 33.143–45). Freccero's analysis of this final image underscores how Dante finds an ingenious image to record his own participation in Incarnation: he is like a wheel that spins in a circular motion around Love and so achieves the perfect motion of eternity; but a wheel also proceeds in a straight line as it makes its circular motion, implying that Dante is both in time and out of time, still fully human as he achieves divine perspective. The poem he writes brings Dante to perfect fulfillment as he fits neatly the pattern of the Incarnation. In so doing he can look on the world of constant change from the perspective of timeless certainty. He occupies that still point of intersection of the timeless with time.

Dante advanced Augustine's understanding of how the Incarnation is the key to human development and fulfillment. They shared a distrust of the arrogance of Platonism, and both called for the individual to listen for God's voice within them. Dante made human desire itself a potentially good and necessary thing in the plan of humankind's redemption and perfection, as it purges desire of its excesses and brings perfected human bodies up to heaven itself. The body is not to be rejected and despised, but it is to be perfected and enjoyed in a heaven of sensual delight.

This is an important point: there is no easy claim to transcendence in the Christian tradition, no disembodied flights of pure mind above the temporal and the material. This tradition is not to be confused with what we call Cartesian humanism or an Enlightenment humanism stemming ultimately from Plato. The Christian tradition is almost as skeptical of such claims of transcendence as the most cynical postmodern debunker might be, but the Christian tradition based on Incarnation finds a way to maintain its respect for the temporal and material conditions of humanity and still hold out hope for transcendence—a much more complex transcendence perhaps but the one figured first in the Gospel stories of Christ and then made central to our literary heritage by Dante.

Uses of the Grotesque: The Vulgar Body in Rabelais

Thus far I have focused on perhaps the two most important literary figures in the medieval period, Saint Augustine and Dante, as they worked to avoid the error of the Platonists, who depicted the body as an obstacle to be overcome, as a source of deceit and even evil to be rejected. The Christian literary tradition that I wish to assemble does not seek to deny the primacy of the body in our lives and in our destinies but centers on the Incarnation as the mystery of faith that allows us to recognize in our material existence the possibilities of perfection and redemption. I want now to look at the texts of two other writers, both of whom would describe themselves primarily as Christians and whose literary texts exhibit an even more urgent compulsion to make the human body prominent in their examinations of the human experience. What distinguishes the imaginative works of Rabelais and Swift from their medieval predecessors is their emphasis on the body as vulgar, even as grotesque and monstrous. Their more urgent emphasis reflects the changing times.

Between Dante and Rabelais, European culture underwent tremendous shifts. The invention of the printing press, the discovery of the New World, the Protestant Reformation, and the Copernican revolution all occurred within fifty years or so preceding the publication of *Gargantua and Pantagruel*, and Rabelais was the first major European writer to show an awareness of these changes in his imaginative texts, especially the revolutionary effects of the printing press on language and authority. As part of this awareness, his descriptions of the human body became excessive to the point of becoming grotesque. *Gargantua and Pantagruel* can be read as a serious meditation of the meaning of the vulgar body in the Christian humanism of the early modern period.

The most obvious attribute of Rabelais' depiction of the human body is its excess and the consequent focus on the body's vulgar nature, "vulgar" in the sense of the body's most ordinary, quotidian, and common functions. Rabelais' focus is so intense that in his art the vulgar becomes the grotesque. The grotesque took form as an artistic category in the sixteenth century. It was just at this time that the term "grotesque" was first used to describe a kind of artistic depiction of the human form that originated with the discovery in 1480 of some unusual figures in underground passages of Roman baths dating back to Nero's reign. These figures presented an amalgam of different kinds of animals magically fused: animal bodies, for instance, with human faces and bird's wings. These images from the grottoes were soon called "grotesque" and "became a well-known motif in both the religious and secular art of the Renaissance" (Adams and Yates, 5–7).

The grotesque as a form and motif is obviously ancient, perhaps even primordial, but it enjoyed a powerful revival in the sixteenth century, and most scholars of the grotesque mention Rabelais as one of its chief practitioners. His representation of the human body in *Gargantua and Pantagruel* occurred at a moment in art history when the grotesque had become an important motif in art and at a time in cultural history that made the grotesque a powerful way of interpreting the radically new conditions facing European culture. For, among its many effects and possible meanings, the grotesque is first a "sudden introduction of chaos into our familiar and relatively knowable world" (51). This aspect of the grotesque makes the familiar world suddenly seem strange and in urgent need of new forms of comprehension. As Wilson Yates has put it, for Wolfgang Kayser, whose pioneering work *The Grotesque in Art and Literature* did much to delineate the field of study, "the presentation of the grotesque is of an *estranged or alienated world*." The estranged world is "a world that is a transformation of our world, a world in which the familiar and natural elements 'suddenly turn out to be strange and ominous'" (17). The grotesque performs the useful function in art and literature of registering the sudden awareness of new conditions that have challenged the prevailing order and leave the culture in a state of temporary but very real and profound confusion. Rabelais' day is such a period, and his use of the grotesque is partly explained by this need to represent estrangement.

Kayser's view of the grotesque is a dark one, calling in from the boundaries darker, demonic forces that the ordinary world has sought to suppress and cast to the margins. We are probably much more familiar with the happier interpretation of the grotesque that Mikhail Bakhtin advanced in *Rabelais and His World*, in which he concurs with Kayser that the grotesque makes the existing world seem strange and broken but diverges from Kayser's thesis by seeing this estrangement as a setting up of the possibilities of a new order of pleasure and community. Bakhtin's critique is complex and manifold, but it lays clear emphasis on the human body as our contact with the world, as what connects us intimately with the material universe:

> The grotesque body is not separated from the rest of the world. It is not a closed, complete unit; it is unfinished, outgrows itself, transgresses its own limits. The stress is laid on those parts of the body that are open to the outside world, that is, the parts through which the world enters the body or emerges from it, or through which the body itself goes out to meet the world. This means that the emphasis is on the apertures or the convexities, or on the various ramifications and offshoots: the open mouth, the genital organs, the breasts, the phallus, the potbelly, the nose. The body discloses its essence as a principle of growth which exceeds its own limits only in copulation, pregnancy, childbirth, the throes of death, eating, drinking, or defecation. This is the unfinished, ever creating body.... (26)

By bringing us rudely back to the material world and our bodies, the grotesque has the capacity to readjust our attitudes toward human existence and value.

With Bakhtin's critique in mind, I want to advance a reading of Rabelais' use of the grotesque that fits the paradigm I have set up in Augustine and Dante, Rabelais as a writer working within the Christian imagination.

It takes little effort on any reader's part to see why Rabelais would be included prominently in the study of the grotesque, for he delighted in presenting images of the body that are excessive and disordered and engaged in the lowest functions of human life. The body is an aspect of human existence that demands attention and perhaps reevaluation in Rabelais' text. According to Bakhtin, "In the imaging of the body, body parts are juxtaposed and connected, defying easy recognition and leveling any sense of one part as private or public, good or bad, repulsive or attractive" (23). In this leveling Rabelais is demolishing the older hierarchies that were employed to interpret and control the body that organized the body in coercive and confining ways. In Bakhtin's reading Rabelais is liberating the body from the mind/body split that was borrowed from the Platonists and used by a repressive culture to tyrannize the body and its desire. Rabelais wants to liberate the body from such tyranny and allow it to recover the exuberance and delight it once enjoyed. According to Yates, "Bakhtin is attempting to uncover a liberating and healing antidote to official culture. Official culture severed the whole, disembodied the self, abstracted life, and created authoritarian structures and status that deny the regenerative powers of nature" (25–26). Bakhtin's reading of Rabelais places him squarely in the context I have already established for Augustine and Dante, as a writer who needs to redress a serious misinterpretation of the role of the human body in human existence and—here I part company with Bakhtin—in God's providential plan for humanity.

The opponents for Augustine and Dante are the Platonists, philosophers who locate truth and ideals in the pure realm of spirit, with the body as an obstacle to the pursuit of the true forms. Something seems more urgent for Rabelais, as if the body has been so denied and invalidated by what Bakhtin calls "official culture" that the process of correction and liberation requires the drastic means of the grotesque. I have been trying to develop my understanding of a "Christian tradition" that does not degrade or devalue the body and our material existence, but there might always have been another tradition within Christianity that lacked the broader and more balanced view I have been describing, one that in Rabelais' time was perhaps becoming "the official culture." The Reformation had already begun producing new religious denominations that would demote the body to a lower place than the one assigned to it in the earlier Christian tradition, the one that produced Augustine at its beginning and Dante in its flourishing. We can call these denominations by a single name, Puritanism, as a shorthand for a Christian view that suspects and even fears the body. Always open to suspicion in any religious understanding of the world, the body is validated by an older and greater Christian tradition centered on Incarnation. And Rabelais continued this tradition, the tradition of Augustine and Dante, into the early modern period.

Rabelais' writing in *Gargantua and Pantagruel* had as one of its aims the subversion of accepted tradition and authority that was already set in motion by the various crises in knowledge of his day, especially the changes in the dissemination of information and ideas made possible by the invention of the printing press in the middle of the fifteenth century. His sense of verbal playfulness may well be attributed to the new means of circulating the written word, for with moveable type any "shit" could be published: Rabelais' delight in scatology and his piling up of massive lists (a list of Gargantua's childhood games, for instance, which cover several pages) can be connected as examples of the grotesque, with the monstrous piling up of words making of language something new and different. In a book on Joyce and Bakhtin, Keith Booker notes Leo Spitzer's insight that for Rabelais "words not only relate to things, but themselves *are* things, with a reality of their own" (48). Even language took on a materiality that could fit his delight in the grotesque. In his emphasis on the body, especially its orifices, Rabelais made sure that his reader cannot evade the body but instead must confront it as a gigantic problem, one that threatens to overwhelm us. For that is what his playful and happy use of the grotesque tends to do; it makes the body something that cannot be ignored. If the official culture was working hard to deny the body a place of prominence, then Rabelais was providing the antidote, making the official world seem strange and absurd and encouraging his readers to examine the body without hierarchical categories or metaphysical prejudices. In fact Rabelais' use of the grotesque may be seen as his urgent attempt to make us account for the literal fact of our bodies in whatever philosophy or worldview we adopt to meet the changing conditions of early modernity.

Rabelais cannot fit into the kind of work that Leonard Barkan has done in *Nature's Work of Art,* which treats the body as symbol or image for understanding our lives. It is the literal fact of our bodies, their sheer and obvious presence in our lives, that occupied Rabelais' interests. The body is not a symbol of cosmic unity or of our spiritual correspondence to nature and natural forces. It is merely part of nature and our very concrete connection to, and our way of participation in, the material world. Barkan's earlier book, *The Gods Made Flesh,* offers a different survey of writers who focused on the representation of the body, following the fate of Ovid in the Middle Ages through Shakespeare. Even this book, with its celebration of the pagan sensibility over a more morbid Christian attitude, misses the Christian tradition of Incarnation that shares more with Barkan's depiction of a pagan sensibility than it does with his fairly stereotypical and limited sense of what a Christian attitude toward the body may entail. The Christian tradition based on Incarnation helps not only to explain Joyce and a modernist humanism but to rescue Christianity from this prevailing and limiting stereotype.

Critics have used Rabelais' writing to advance their own desire to deny transcendence and promote a healthy materialist attitude toward our lives. Up to a point it does accomplish the latter, and this is what Bakhtin emphasizes with his myth of carnival. The body is liberated from the stranglehold of a puritanical official culture, and the culture is thus transformed into something higher: the vision that carnival inspires. What Bakhtin's celebration of liberation and transformation misses is the Christian aspect of Rabelais' text, which is prominent and difficult to ignore. My reading of Rabelais accepts most of what Bakhtin has suggested and adds to it an emphasis on Rabelais' effort to remake, or reform, Christianity: the church had become so degraded and corrupt in its history that Rabelais used the grotesque to break down the familiar world that had been largely created by this institution and to reestablish a happier sense of the Christian life.

Despite the efforts of its theologians and secular writers, Christianity had become a religion that denied the body and made of it an object of sinful desire to be overcome. Along with his fellow Christian humanists Erasmus and More, Rabelais worked to bring the body back into consideration in our understanding of the Christian life. Rabelais' broad and often vulgar humor concerning the human body and its functions has a serious purpose, to force the body back to the center of our thinking about ourselves and our destinies. Most of the representations of the body are both exaggerated in size and focused on what are normally considered its lower functions, sexuality and scatology. There is one passage that has an unusual context, even for Rabelais, that might open the way to Rabelais' sense of his Christian purpose in the book:

> Gargantua now woke about four o'clock in the morning and, whilst he was rubbed down, had some chapter of Holy Writ read to him loudly and clearly, with pronunciation befitting the matter; and this was the business of a young page called Anagnostes, a native of Basche. Moved by the subject and argument of that lesson, he often gave himself up to worship and adoration, to prayers and entreaties, addressed to the good God whose majesty and marvelous wisdom had been exemplified in that reading. Then he went into some private place to make excretion of his natural waste-products, and there his tutor repeated what had been read, explaining to him the more obscure and difficult points. On their way back they considered the face of the sky, whether it was as they had

observed it the night before, and into what sign the sun, and also the moon, were entering for that day. (1, 23, 87)

The body of the giant Gargantua is juxtaposed with the reading and study of Holy Writ. His gigantic body is being rubbed down as he hears the passage the first time; his spiritual response to the scriptures, to worship God, is joined to his more "natural" response to excrete waste products. His tutor reads the passage a second time and expounds upon it as Gargantua excretes the waste. This is one of the many passages in which Rabelais makes the body and its functions nothing more than part of the ordinary routine. It is part of his strategy to make the body something that is always making demands on us and whose demands must be respected, even when inconvenient or when something "sacred" is occurring. But it is more than that. This passage is meant to remind us that the human body is never neglected in Holy Writ, neither in the Hebrew Bible, where the historical destiny of the Jews is the main topic of both the historical and prophetic books, nor in the New Testament, in which the bodily Resurrection of the Christ is the great accomplishment. Gargantua is perfectly comfortable in his body and feels no contradiction between his sacred and secular activities.

In the hands of a different writer, this passage might provide the opportunity for reductive mockery, as defecation and urination are placed next to worship and adoration, debunking the higher behavior and reducing it to the lower. In the analyses of contemporary critics, a passage such as this might be twisted out of its good humor and made to seem a scathing critique of religious practice. Rabelais gives the page who reads scripture to Gargantua a name that clinches my point: "Anagnostes" indicates someone who is not agnostic, who is poised perhaps even to combat such doubting. Rabelais is not demeaning the sacred by means of the vulgar but merely placing the two on the same plane of importance in order to begin a reevaluation of the relation of the body to the spirit, a reevaluation of the body's role in our spiritual itinerary. Going to the outhouse and reading sacred scripture brings the most vulgar aspect of our humanity into contact with our highest aspirations. There is no contradiction or opposition or hierarchical demotion of the one in favor of the other. As the theorists of the grotesque understand, Rabelais was breaking down old hierarchical orders and bringing what was in binary opposition onto a level plane where they can realign themselves in a new way.

And that new way is the old way of Augustine and Dante, the way in which Christian writers were able, under the influence of the Incarnation, to see the body as perfectible and as a necessary part of our lives as Christians, both in this life and in the next. Like Erasmus and More, Rabelais works to make the traditional Christian values seem new, vital, and happy. The body, which had been elevated in Christian theology, had become entangled in a morbid and puritanical interpretation that Rabelais sought to demolish; once freed from that, the body can be restored to its rightful place as the necessary site of our redemption.

There is a binary opposition at work in our attitudes toward the body and toward ideals that needs to be identified and corrected. What may, following Augustine, be called Platonism tends to degrade the body while seeking to promote transcendence; and the postmodern sensibility seeks to deny transcendence by promoting the body. The Christian tradition based on Incarnation allows us to avoid the either/or of such binaries and affirm a both/and: the body need not be denied as one follows a paradigm leading to transcendence. Rabelais has become a congenial figure for the postmodern turn of mind, in no small part because of the groundbreaking work of Bakhtin, in that Rabelais exhibits so many characteristics of the postmodern, including—and maybe especially—a sense of the comic that is devastating mockery.

Rabelais mocks everything and anything, almost always evoking a laughter that deflates the grandiose and debunks the pretentious, but never does he mock the scriptures or the behavior of the giants—whether it is Grandgousier, or Pantagruel, or Gargantua—when they are called on to act as Christian princes. This actually occupies a significant part of book 1, the focus of this analysis. The behavior of Grandgousier and Gargantua is in marked contrast to that of Picrochole, who uses the most trivial of conflicts between his bakers and Grandgousier's shepherds as an excuse to begin a military campaign of world conquest. The ambition of the "normal" prince Picrochole is enormous and gigantic, and the behavior and attitude of the giant princes is modest and merciful. Picrochole's advisers goad their prince to begin a campaign reaching to Babylon, and he is easily incited by his gigantic ambition to do so. It is Picrochole who says that the end of their campaign, its goal, is to allow them to come back home and take their ease; the one who points out that they can do this right now without the warfare is called a "fine dreamer" who wants to hide in a chimney corner. The "normal" prince is the one whose ambitions are grotesque.

And the behavior of the ones whose bodies are gigantic is modest. They act in conformity with Christian virtues of mercy and peace. When Grandgousier hears that the quarrel began over four or five dozen cakes, he orders that five cartloads of cakes—and a large sum of money besides—be sent as a peace offering, "For I very much dislike making war" (1, 32, 107). This sign of Christian virtue is interpreted by Picrochole's minister Touchspigot as a sign of weakness that spurs the ambition for world conquest. Grandgousier had already written a letter to his son in which he describes the proper attitude of a Christian prince toward warfare: "My intention is not to provoke, but to appease; not to attack, but to defend; not to conquer, but to guard my loyal subjects and hereditary lands which Picrochole has invaded in an unfriendly manner, without reason or excuse, and where day by day he pursues his furious enterprise with excesses intolerable to free-born men" (1, 29, 103). The Christian prince must use violence on occasion, but its use must be reluctant and defensive. When the warfare is described, there is the typical Rabelaisian delight in excess, as Gargantua's mare demolishes an enemy castle with a torrent of urine, as Gargantua mistakes the cannonballs meant to fell him for annoying flies to be swatted away, as he combs the cannonballs out of his hair, and as he eats six pilgrims by mistake when he eats some lettuce. Eventually Grandgousier deals with these pilgrims and with his vanquished enemies, and the same Christian benevolence is displayed. In Rabelais' version of the grotesque, Christian virtue and grotesque exaggeration are part of the same vision.

Rabelais made use of the popular Renaissance motif of the grotesque in order to present as new and strange and wonderful the familiar teachings about the proper behavior of Christian princes, which is the one thing he spares from his ribald and absurd mockery. In setting free the pilgrims from Picrochole's country, Grandgousier says, "Go your ways, poor men, in the name of God the creator. May he be a perpetual guide to you, and don't be so ready to undertake these idle, useless journeys in the future. Look after your families, work, each man at his vocation, instruct your children, and live as the good apostle St Paul directs you" (1, 45, 137). There is no hint of mockery in these injunctions, but the simple and direct eloquence of a good prince showing mercy. Similarly he is merciful to Touchspigot, who had been false to both Grandgousier and his own prince, and to all the vanquished people taken captive in the war. Gargantua sends the vanquished back home with safe escort and a gift of three-months' pay, treating them with the same kindness that his father had shown in similar circumstances and who had explained to his counselors, "that if he treated them with any kindness, this was no more than he was by duty bound to do" (1, 50, 147). Such mercy and kindness are what Christian princes are obligated to perform, and in Rabelais' world, the giants, whose bodies had been the source for his use of the grotesque, are the ones with the Christian sensibility, which is Rabelais' way of making such behavior seem outlandish and rare, even though it was the familiar teaching of conventional doctrine.

The first book of *Gargantua and Pantagruel* ends with Gargantua's rewarding Friar John by building a new abbey to be founded on the friar's own rules and regulations. Once again Rabelais' writing spares from ridicule and mockery a certain set of what can only be called Christian ideals. Bakhtin wants to see in the Abbey of Thélème a vision of a happy communal life of a new order based on democratic ideals; if we adjust that formula from carnival to a vision of heaven

I can concur. For the abbey that Friar John constructs can only be a goal to be realized in a Christian afterlife.

The fifty-fourth chapter of the first book of *Gargantua and Pantagruel* is devoted to an inscription over the great Gate of Thélème. This inscription is meant to remind us of the fearful words inscribed above the gates of hell in the third canto of Dante's *Inferno:* "Abandon every hope, ye that enter." Above the gate at Thélème there are words of moral judgment, telling those who read it who may enter and who may not. Told to "enter not here" are "vile hypocrites and bigots, pious old apes, and puffed-up snivelers"; "lawyers insatiable, ushers, lawyers' clerks, devourers of the people, holders of office, scribes and Pharisees, ancient judges who tie up good citizens like stray dogs with cord on their necks"; "miserly usurers, gluttons and lechers, everlasting gatherers, tricksters and swindlers, mean pettifoggers" (1, 54, 153). This is a list of "sinners" we might indeed find in Dante's hell, which is obviously much more organized and detailed than this. Nonetheless, in one bold stroke, Rabelais indicated a judgment like Dante's to be delivered before entry is allowed into the abbey. We are also told who may enter: noble gentlemen, ladies of high lineage, and

> You who preach with vigour
> Christ's Holy Gospel, never mind who scoffs,
> Here you will find a refuge and a tower
> Against the foeman's error, the picked arguments,
> Which falsely seek to spread about their poison.
> Enter, here let us found a faith profound,
> And then let us confound by speech and writing,
> All that are foemen of the Holy Writ.
> Our Holy Writ and Word
> For ever shall be heard
> In this most holy spot.
> Each wears it on his heart,
> Each wears it as a sword,
> Our Holy Writ and Word. (1, 54, 154–55).

In the Abbey of Thélème we will find noble men and ladies, preachers of the Gospel, and no one else. The Gospel must be preached with vigor and confidence, and it is the profound foundation of the abbey. There is no trace of condescension or mockery here, and when one considers that it is Friar John of the Hashes, the vigorous and athletic opponent of all pious fraud and cowardice, who makes these rules (or for whom, at least, the rules were made), such words are even more fully safeguarded from mockery. The abbey is "a refuge and a tower" against the scoffers, against those who want to make of the Gospels something less than God's word to be trusted and lived by. The great scoffer wants this one thing only to be safeguarded from scoffing.

Because the Gospels provide this sure foundation, the men and women who are allowed entry into the abbey have no rules to follow but one:

> All their life was regulated not by laws, statutes, or rules, but according to their free will and pleasure. Those rose from bed when they pleased, and drank, ate, worked and slept when the fancy seized them. Nobody woke them; nobody compelled them either to eat or to drink, or to do anything else whatever. So it was that Gargantua had established it. In their rules there was only one clause:
>
> Do what you will
>
> Because people who are free, well-born, well-bred, and easy in honest company have a natural spur and instinct which drives them to virtuous deeds and deflects them from vice; and this they called honour. (1, 57, 159)

This is not a Rabelaisian call to licentious behavior, nor is it a vision of a communal world based on the chaos of carnival. Rather it may be read as Rabelais' version of Dante's *Purgatorio,* where Virgil crowns and miters Dante and tells him to take pleasure henceforth as his guide, that not to act upon his will would be the only fault. Those who are purified in Dante's world—and those who have been allowed entry into the Gospel-based world of Thélème—can, in fact must, do whatever they will because whatever they will is good, and they only will the good. It is with a vision of a perfect Christian world that Rabelais ends book 1.

Such hopes are no longer part of the official culture because that culture has become stultified and corrupt, and without a healthy sense of the body and our material existence, official culture cannot imagine this heavenly kingdom. Rather these hopes exist on the other side of mockery, fresh and new and vital for a culture needing a firm grounding in a visionary ideal. As a counter to the sterility of official puritanical culture, Rabelais presented the grotesque as his way of restoring what has been lost: the high hope of a perfect Christian life in a bodily heaven of the Resurrection.

Monsters and Modernity: The Vulgar Body in Swift

Rabelais thus fits into the Christian imagination of the Incarnation, and his work bears striking resemblance in this regard to another writer who would certainly have seen himself first and foremost as a Christian and who also placed the grotesque body in the foreground. Jonathan Swift was similarly obsessed by the need to depict the human body in its most vulgar activities and with the kind of exaggerated representation we have been calling grotesque. In the two hundred years between Rabelais and Swift occurred the political and intellectual developments that, following Toulmin, I have called the origin of modernity. Like Toulmin, Charles Taylor has insisted that the Cartesian philosophical contribution to Plato's mind/body split was to sever the body and mind as fully as one can, creating a complete chasm between the two, locating truth in the mind or soul and locating temporal relativity and misleading observations in the body (145). The Platonic split between soul and body is reinforced and exaggerated, and the body suffers a severe diminution of its status in the radical dualism of Cartesian philosophy. Swift is the first great writer in this Christian tradition after Descartes.

In a section of his book called "From Humanists to Rationalists," Toulmin presents the writings of Montaigne as the epitome of humanist attitudes toward the body, arguing that Montaigne and his fellow humanists had a healthier and more realistic attitude toward the body than the later, modern rationalists: "For Montaigne, part of our humanity is to accept responsibility for our bodies, our feelings and the effects of the things we do, given those bodies and feelings; and we must do so, even if we cannot always keep these things under complete control" (40). According to Toulmin, the rationalists saw the body not as a basic part of who we are but as something opposed to the self, and that the only parts of us that are truly ourselves are our thoughts and abstractions. We are not responsible for our emotions: "Feelings are not something *we do*. They are what *our bodies do to us*" (40). Feelings, in Toulmin's formulation, have been separated from the true self as the body has been severed from the mind. "In separating rationality and logic from rhetoric and the emotions, we are unwittingly committed to the basic agenda of modern philosophy" (41). The humanists had a broader and more comprehensive attitude toward humanity, including the mind and its rational powers but also emphasizing the body and the feelings that are attached to the mind, which Erasmus ascribed to the rule of Folly. With the advent of modern philosophy with Descartes and of the modernity he set in motion, the basic definition of the human being was been narrowed to include only our rational powers, either neglecting or degrading the material nature of human being. In this transition from humanists to rationalists, there is a loss of status for feeling and passion.

No one can accuse Erasmus or More, Montaigne or Rabelais, of not valuing intellect and learning. Yet, with both sets of humanists, the foundation is feeling. As Wallace Stevens later wrote quite clearly, and with the excitement of an important discovery, "That's it: the more than rational distortion, / The fiction that results from feeling. Yes, that" ("Notes toward a Supreme Fiction").

Much has been written about the eighteenth century as a period in which passion and feeling struggled for a place in cultural theory, and the rise of the novel, with its emphasis on the individual and his or her ordinary life, also gave rise to the sentimental novel and the sentimental hero. The Age of Reason, it might be said, led to a severing of passion from the rational powers and led some writers to make of passion something higher than reason. It is an age beset with problems of how the rational mind confronts nonreason, as Foucault repeatedly demonstrated.[5] In a survey of the treatment of the body by the Christian imagination, the place of Jonathan Swift should be clear: responding to the problems set in motion by modern philosophy and modernity, his treatment of the body is more urgent than even that of Rabelais, and usually less happy and joyful. It is as if Swift recognized that the human body is in danger of being relegated to a position of such unimportance, or of such ridiculous and unearned importance in the hands of sentimentalists, that he had to force it back into the scene of cultural commentary by excess and ugliness. If we are to live in an Age of Reason, we must recognize that reason has a very strange dwelling, one that neither obeys reason as its master nor disappears when asked so reason can perform its important tasks unimpeded. If the postmodernists' problem with modernity is its naive belief in the ability of reason to master material conditions and lead us on a path of rational progress toward a brighter future, then we can claim that the early modern humanists provide a model for a more comprehensive attitude toward human being and that the Christian writers considered here share an attitude toward the body that we would normally assign to the postmodern critique, as something that modernity has tried to control and confine in its rational march toward progress.

For *Gulliver's Travels* Swift invented a narrator who journeys to a variety of places, and among the many aspects of European rationalist culture that Swift satirized is the problem the body causes for rational society. In the land of Lilliput, Gulliver is a giant, and he presents a gigantic problem to the Lilliputians: the difficulty of keeping Gulliver well fed and of keeping the city clean require tremendous resources, both financial and in terms of labor. No civilized space can be maintained without a great deal of attention being paid to the body, both what it needs and what measures must be taken to maintain cleanliness and safety because of its nature.

The arrogance of the Lilliputians is also satirized; they believe that they can master the giant's body and maintain proper control over his power. Book 1 presents the human body as an enormous problem to be confronted by a relatively diminutive faculty, which proves incapable, despite the most tremendous efforts, of mastery over the body.

Book 2 brings us to a place where Gulliver must confront giants, and the focus on the body in Brobdingnag is not on the problems it presents to human society but on its ugliness. This is the darkest section of *Gulliver's Travels*, even darker than the ending, where Gulliver turns his back on human beings in general and his family in particular because of his experiences with the Houyhnhnms. The Brobdingnag section is darkest because it presents scathing critiques of the human, both as an ugly creature and as an arrogant one. Because of his small size, Gulliver gets a close-up look at the human bodies of these giants, and he does not like what he sees: "the most horrible spectacles that ever an European Eye beheld. There was a Woman with a Cancer in her Breast, swelled to a monstrous size, full of holes, in two or three of which I could have easily crept, and covered my whole Body. There was a Fellow with a Wen in his Neck, larger than five Woolpacks, and another with a couple of wooden legs, each about twenty Foot high. But the most hateful Sight of all was the Lice crawling on their Cloaths" (93–94). One might argue that these were close-up views of disease, deformity, and poverty, not of the human being at its best and highest, or even in a "normal" or "natural" state. But even the sight of female beauty, when viewed close up, is repulsive to Gulliver: "For, they would strip themselves to the Skin, and put on their Smocks in my Presence, while I was placed on their Toylet directly before their naked Bodies, which, I am sure, to me was very far from being a tempting Sight, or from giving me any other emotions than those of Horror and Disgust. Their Skins appeared so coarse and uneven, so variously coloured when I saw them near, with a Mole here and there as broad as a Trencher, and Hairs hanging from it thicker than Pack-threads; to say nothing further concerning the rest of their Persons. Neither did they scruple while I was by to discharge what they had drunk, to the quantity of at least two Hogsheads, in a Vessel that held above three Tuns" (99). The beautiful ladies of the court of Brobdingnag fill him with "Horror and Disgust" because of the "natural" and "normal" flaws of the body that we usually do not have the opportunity to see. Swift's satire makes even the most beautiful human body seem repulsive in this second book, as if to suggest that our very normal and natural state is monstrous.

This viewpoint is at the heart of Swift's severe and unsparing satire against the body in *Gulliver's Travels*. As Dennis Todd has pointed out in his study of eighteenth-century monsters, for Swift the emotional response of viewing the monstrous is to see "how closely the monstrous verges on the normal" (157); actually the normal verges on the monstrous. In Swift's satire, there is no normal body but only the monstrous. Humankind is by its very nature monstrous, and our desperate attempt to create the category of the normal is a sign of our need to exert reason's power over the body, which can never truly come under its sway.

Todd's chapter on Swift is useful to this study because Todd makes the term "monster" relevant to Swift in the way the term "grotesque" was central for Rabelais. Todd notes the popular diversion of monster shows in Swift's London and suggests that the monstrous was an important category to Swift because it poses fundamental questions about identity and our definitions of our humanness (see especially 156–61). The failure of the distinction between monstrous and normal is a conclusion Todd approaches but never quite makes. We would like to think that the monstrous is a subordinate category to the normal, a deviation from the prior term or its lack. But Swift made the monstrous the "first" term in this binary opposition, as the "normal" state of our bodies that then leads to the desperate erection of the category "normal" to give us refuge from our monstrous selves. The giants in Brobdingnag are more kind and decent than the "normal" humans Gulliver recalls and recounts to the king of Brobdingnag. Gulliver tries to impress the king with the virtue and importance of European men, and after Gulliver's historical account of European affairs, which is intended to impress, the king makes this judgment: "I cannot but conclude the Bulk of your Natives, to be the most pernicious Race of odious little vermin that Nature ever suffered to crawl upon the Surface of the Earth" (111). The normal humans are monstrous in their violence; the monstrous humans are admirable in their modesty and decency; the boundaries have been erased, and the very meaning of the term "human" called into question.

The movement from the grotesque in book 1, where the body is a gigantic problem, to the monstrous in book 2, where deformity becomes the body's normal state, is rendered more complex in book 3, where in Laputa the Cartesian mind/body split is satirized. It is as if Swift were implying that to sever the mind from the body as neatly as modern philosophy does is in itself monstrous and makes of the once fully integrated human being a monster dominated by reason. The rulers of this land live on a floating island, separated from the fertile and lush land below and ruling it with awkward but very real power. Their devotion to pure intellect and abstract thinking has rendered them almost completely useless for practical affairs. Their clothing is ill-made because of their devotion to abstract principles, as are their houses and furniture; they are unable to hold conversations with each other without the intervention of their flappers, whose occupation is to hit them on the head to break them out of their reverie and remind them of something at hand. For all their devotion to reason, they have no peace of mind but are instead wracked with constant apprehension derived from their observation of celestial phenomena. They neglect the pleasures of human existence and suffer their wives to engage in adulterous sexual liaisons right beneath their noses. Swift's lampoon of the pure mind is a powerful corrective to naive claims about transcendence.

In fact, through his creation of Laputa, Swift denied the complete transcendence of the Platonic or Cartesian. The floating island cannot move beyond the boundaries of the land below, from which the island's inhabitants receive the resources that sustain life, nor can the island go higher than four miles above the land. Hard as they might try, those who want to leave the body ultimately find they are unable to break entirely free. We are inextricably tied to a body that we would want to escape or, if escape is impossible, at least to master. And when those below rebel, those who rule from above show themselves to be ruthless in the exercise of their power. They can block the sun and rain from the land and thus threaten those below with famine and disease. If the crime below is serious enough, those on the island can pelt those below with great stones, forcing the inhabitants below into cellars or caves; and if the offense is so great and the resistance so severe, those above can crash the island on the land below, destroying it and its inhabitants. But as this punishment also destroys the resources that maintain life on the island, this is only the last resort and rarely taken into consideration. The mind is ruthless in trying to assert its mastery over the body, and it finds the body uncongenial to its devotion to reason as well as a constant threat for rebellions and requiring constant vigilance. This is a scathing critique of the rationalist humanism of the Enlightenment.

The world created by the split of the mind from the body is indeed monstrous, and it sets up the last of the four books in a suggestive way; for the land of the Houyhnhnms brings us to another place where the rational mind has been severed from the human body. This time it has been placed into the bodies of horses, where the sight of this mixture of beastly body and rational power strikes us as an instance of the grotesque and lurches us toward the recognition that the placement of reason in our own material bodies is no less odd or strange than its placement here in the horses. Swift underscores the problem by creating the Yahoos, creatures with human bodies but without humans' rational powers. Todd's analysis of the monstrous in *Gulliver's Travels* spends more time discussing the monstrousness of the Yahoos than any other of Swift's creatures, and one can understand that they are its most visible emblem. But the Houynhnhms are more monstrous than the Yahoos, for in watching the operation of reason in an animal without opposable thumbs, we are brought to Swift's fullest critique of humanity. The only thing that separates the Houyhnhnms from human being is that humans can use reason to build things, while the Houyhnhnms are unable to develop the practical science and technology that were threatening to turn Europe into a monstrous version of itself. The Houyhnhnm world of pure reason might seem a bit cold and open to the same critique that More made of the rational thinking that set up the laws and practices of Utopia. The Houyhnhnms, like their Utopian counterparts, do not allow passion to play a dominant role in their institutions, and the way in which the family unit has been disassembled and recast in more rational mode might strike one either as a progressive way of breaking out of a pathological entity or as a too-rational denial of the importance of nurturing and love. But, also like Utopia, the land of the Houyhnhnms suffers from far less pain and violence than the human world Gulliver comes from and returns to, and the Houyhnhnms' world is, for Gulliver at least, a far better place than the England he must readjust to. Without the ability to make things, the Houyhnhnms do not have the luxury items that fuel our greed and have made us monstrous. Without the ability to begin what soon became the Industrial Revolution, the Houyhnhnms' cannot create a system of economic exchange like the one that will make of the human world a deformed and degenerate place. Swift's satire plays along a very fine line. We want to disapprove of the coldness of the reasonable horses but cannot help but admire their more just world.

When Gulliver is at home, he reflects on the human being as a "lump of deformity" that makes him sick to be near. Swift tried to deny the charge that he himself was a misanthrope, as in his November 26, 1725, letter to Alexander Pope: "I tell you after all that I do not hate Mankind, it is vous autres who hate them because you would have them reasonable Animals, and are Angry for being disappointed. I have always rejected that definition and made another of my own." Swift wanted to correct our understanding of humanity, not as a rational animal but as one capable of reason: "I have got Materials Towards a Treatis proving the falsity of that Definition *animal rationale;* and to show it should be only *rationis capax*. Upon this great foundation of Misanthropy (though not Timons manner) The whole building of my Travells is erected" (Swift to Pope, September 29, 1725). Humans are not essentially rational but merely capable of exercising rationality; it is not the foundation of our deepest nature but something we have the capacity for, at times and for diverse ends. Misanthropy results not from this view but from seeing human being as essentially rational and then hating them for failing to live up to that nature: "Therefore sit down and be quiet, and mind your Business as you should do, and contract your Friendships, and expect no more from Man than such an Animal is capable of, and you will every day find my Description of Yahoes more resembling. You should think every Man a Villain, without calling him so, or flying from him, or valuing him less. This is an old true Lesson" (Swift to Thomas Sheridan, September 11, 1725).

Swift's various depictions of the human body as problem for reason have as their goal not misanthropy but a redefinition of human being, one that includes the body and its passions as part of the essential nature of humanity. He wanted to correct the Cartesian error of defining human being as essentially reasonable and rational, for that is the actual cause of misanthropy. We are in danger of losing our proper sense of human identity in the overvaluation placed on reason in modernity, and Swift worked with the grotesque and the monstrous to complicate the construction of our identity as rational animals. In his recent study, Frank Boyle sees Swift as the "nemesis" of modernity, as its most bitter satirist. Placing Swift's reaction to the development of the agenda of modernity in the context of Stephen Toulmin's understanding of modernity, Boyle claims that Swift "presented Modern readers with what he understood as the contradictions—dangerous, and potentially antihuman—inherent to Modernity" (xii). Boyle even wants to connect Swift's antimodern satire to Toulmin's humanist heroes (118–19). Boyle's work corroborates of my sense of Swift as within the tradition of the early modern humanists, whose understanding of humanity was more comprehensive, always including feeling as one of its central components. On the other side of Descartes, Swift continued that tradition and also the tradition stemming from earliest Christian writing about the prominence of the body in our understanding of the human being. Swift reacted against modernity's separation of passion and feeling from rationality and logic and needed to employ the monstrous as a way to announce the urgency of his position. A Christian humanist, he worked to oppose the rationalist humanism of the Enlightenment.

Ulysses as Epitome of a Modernist Humanism

This sketch of the Christian imagination or the Christian tradition based on Incarnation provides a context within which to study Joyce's *Ulysses*, an approach I anticipated and came close to in my *Joyce's Modernist Allegory*. But the context makes a crucial difference in what can be said about the single most important modernist literary text, perhaps the single most important text of any kind in establishing the modernist responses to modernity. The context of my previous analysis was Joyce's critique of the novel as a genre, his sense that the novel was no longer adequate to his purposes of presenting something heroic and true in the figure of Leopold Bloom. Dealing with Bloom as an emerging figure in various genres—the naturalistic novel, the romantic novel, the epic, and finally what I call "modernist allegory"—I argued that Joyce's effort was to find a language and a style capable of elevating Bloom to the status of hero, that Joyce wanted Bloom to follow the paradigm of Christ, who fully in the body was able to overcome the pull of gravity and ascend to heaven.

I noted Joyce's exquisite sense of comedy when the narrator of the "Ithaca" episode reports that the last time Bloom weighed himself was on the feast of the Ascension, and I took this as an indication of Joyce's purpose, to suggest in Bloom a love and forgiveness so lofty that he is in unconscious imitation of

Christ and capable of being raised to the stars as an heroic figure for the age. I still believe all this to be true about *Ulysses,* and I want only to supplement that argument by showing how *Ulysses* can be read in this Christian context as a cornerstone of a modernist humanism as well.

The "odyssey of styles"⁶ that Joyce enacted in *Ulysses* is a perfect manifestation of the postmodern aspect of modernism that has been all too often ignored in the convenient mischaracterization of this period and its texts by those who have their own postmodern agenda to pursue. For Joyce tried out, only to debunk and reject, style after style as he searched for a language capable of presenting the "truth" about, and the "truth" that is in, Bloom. *Ulysses* is a text in search of a style capable of presenting the truth, and its greatness lies both in its "postmodern" exposure of language as mystifying and fraudulent and in its "modernist" faith that a truth still can be presented, that a language can be found fit for the job of presenting Bloom as a Christian hero. In this broad and comprehensive way, Joyce's *Ulysses* not only fits my paradigm for a modernist humanism, but it is also the text that most fully exhibits its most fundamental impulses. Joyce does more than any other author of this or any other period—with the possible exception of Dante—to expose language as inherently fraudulent; yet Joyce did not feel at all satisfied in merely showing up and debunking any conceivable attempt to set up an ideal for one's culture. He worked long and hard to be able to present Bloom as an emblem of Christian love and mercy. Joyce did not want to leave his culture merely demystified and empty, allowing greater demons to fill the void. It is the artist's job to fill that void with an ideal capable of constructing a better culture.

Which brings us back to Bloom, the most fully embodied character in all literature. That Joyce was a keen student of literary history and included much of that history in *Ulysses* is well known, and Augustine, Dante, Rabelais, and Swift are among Joyce's most cherished precursors. Joyce worked in *Ulysses* to retrieve a Christian tradition that allowed him to counter the Platonism that had for centuries misled Western culture in how to construct a satisfying and successful humanism, fulfilling this Christian tradition of the vulgar body in his presentation of Bloom as an incarnation of Christ.

"Christ was a jew like me"

Like the other Christian writers sketched earlier in this book, Joyce was interested in rescuing Christianity from the degraded condition it had fallen into. What may be surprising to some readers is that even his decision to give Bloom a Jewish identity is part of this same ambition.

Among the many reasons for giving his modern Odysseus a Jewish identity is Joyce's interest in "reveal[ing] the Judaic foundation of Catholicism through Bloom," as Beryl Schlossman has put it (26). Schlossman is the critic who comes closest to my argument that Joyce was committed to a renovation of a Christian tradition in *Ulysses*. At times she is on the verge of recognizing that the return to a Judaic foundation is a way of renewing Catholicism, as when she says, "In Joyce's characterization of Bloom, the Judaic element precedes and founds the symbolic dimension located in Catholicism" (35), or when she says that the Jewish people should be "considered the womb of Catholicism" (59); but she fails to see that Joyce's central critique of his culture's version of Christianity is its having been Platonized to denigrate the body and its place in the Christian paradigm. This failure is most evident when she says, "Modern realism emphasizes sensation, materiality, and the body, thereby relegating Catholicism to the past" (12). Joyce's desire to rescue Catholicism from such misunderstanding of its deepest mystery, is apparent in his making Bloom a Jew like Christ, one fully in the world and of the world, in the flesh and of the flesh, but also capable of rising above it in a divine elevation. One does not have to choose between modern realism and Catholicism. Joyce wanted us to understand that Catholicism is as fully committed to the body and materiality as the most rigorous naturalism, of which he was the great master, could be.

Shlossman again comes close to seeing this when she describes Joyce's dissatisfaction with the Irish Renaissance of his day, represented most fully by George Russell and his acolytes in the "Scylla and Charybdis" episode. She sees Joyce as turning to Bloom as a Jew to counter the sterility and oppression of this Platonic Irish culture (19–20); yet she implies that it is Judaism, not a corrected and renovated Christianity, that can resolve this error. She is correct in thinking that Judaism values the body and material history, as opposed to Russell's enervated Platonism; but the deeper point is that Catholicism also values these, a Catholicism cleansed, so to speak, of the Greek error and returned to its proper Jewish foundation.

It is ironic that both Schlossman and Robert Boyle have emphasized Joyce's use of the Christian mystery of the Trinity in *Ulysses,* and of course there is much in Joyce's text that justifies their emphasis. But it also seems clear that Joyce's use of the mystery of the Incarnation is even more central to *Ulysses*. For this is the mystery that allows us to value the body and the material conditions as fully as the Jewish tradition does—in that Christ was fully human and lived at a particular moment in human history—and also to value the spiritual and the transcendent, in that Christ is also divine. It is not a choice between a Jewish fidelity to the body and a Platonized Christian flight to disembodied transcendence; like the Christian tradition I have been describing, Joyce's renovated Christianity has both. Greekjew meets Jewgreek in the mystery of the Incarnation.

In "Cyclops," Bloom makes the claim that "Christ was a jew like me." This is comic because Bloom has it backward; one ought to say "I am a Jew like Christ," giving Christ the position of privilege in the comparison. But the comic error is also deeply serious, as errors always are with Joyce. Joyce wanted to reclaim Christ and renovate the Church by returning Christianity, specifically Catholicism, to its Jewish foundations through the character of Bloom. Ira Nadel has noted that in Joyce's Trieste library was Edouard Dujardin's *The Source of the Christian Tradition: A Critical History of Ancient Judaism* (80). By making Bloom a Jew like Christ, or by making us see Christ as a Jew like Bloom, Joyce is returning us to the source, to the foundation, as a way of getting Christianity back to its proper values. Among the other effects of giving Bloom a Jewish identity, this effort to renew a Christian ideal of love is paramount.

Countering Plato: Stephen's Art and Aesthetics

Joyce created a version of himself as youthful artist in *Ulysses* in order to set up our reading of Bloom. One of the most important episodes in the text for the development of Stephen's aesthetics is "Scylla and Charybdis," in which Stephen explains to a small and dwindling audience his theory of creation for Shakespeare's *Hamlet,* and by extension a theory of artistic creation for all great art. But as important as Stephen's theory about that particular play is, we should begin with the moment in which Stephen thinks about his relation to the most prominent man of letters in his small audience, one of the most influential men in Dublin at the time, the poet George Russell, pen name Æ. When he senses that Stephen's theory is going to be highly biographical in nature, Russell tries to quash such speculation: "All these questions are purely academic, Russell oracled out of his shadow. I mean, whether Hamlet is Shakespeare or James I or Essex. Clergymen's discussions of the historicity of Jesus. Art has to reveal to us ideas, formless spiritual essences. The supreme question about a work of art is out of how deep a life does it spring. The painting of Gustave Moreau is the painting of ideas. The deepest poetry of Shelley, the words of Hamlet bring our minds into contact with the eternal wisdom, Plato's world of ideas. All the rest is the speculation of schoolboys for schoolboys" (9. 46–53). This is Joyce's way of bringing his text into line with the persistent problem of the Christian imagination, the temptation of spiritual writers to want to flee from the concrete, local, and material reality of human life toward "Plato's world of ideas." Commentators on this episode have long recognized that Stephen is trying to navigate a course between two dangerous extremes, and one of these extremes is the Platonism of the Dublin literati who want an art that eschews the historical and flees to the timeless, "formless spiritual essences." (The other equally dangerous extreme is the cynical mockery of naturalism as epitomized by Buck Mulligan.) Stephen knows the aesthetics of a Russell, who mocks the clergyman's anxiety about "the historicity of Jesus." This snide comment, intended to reduce Stephen's status as an intellectual, reveals much about Russell's aesthetics and also brings in the mystery of the Incarnation, which posits that the eternal wisdom took on human flesh and dwelt among us as a man. The historicity of Jesus is an essential consideration for Christians, for in the Incarnation the gap between the divine and human is bridged; the possibility for humans to share in eternal wisdom exists only because of his historicity. To ignore Jesus's body and care only for the divinity is to err in the same way that some of the heretics Stephen had been thinking about in "Telemachus" had erred. Stephen's insistence on the biographical specificity of artistic creation is his response to such flights to the formless, flights to the eternal that deny the validity or importance of the material conditions of human existence. Artists create not out of formless essences that they intuit with their pure intellects but out of the passions that are aroused by living in the body and within material reality. According to Stephen's speculations, Shakespeare's deep need for vengeance is what inspired *Hamlet,* and whether or not Stephen believes his theory, or whether or not Joyce does, what this theory advances for *Ulysses* is the primacy of the body and its passions and the impossibility of great art being created by Platonists who disregard and even deny the body.

Earlier in the day, Stephen has had an interior debate with William Blake, probably the greatest poet to have created out of such disregard. Stephen, like his creator, has great respect for Blake, but his flights to the eternal were reckless: "Fabled by the daughters of memory. And yet it was in some way if not as memory fabled it. A phrase, then, of impatience, thud of Blake's wing of excess. I hear the ruin of all space, shattered glass and toppling masonry, and time one livid final flame. What's left us then?" (2. 7–10). In Blake's apocalyptic writings, time and space have been shattered as he presents, we may say, "formless, spiritual essences," and such attempts to fly upward without the body are doomed to fall back down, with a thud. Blake was impatient and excessive; what is required is a patient art capable of locating within time and space the eternal and divine. Stephen's best-known line—"History is a nightmare from which I am trying to awake"—is followed up immediately, though silently, with a comment that balances it: "What if that nightmare give you a back kick?" History cannot be ignored in favor of timeless essences, for history can give you a back kick and send you sprawling—all this in an episode in which anti-Semitism is presented as a nightmare on the horizon that will indeed kick back.[7] From these two episodes, one can gather Stephen's fundamental aesthetic position, that art must deal with the here and now and that, if the timeless is to be reached, it cannot be done without taking into account the severe constraints of history and our material conditions of existence.

Through Stephen's aesthetics, one may discern that Joyce did not advocate an art that ignores history, a kind of literary art that seeks to escape from specificity and the local and the concrete in favor of the timeless and ethereal. When a critic as insightful and as forceful as Alan Sinfield describes modernism as a kind of art that eschews the temporal and the local, one must pause to wonder if he gave any real attention to *Ulysses*, which would in so many ways have corrected his assessment. Even if he would like to draw a distinction between modernism as actually manifested in the texts and modernism as an academic construction of the cold war aiming at a taming of the real impulses of the texts it wants to domesticate, then this distinction should be announced and the modernists texts retrieved from such gross misrepresentation. Sinfield sees in modernism an aesthetic that so highly prizes design and technique that it distinguishes art from journalism, high art from popular entertainment, in an effort to unloose the art from its material conditions of production. Many recent accounts of modernism have been inspired to correct this error, and they almost always cite Andreas Huyssen's notion of "the great divide" between the high and the low, the elaborately artful design of serious art and the popular art forms that reached the people. But a glance at *Ulysses* would force a postmodern critic to see how Joyce includes popular music, journalism, popular literature, and magazines as he pursues his modernist aims. There is arguably no text and no artist who delights more in depicting the local in its exact and real dimensions as Joyce in *Ulysses*. Hugh Kenner has emphasized this aspect of Joyce's text more than anyone else, and the anecdotes from Ellmann's biography about Joyce's efforts to check some facts about Dublin geography and denizens abound. Which is not to say that *Ulysses* is not highly designed and technically elaborate; no text is more so. What studying *Ulysses* forces on the postmodern critic is its sense of the local and the concrete, of the popular and the lowly, as an essential part of the modernist aesthetic.

Sinfield opposes an idealist aesthetic of literature in which "literature is envisaged as 'rising above' its conditions of production and reception; as transcending social and political concerns and other such mundane matters. The argument most often presented for this is that great art has endured the test of time" (27–28). Instead he calls for an aesthetics that is materialist and a literature that is interventionist, a literature that actively seeks to contest the conditions of plausibility that render one story true and central and another outlandish and marginal.[8] Joyce's aesthetics, as Stephen suggests, is both. It is interventionist in that Joyce tried out various styles and techniques for storytelling, exposing one mode of representation after another as partial, fraudulent, and inadequate to his deeper purpose, the discovery of a language capable of presenting a truth. Joyce exposed the conditions of plausibility of the styles and techniques his culture had developed, and in one most outrageous episode he presented the entire history of prose fiction. This is his postmodern critique, as he intervened in his culture and tried to establish new conditions for a new story.

In "Aeolus" Stephen tells a story that is instructive in this regard. For it has the scrupulous meanness of a story from Joyce's naturalistic collection of stories, *Dubliners,* but with an ending that suggests something more. His story of "two Dublin vestals" going up Nelson's Pillar to enjoy the view of Dublin is told with exacting precision, describing their itinerary in great detail. Professor MacHugh, who is Stephen's chief audience for this performance, says as Stephen piles detail upon detail, "Yes, I see them." And "I see the idea. I see what you mean." Then, when Stephen reveals his title, the professor exclaims in rapid succession, "I see." "I see." "I see." In an episode devoted to rhetoric and noise and to listening in general, for a story to make its hearer see is a feat. What Professor MacHugh sees at first is the two women and their concrete manifestation in a very real locale, but what he sees at the end is Stephen's ultimate point, his "vision," for Stephen has begun his story with the claim "I have a vision too." For Stephen's story, as precise and concrete as it is, has no point until he reveals his title, "A Pisgah Sight of Palestine or the Parable of the Plums." What is indicated is the failure of the two elderly women of attaining a vision, as Moses did at Pisgah. They crane their necks and see the churches that, from their perspective (both literally and figuratively), dominate Dublin. But they dribble plum juice out of their mouths and spit the plum stones slowly out between the railings. It is a vulgar ending that contrasts with the loftiness of the title. This is Stephen's way of indicating the possibility of seeing, in a specific place (Dublin) and at a specific time (Thursday, June 16, 1904), what can be called only a vision. If one is to see, it must be a specific place and in a specific time. The local and concrete are not eschewed or escaped but embraced as a necessary part of Joyce's visionary aesthetics.

Bloom and the Vulgar Body

Joyce's ultimate purpose was to elevate Bloom to the status of Christian hero, as a manifestation of the Incarnation in his kindness, mercy, and love. From the very first words that describe Bloom, we follow the most fully embodied character in literature: "Mr Leopold Bloom ate with relish the inner organs of beasts and fowls. He liked thick giblet soup, nutty gizzards, a stuffed roast heart, liver slices fried with crustcrumbs, fried hencods' roes. Most of all he like grilled mutton kidneys which gave to his palate a fine tang of faintly scented urine" (4. 1–5). Not only do we know, as the very first thing about Bloom, his eating preferences, but we eventually watch him eat, three complete meals. In the course of the novel we watch him defecate, urinate, and masturbate. We even find out, in the homecoming episode, Bloom's height and weight (5 feet 9 ½ inches tall and 158 pounds) and that he has a full build, a mustache, and olive complexion. We learn things about Bloom's personal history—for instance his middle name (Paula), his childhood nickname (Mackerel), the number of times he has been baptized (three, once by a Protestant cleric, once by a Catholic priest, and once by some schoolboys as a childish prank, one that might even be anti-Jewish in nature); names of childhood friends; the place where he and Molly first met, where they first made love, where they lived at different points in the marriage, and so on. We discover things about his financial circumstances that we surely know about no one else in literature or in life: an insurance policy for his daughter, Milly, with a cash value of more than 133 pounds on this date; his bank account, 18 pounds, 14 shillings, and sixpence; 900 pounds of stock; and a grave plot paid for in full. These are just some of the many details we learn about Bloom, and by the time the novel is over, we know more about Bloom, with precision and exactitude, than any other character in literature. But why?

Kenner has noted that we learn most of the details about Bloom late in the text, in "Ithaca" and "Penelope" especially, and he calls this an "aesthetic of delay,"[9] suggesting that part of Joyce's sense of art was to continue to "flesh out" his hero with a facts and details about his unique personal circumstances and material condition as he elevates him to the heights of epic or allegorical significance. As the novel moves away from naturalism and toward symbolism, as it moves away from realistic depiction to symbolic figuration, Joyce made sure that readers would never ignore the materiality of his hero, loading the late episodes, especially "Ithaca," with facts and details about Bloom's body and existence. If Bloom is to rise to the heights of such lofty meaning for this text and for his culture, it will be as a fully embodied character, a character whose body and material circumstances will be taken up, against gravity, to such heights.

There is one episode in particular that deserves special attention, for in "Lestrygonians" Joyce presented the human body as an eating and defecating machine. It is the hour between one and two in the afternoon, and Bloom feels his energy running down and feels the need to eat: "This is the very worst hour of the day. Vitality. Dull, gloomy: hate this hour. Feel as if I had been eaten and spewed" (8. 494–95). He continues to walk about aimlessly, and then recognizes that he has come to a place where he may take lunch: "Duke street. Here we are. Must eat. The Burton. Feel better then" (8. 640). In this episode the human body is presented as a machine that requires food as energy and that releases waste products as part of the mechanical process of digestion. As Bloom thinks about the "naked goddesses" "standing in the round hall" of the library museum, he thinks about the differences between the human body and the bodies of the classical gods and goddesses: "Quaffing nectar at mess with gods golden dishes, all ambrosial. Not a tanner lunch we have, boiled mutton, carrots and turnips, bottle of Allsop. Nectar imagine it drinking electricity: gods' food. Lovely forms of women sculped Junonian. Immortal lovely. And we stuffing food in one hole and out behind: food, chyle, blood, dung, earth, food: have to feed it like stoking an engine. They have no. Never looked. I'll look today. Keeper won't see. Bend down let something drop. See if she" (8. 925–32). In these musings, the human body has been reduced to a mere machine to be stoked, while the gods and goddesses have bodies that enjoy a higher kind of food and may not even need to defecate. It is funny that Bloom plans to test this hypothesis by going round to the library museum and seeing if any of the statues of the gods there have an anus, as if that would prove anything. Perhaps it would prove that in our imaginings, the gods and goddesses are purer and not defiled by the need to release wastes. Perhaps it would prove that, when we imagine the divine, we imagine something without the human form that we carry about with us and that drags us down when it needs food and carries us along on its mechanical ways of desire. For Booker, this moment is a sign of Joyce's Rabelaisian intentions: "Bakhtin's work on Rabelais has taught us that an emphasis on the 'lower bodily stratum' can subvert the pretensions of authoritarian discourse in powerful ways" (25–26). For Joyce and his day, the authoritarian discourse that had to be subverted was—ironically—the Cartesian discourse that assumes a disembodied rational self and not the Christian discourse of Incarnation. The Enlightenment separation of the mind from the body and its passions ruled Joyce's day, and it has affinities with the Greek culture that the statuary of the goddesses belongs to. So Booker is right, but not in the way he intended, when he makes Bloom's curiosity about "the presence of absence of posterior rectal orifices in the case of Hellenic female divinities" (*Ulysses*, 17. 2077–78) Joyce's way of taking issue with Greek, that is Platonic, culture. Yet in the Incarnation, Christ has just such a body as ours. The vulgar body that we carry about is in no way different from the body of God made flesh. At least in *Ulysses*, the pagan gods that seem to indicate a delight in the flesh actually disdain the flesh much more than does the Christian God of Incarnation or the tradition of Christian writing that *Ulysses* culminates. To return to this Christian tradition is Joyce's subversive act, and in this way it is precisely Rabelaisian.

The first place Bloom stops at is so disgusting that he cannot bear to eat there. The men who do eat there are compared to animals: "His heart astir he pushed in the door of the Burton restaurant. Stink gripped his trembling breath: pungent meatjuice, slush of greens. See the animals feed" (8. 650–653). In this episode physical needs are either mechanical or animal, and in both comparisons the dignity of human being is neglected or debunked. The Darwinian context is brought into the text as Bloom leaves the Burton: "Every fellow for his own, tooth and nail. Gulp. Grub. Gulp. Gobstuff. He came out into the clearer air and turned back towards Grafton street. Eat or be eaten. Kill! Kill!" (8. 701–3). When it comes to food, we are no different than the animals, a point underscored at the beginning of this episode when Bloom feeds the seagulls, who devour the bread that Bloom casts on the water. That our need for food connects us to the animal world is a central point in Bakhtin's reading of Rabelais: "The unfinished and open body . . . is not separated from the world by clearly defined boundaries; it is blended with the world, with animals, with objects" (26–27). In this episode of *Ulysses*, human nature is blended with machines and animals, no longer distinctly separate and dignified by that separation.

Whether the analogy is to machines or animals, this episode underscores the demands of the body on our moods and on our mental states, demands that must be attended to and appeased. Bloom even wonders if "peace and war depend on some fellow's digestion" (8. 752–53) as the body determines even such important decisions of statesmanship. What is also implied in this episode is that sexual desire, specifically Molly's unsatisfied desire, which is leading her to her affair with Boylan, is also something that demands attention and cannot be denied:

> Walking down by the Tolka. Not bad for Fairview moon. She was humming. The young May moon she's beaming, love. He other side of her. Elbow, arm. He. Glowworm's la-amp is gleaming, love. Touch. Fingers. Asking. Answer. Yes.
> Stop. Stop. If it was it was. Must. (8. 587–92)

Shortly after this image from a day several weeks earlier, Bloom indulges in a brief memory of some happier days from much longer back, hoping to use memory to fight against his present unhappy circumstances with Molly. Bloom, however, is not inspired by memory to go back home to intervene in Molly's life. Instead he thinks, "Useless to go back. Had to be. Tell me all" (8. 633). This is Bloom's fundamental attitude toward the affair all day long, to be sure, but here it is part of a critique of the body as an undeniable force, as an engine that drives us along tracks that we do not necessarily want to be on. Bloom acknowledges that there is a necessity to Molly's affair, almost as if it were not a free choice of her own. The body has needs that cannot be denied, needs that drive the plots of our lives.

This episode presents the body at its most powerful in determining the direction and shape and meaning of our lives, against which the mind is not capable of mastery or control. One of the most important features of Bloom is his utter passivity, especially regarding Molly's affair: he is not a man of action; he is not a man who seeks to be master of his own household; he is not a man who seeks to exert his will against circumstance and change the course of events, even the events of his own life. "Ulysses" and "useless" are almost anagrams, and Bloom's understanding of the uselessness of most efforts to exert will or exercise autonomy is what characterizes him and what might seem to disqualify him from being considered a hero. Most heroes, especially in epics, are strong-willed men who rise above circumstance and impose their wills on the course of events. But Bloom is almost utterly passive, allowing events to unfold as they must and allowing the needs of the body to drive the plot of his day. Much of this book depicts the power of the body and our material nature to limit and define our sphere of activity and our sense of the possible.

In this episode even memory, an act of the mind independent of the body, is unable to exert a happy pressure back against circumstances and bring Bloom any solace. Bloom thinks about his past life with Molly several times this episode, and each time an image from the past merely marks the difference between time past and time present: "I was happier then. Or was that I? Or am I now I? Twentyeight I was. She twentythree. When we left Lombard street west something changed. Could never like it again after Rudy. Can't bring back time. Like holding water in your hand" (8. 608–11). The lack of a stable and permanent "I" might be worth noting here, as well as the lack of a personal pronoun letting us know who could not like the sexual act after Rudy's death, Bloom or Molly. What is certain from this passage is that the present time seems much diminished from a happier past. Earlier in the episode Bloom tries to please himself with calls to "remember her laughing at the wind"; "remember when we got home raking up the fire." "Happy. Happy. That was the night. . . . " (8. 191, 194, 200–201). Then there is Bloom's detailed and lengthy recollection of the first time he and Molly made love on Howth, which contrasts powerfully with the same recollection from Molly's memory that ends the novel. In "Penelope" it is happy and exuberant and affirmative; in "Lestrygonians" it is only a sad marker of the gap between a happier past and a depressing present: "Me. And me now. Stuck the flies buzzed" (8. 917–18). In this episode Bloom is brought downward from any good mood or happy thoughts by the material circumstances that define his life and that seem to confine him, as he feels as paralyzed here as any character from *Dubliners*. In this episode human agency and will are made to appear weak and futile, as the mind is powerless to counteract the passions and needs of the body. "Lestrygonians" presents the body as a monster that is too powerful for the mind to subdue or control.

The Grotesque and the Monstrous: Changing Styles in *Ulysses*

Named after the monstrous cannibals who devour some of Odysseus's men, this episode is called "Lestrygonians" because in it the body becomes monstrous, becoming more powerful than the self or the mind that it houses and that ought to control and direct it. This episode represents Joyce's way of responding to and opposing a Cartesian or Enlightenment modernity that wants the mind to be master of the human self and its destiny, controlling and directing our lives in space and time toward a rationally conceived set of goals and projects. But it is really not true to say that the body is monstrous in this episode; it does not become monstrous, as it did in *Gulliver's Travels,* nor does it become grotesque as in did in *Gargantua and Pantagruel.* The body is most accurately called "vulgar" in Joyce's text because it pays lots of attention to the lower functions that polite society likes to ignore and cover over. Bloom presents a vulgar body in the sense of its being common and low. What are more properly monstrous and grotesque in *Ulysses* are its styles. Joyce's ingenuity in *Ulysses* can be found partly in his decision to make the ways of narrating his story grotesque and monstrous, challenging the reader's ability to recognize the humanity of the characters so depicted.

Joyce completely demolishes the notion that any mode of narrative representation can be a neutral window onto the world or into the heads of his characters. The opening six episodes, all told in a uniform style of lucid naturalism and interior monologue, seem to be perfectly in keeping with the traditional novel's devotion to realistic depiction; but when we review what we have come to call, after Michael Groden, the initial style of *Ulysses* from the point of view of the later episodes of stylistic extravagance, we are led to consider that none of the styles, including that initial style, captures reality any more fully or any more truly than any other and that there is something misleading even about the opening naturalistic style. For that style, already cast in doubt from the seventh episode on and then abandoned fully after the tenth episode, is so devoted to the body and its demands that it cannot but debunk, puncture, or deflate any attempt to elevate humankind in or through the characters of Stephen and Bloom. Each of Bloom's first three episodes in the initial style end with deflation: with sadness at Dignam's death in "Calypso," with Bloom's anticipation of his body in the bath at the end of "Lotus Eaters," and with funereal morbidity about our general mortality in "Hades." Bloom's thoughts about the law of falling bodies at the beginning of "Lotus Eaters" are an indicator of the tendency of this part of *Ulysses.* No matter how much Joyce wants to elevate his characters, the weight of their bodies brings them crashing down to earth. Presiding over this festival of debunking is the greatest mocker in all literature, Buck Mulligan.

By creating Buck Mulligan and placing him as the opening voice and sensibility of *Ulysses,* Joyce set in motion an often antic comedy that seems to delight in debunking and deflating. In effect Joyce established a figure of Folly, someone who casts doubt on any figure of pretension or any position that has become so rigid and conventional that it assumes a dignity it no longer deserves. Attitudes toward Buck Mulligan vary, and too often he is castigated as the gay betrayer of Stephen's brooding imagination. However, Robert Bell's *Jocoserious Joyce* presents Mulligan in a happier light: "Buck persistently burlesques everything abstract, ethereal, or idealistic. Nothing is left unchallenged; everything is open to travesty, parody, mockery. The tug downward is insistent in *Ulysses,* and Buck Mulligan is the apostle of gravity" (21). That Buck Mulligan is fun to watch and that he would be a better companion than Stephen Dedalus seem beyond dispute, and Bell does well to make of Mulligan a figure of fun and frolic. Like the actions of the fools in the early modern period, Buck Mulligan's antics have as their purpose the debunking of pretension and clichéd principles. Yet Bell goes too far in claiming that "the text eventually approaches Buck's view" (21). It is one thing to rescue Buck from Stephen's morbid dislike, and it is quite another to make him the presiding spirit over the entire novel. Rather Buck Mulligan is the happy embodiment of the postmodern critique that wants to expose as empty and fraudulent any claim to permanent and absolute value the text might try to offer. He is the postmodern challenge to the modernist ambition.

Buck Mulligan's fun is rooted in an attitude toward the body that one can only call naturalistic. Putting aside for a moment his mockery of the Eucharist and the Ascension, let us first examine his attitude toward Stephen's mother's death. When Stephen explains that Mulligan gave offense when he said to his aunt, "*O, it's only Dedalus whose mother is beastly dead,*" Buck launches into a defense of his attitude: "And what is death, he asked, your mother's or yours or my own? You saw only your mother die. I see them pop off every day in the Mater and Richmond and cut up into tripes in the dissecting room. It's a beastly thing and nothing more. It simply doesn't matter" (1. 204–7). Mulligan's vantage point is that of the medical man, the man of science who sees the human being as nothing more than a beast whose body eventually dies. He represents the Enlightenment modernity that places its faith in science and reason to evaluate all human existence. Darwin placed humanity strictly within the context of nature and natural selection, and Mulligan occupies that space as well, the same space as Nietzsche, that other great debunker with whom Buck identifies himself several times in the episode. From the vantage point of nature and man's beastly body, any pretension can be mocked, and Mulligan does it with wit and charm. But he sees nothing beyond his scientific debunking: "It's a beastly thing and nothing more. It simply doesn't matter." He can only see humans as Darwinian beasts, and he neglects any other possible way of evaluating life and death.

So Stephen is ultimately correct in his assessment of Mulligan, and he is the opposite danger from the disembodied Platonism that Stephen must sail by in "Scylla and Charybdis." For if Russell and Blake advocate an art that leaves the body for the ideal realm, Mulligan's art—for he is also a poet, and unlike Stephen a poet invited to George Moore's this evening—is one that punctures every ideal and brings us back to the body. Mulligan's is the opposite error of the Platonists of Augustine and the Cartesians of Swift and the sloppy Romantics of Joyce's own text: Mulligan's aesthetic wants to make the body and material culture in general the ultimate perspective from which to view life and assign values. The difficult path Stephen's art must discover is a way to locate the ideals of Blake within the bodily and material. The Incarnation resolves the dualism that has plagued Western culture and allows a double focus on both the temporal and the timeless, the body and the mind.

"Lestrygonians" is written, one might say, under the sway of Mulligan's aesthetic, and its style is monstrous because the kind of life described within its perspective is not a human life but one that only has the outward appearances of humanity. Any claim to agency or will has been hollowed out by the monstrous exaggeration of the body's position in assessing human life. If Platonists fear the body too much, it might well be because the body can take over a life and direct it to lower destinies than are possible. But to deny the body is to provide the mind with unimpeded claims to autonomy and authority that cannot hold up under scrutiny.

Joyce's most ingenious contribution to the Christian tradition of Incarnation might well be in his decision not to create any monstrous figures in the text (though we perhaps glimpse some in "Oxen"), but to make the styles themselves a series of monsters that Bloom—or his reader?—must confront. It seems safe to say that all the stylistic experiments are grotesque and monstrous exaggerations of "normal" narratives and that Joyce has made his hero wander through a series of encounters with monsters in which Bloom must retain his humanity.

The "Cyclops" episode might be the one best suited for this demonstration, as it presents in its title a monster from the Homeric epic that Joyce has transformed into a stylistic device threatening Bloom's humanity. This is also the episode that is most "Rabelaisian," in that it contains the kind of excessive language and exaggeration one typically associates with Rabelais. The lists that the parodic narrator presents are perhaps the closest Joyce comes to imitating Rabelais, and the delight in the mere listing suggests that words have indeed become things to play with and enjoy in and for themselves, as Spitzer says. But what is monstrous or grotesque in this episode are its alternating narrators: the lofty parodic narrator, whose main task is to provide inflated stories tangential (at best) to the "real" action of the episode, and in which the absurd lists are presented; and the mean unnamed narrator from whom we receive the main action of the episode. The lofty narrator uses language so excessively and devises styles that seek so urgently to beautify and ennoble that he cannot be trusted to give us anything like a reliable account. His depiction of a hanging is so sweet and sentimental that it is outlandish; his description of the citizen as a giant-sized hero is simply impossible; his list of Irish heroes is absurd; his description of the dog Garryowen's poem is just plain silly. These parodies of the high and lofty, which according to Groden were part of Joyce's original conception for the episode, before he thought of the main action in fact, indicate that attempts to use lofty language to describe heroic behavior no longer work in a modern world of reason and realism. Such attempts are exposed as fraudulent. They also force us to think about the narration presented by the unnamed "I," whose meanness and spite are emphasized by the contrast. He is no more to be trusted than his opposite; if the one wants to raise his subject matter to lofty heights of sentiment and sublimity, the other wants to reduce events and personality to their lowest possible motivations. And the "I" hates Bloom most particularly. The "Cyclops" in this episode is this "I" who only hates, while the lofty narrator's attempts to rescue Bloom from the monster with "poetry" look ridiculous and impotent. The narrator of the main action hates Bloom and wants us to do so as well, and, because of the lofty narrator's ineptitude and loss of credibility, Bloom must resist or evade this reduction merely by force of his personality. The twin stylistic monsters provide the context in which Bloom emerges as a most decent human being.

This is the first episode in which we are not privileged with looks inside Bloom's head, but we as readers of the novel up to this point have come to know him well, and we rely on that knowledge of his personality to push back against the monstrous meanness of this episode. Perhaps nothing Joyce does is as effective in providing the illusion of Bloom's "reality" as a character than stepping outside Bloom's consciousness and allowing him to stand on his own, in the midst of competing one-eyed monsters who cannot see the truth before them. And Bloom in this episode is at his most active and passionate, as if he were fighting these monsters. What he does in this episode is reject the meanness and hatred of Irish nationalism and advocate love in its place.

After Bloom's defense of love, the citizen sarcastically calls Bloom a new apostle to the gentiles, and in that sarcasm is the clue to the episode, for Bloom is indeed like Saint Paul in that both preach love in a hostile context. Paul's famous and beautiful definition of love occurs in the thirteenth chapter of his first letter to the Corinthians, a church that was divided by its own spite and aggressiveness. Bloom's definition of love is hardly eloquent—"Love, says Bloom.

I mean the opposite of hatred"—but it is enough for this text that the word be uttered plainly. It takes great strength to oppose the citizen with the sure but modest conviction that Bloom demonstrates throughout the episode, and he is able to overcome the threats of the unnamed narrator who would like to get us to hate Bloom too. He rises above his narrators and remains fully human as he advocates the emotion that makes us capable of being fully human, the feeling of love, "the word known to all men."

Which is quickly and roundly mocked by the citizen. When John Wyse Nolan reminds the citizen that we are told to love our neighbor, the citizen responds contemptuously, "That chap? Beggar my neighbor rather is his motto. Love, moya! He's a nice pattern of a Romeo and Juliet" (9. 1490–92). The citizen, like the nameless "I" who narrates, wants to see Bloom as a miserly Jew, and it is left to the reader to recall that Bloom not only promised to give five shillings to the widow Dignam but already put the money up. Furthermore, to the citizen and the narrator who champions him, love is sexual love of the adolescent sensibility, and not the larger charity we are called on to feel and live by. In Bloom's defense, the lofty narrator then launches into an absurdly sentimental period about love: "Love loves to love love. Nurse loves the new chemist. Constable 14A loves Mary Kelly. Gerty MacDowell loves the boy who has the bicycle. M.B. loves a fair gentleman. Li Chan Han lovey up kissy Cha Pu Chow. Jumbo, the elephant, loves Alice, the elephant" (12. 1993–96). The famous elephant pair of Jumbo and Alice makes the list clearly silly, and the ending is a hackneyed reference to God's universal love: "And this person loves that other person because everybody loves somebody but God loves everybody" (12. 1500–1501). Language has become so conventional and clichéd that words such as "love" have become almost indefinable, almost inexpressible. Bloom's mere assertion of love in this context is enough to make him admirable. Joyce's lesson from Dante is that language is inherently fraudulent and from Rabelais that words such as "love" have lost their authority and have become mere things in the world. Despite this skeptical context, Joyce managed to make the mere assertion of the word almost a heroic feat in itself. It all comes down to a simple goal for the most complex modernist projects, how to make love authentic in a thoroughly cynical age.

The stylistic monster does not defeat Bloom, but instead he resists it with this word, which perhaps has a power to slay such threats to our humanity. It is the word Stephen asks his mother about, the mysterious word known to all men. Bloom slays the monster that wants to debunk him and reduce him to a figure of pathetic impotence; he does so by rising up to defend our humanity by means of this word. From Rabelais onward the status of the word has become degraded, and in Joyce's own day it may justly be doubted, as Saussure was teaching, that a word such as "love" has any referent outside language. Yet Joyce used all his artistry to make the word powerful again. Bloom, bravely and with confidence, is able to utter the word love, and it may indeed be enough to slay the monsters.

This is the one episode where Bloom explicitly identifies himself as a Jew; in fact, in recounting this scene to Stephen later, he claims that he is really not a Jew, and earlier in the day he never thinks of himself as affiliated with any religion. But here, when he is being persecuted as Jew, he makes the famous remark "Christ was a jew like me." This identification may seem impossible to sustain and to be debunked by the way the episode ends, with the clearly absurd comparison of Bloom to Elijah, which is comically deflated. But the identification of Bloom as a Jew like Christ is one that Joyce tries to make again, and it is in the preaching of love that Bloom is most Jewish in the way Christ was.

While one may say that all the later episodes present some sort of stylistic monster threatening Bloom's humanity, the other episode that does so most boldly and clearly is "Circe." This episode brings a distinctly twentieth-century threat to the Enlightenment version of humanism that rests on the faith in a rational self in control of its destiny, for in "Circe" an antic Freudian whirl of outlandish and nonrational images from the unconscious confront Bloom and Stephen. While madness itself is not new to this period, Freudian psychoanalytic theory was, and it was able to array itself in the guise of science to proclaim that consciousness is but a small part of our psychic life and, more alarmingly, perhaps an ineffectual part compared to unconscious forces in guiding and determining our nature and our destinies. The implications of Darwinian theory threaten human agency in "Lestrygonians," while in "Circe" Joyce anticipated how Freudian theories of the mind challenge humanist assumptions about agency and autonomy. We know what Althusser does with ideology in limiting free agency and will, and what Lacan does with the unconscious in the postmodern critique. Joyce and his contemporaries were able to anticipate the implications of theories of the unconscious on our understanding of humanity and the rational underpinnings of humanism.

But Joyce's hero comes through his series of hallucinations pretty much unscathed, which is more than we can say for Stephen. The text and the reader can be seen as the ones undergoing the hallucinations, as we must allow our worst thoughts about Bloom—he is weak and passive; he is a sexual pervert and masochist; he enjoys being cuckolded—to be expressed and purged from the text so that we can then proceed to see the very different kind of hero Joyce was trying to present in the Nostos. If we want to see Bloom's unconscious forces rising against him, threatening to take over his life and bringing him on a track he would wish to avoid, then the action of this episode allows us to conclude that

Bloom is not at the mercy of his unconscious and that he remains pretty much the same man we have seen all day long: kind, practical, and quick-witted. Joyce's remarks about the unconscious—particularly that he is much more interested in consciousness—help us draw the conclusion that his hero has enough integrity to withstand the nonrational onslaughts from his unconscious mind and remain steady and stable. Bloom rises to assert the conscious and rational will against the powerful forces of the unconscious, and he is ready to act humanely at episode's end to rescue Stephen from the hands of civil authority. Circe's power to transform men into pigs falls harmlessly on Odysseus and on his modernist manifestation. He has something that renders him immune from the magic of this kind of metamorphosis. The moly that protects Bloom from Circe's degrading powers is the word "love."

So the grotesque and monstrous images that form much of "Circe" do not transform Bloom, or reduce Bloom, or even make him waver and falter before their power. Poor Stephen—whether because he is younger, or very drunk, or just not as good a man yet as Bloom—suffers a different fate. Stephen's hallucination is not something internal and just for our viewing; he himself sees it and talks to it and confronts it, attacking it with his ashplant as if he were wielding Siegfried's sword and battling a monstrous nemesis. Bloom is left to clean up Stephen's mess with the mistress of the brothel, and, when he catches up to Stephen, Bloom finds him in an altercation with a British soldier. Stephen's internal demons are so strong that they bring him face to face with a power from history, represented by the soldier, who in the end knocks Stephen unconscious. So Stephen has learned what he already suspected, you cannot flee history and if you try to it may just give you that back kick. Bloom saves Stephen from a night in jail and brings him home. Stephen's destiny has been affected by his unconscious, and it brings him into a new plot, one that includes Bloom.

Joyce used the monstrous and grotesque images of the unconscious for at least two relevant purposes here: to show Bloom's utter decency and equanimity, as these violent forces do nothing to make him even stumble; and to drive Stephen into the arms of Bloom, who then acts in the fatherly way the end of the episode suggests. Not only can these monsters not slay Bloom, they bring him to a role he had always hoped to play, father to a talented son. The artist-son will now be able to witness in this strange man the Incarnation of Christian love.

Bloom's Ascension

One of the best-known of Joyce's letters is the one he wrote to Frank Budgen in early 1921, as he was writing "Ithaca" and "Penelope": "I am writing *Ithaca* in the form of a mathematical catechism. All events are resolved into their cosmic, physical, psychical, etc. equivalents, e.g. Bloom jumping down the area, drawing water from the tap, the micturition in the garden, the cone of incense, lighted candle and statue so that not only will the reader know everything and know it in the coldest baldest way, but Bloom and Stephen thereby become heavenly bodies, wanderers like the stars at which they gaze" (*Letters,* 1:159–60). What is important here is Joyce's odd statement that what allows Bloom to become a heavenly body is that the reader knows everything about him. The cold, bald style of "Ithaca" presents more facts about Bloom than the rest of the novel taken as a whole (with the exception of "Penelope," in which Molly also gives us plenty of details), and somehow knowing these facts allows or enables Bloom to rise against gravity and ascend to the heavens.

"Ithaca" resolves the technical problems of *Ulysses* because it eschews all the usual poetic and literary practices and plainly informs the reader of the facts that we need to know, of some facts that are interesting but not essential, and of some facts that seem simply irrelevant. It is so plain and direct—and so nonliterary— that many readers have failed to note what may be the key "fact" of the novel: that in Bloom, Stephen sees "the traditional figure of hypostasis" (17.783). The reader does indeed know everything, including the books on Bloom's bookshelves and the contents of his desk drawers, the intricate pathway of water through the Dublin water system to Bloom's tap, and the advantages of night shaving. The reader knows too much, too many details, many of them of little if any importance in resolving the plots of this text (such as the advantages of night shaving). In the midst of so many facts, all told with the same cold, bald certainty, one might easily fail to notice something as cataclysmic as Stephen's claim to have seen in Bloom the Incarnation. This narrator does not know how to focus, how to emphasize, how to bring something of huge significance into the foreground. In sheer length, the two pages on the movement of water through Dublin dwarfs the statement of Stephen's vision.

Stephen's aesthetic has prepared him, and us, for his moment of vision. Stephen was looking for a kind of art that would avoid the extremes of the disembodied Platonism of Russell and the crude naturalism of Mulligan. His "Pisgah Sight of Palestine or the Parable of the Plums" depicts with precise image and local detail the failure of two Dublin women to see a vision from the top of Nelson's Pillar. Stephen says to begin his story, "I have a vision too," and those words prove prophetic when he sees in Bloom the manifestation of love and kindness.

For that is what we may infer from this "fact" of Stephen's vision of the traditional figure of hypostasis. We are no longer inside the characters' minds, so we cannot know for sure, but it must have struck Stephen as an unexpected surprise for this strange man to come to his rescue, to take such good care of him, and to bring him gently to his home until he could recover. Knowing Stephen as we do, we might be a bit surprised when he waits a full four minutes for Bloom to jump down the railing, get in through the back door, find and light a candle, and come to the front door to let Stephen enter. In an episode of pure facts and with no narrative focus at all, we are left to infer that Stephen really wants to come inside this man's house and see more of him. Perhaps Stephen is remembering his dream from earlier in the day, of a man welcoming him in to his home with a red carpet spread, and in whose presence he flew, easily flew. Perhaps Stephen is seeing those dreams as prophecy of an important event, such as an experience of the Incarnation would be. The coincidence between Bloom's and Stephen's dreams, and the coincidence in these dreams becoming true as Stephen is brought into Bloom's home, are signs of Joyce's elaborate design in making of the random and accidental part of a larger, almost providential plot. We fill in plot and motivation in this cold and bald episode of facts and details, until we are stunned by Stephen's vision.

For that is how Stephen's vision in "Ithaca" ought to be read, as a stunning surprise, as an eruption into the quotidian of the divine in the person of Leopold Bloom, who by his kindness and loving action is an incarnation of Christ. We should recall that back in "Nestor" Stephen rejected Mr. Deasy's understanding of history as a progress culminating in the manifestation of God: "All human history moves towards one great goal, the manifestation of God" (2.380–81). This nineteenth-century, Hegelian view sees history as moving steadily toward greater light and goodness, an Enlightenment view if ever there were one. Instead, for Stephen, God is a sudden eruption, joyous and spontaneous, into time and space: "That is God. . . . A shout in the street" (2. 383, 386). This is the view of history that the Christian belief in Incarnation makes possible, valuing space and time as the conditions for God's participation in human affairs but not in the excessive manner of the Enlightenment, in which the very process of history itself is how God will be made manifest, in which man's thinking and acting are agents that in the end will make God manifest in human history. Stephen's Christian view avoids the error of Blake and the Dublin literati led by George Russell, who want to flee history, and the opposite error of Mulligan's naturalism, which wants to deny the divine and values only the material and natural. It also avoids Deasy's error of excessive valuation of history that nineteenth-century, Enlightenment thinkers such as Georg Wilhelm Friedrich Hegel, Karl Marx, and Charles Darwin advance.

Mulligan's role in final episodes of *Ulysses* is larger than ever, even though he is not present in any material way. For, while Robert Bell is wrong to claim that *Ulysses* approaches Mulligan's attitude of mockery and debunking, his role as unconscious prophet of the text's climax assumes prominence. Buck's Christian name is Malachi, which means "messenger." Buck is the namesake of the last prophet in the Christian Old Testament. Malachi's prophetic book is primarily a diatribe against the bad priests who shepherded God's people in his day, and Mulligan begins his day as the sort of mock priest against whom the prophet made dire warnings. The ending of the book of Malachi offers a remarkable piece of prophecy that Joyce used in manifold ways: "Lo, I will send you Elijah, the prophet, before the day of the Lord comes, the great and terrible day, to turn the hearts of the fathers to their children, and the hearts of the children to their fathers, lest I come and strike the land with doom" (Mal. 3. 23–24). If Mulligan is a prophet in spite of himself, if he is prophesying future things of which he is unaware (as Isaiah prophesied the birth of Christ when he thought he was describing the birth of Hezekiah), then Mulligan is prophesying that Bloom and Stephen will come together as father and son, and a reconciliation between the old and the new will be achieved in their union. But more important, he is predicting the coming of Elijah before the coming of the Lord on the great and terrible day of his manifestation. And Elijah plays an important role in *Ulysses*.

This theme begins in the opening lines of "Lestrygonians," when a young man hands Bloom a throwaway advertising a sermon that evening by an American preacher. Bloom is reading the throwaway: "Elijah is coming. Dr John Alexander Dowie restorer of the church in Zion is coming. Is coming! Is coming! Is coming" (8.13–15). Dr. Dowie must think of himself as the Elijah from Malachi's prophecy, restoring all things before the coming of Christ. Bloom mistakenly identifies himself with Christ in this scene, as he reads the throwaway and says to himself, "Bloo. . . . Me? No. Blood of the Lamb" (8. 8–9). But in Joyce mistakes and accidents are "portals of discovery," and what gets said in jest often comes true in strange but perceptible ways. Bloom made an unconscious prediction of the outcome of the Gold Cup race earlier in the day, at the end of "Lotus Eaters," when he wants to get rid of Bantam Lyons and tells him to keep the newspaper, "I was just going to throw it away" (5.534). Lyons hears a tip, for a horse running in the race is named Throwaway, and—as in the reality of June 16, 1904—the twenty-to-one dark horse Throwaway in fact wins the race. Bloom is completely oblivious to this outcome, but the "Ithaca" narrator sees great significance in this accident.

Asked when earlier in the day Bloom received "previous intimations of the result" of the race, the "Ithaca" narrator mentions several, including "outside Graham Lemon's when a dark man had placed in his hand a throwaway (subsequently thrown away), advertising Elijah, restorer of the church in Zion" (17. 327, 331–33), as well as in the earlier scene when Bantam Lyons asked to borrow Bloom's copy of the newspaper, which Bloom was about to throw away. His inadvertent tip to Lyons and the throwaway "advertising Elijah" are connected here, and the "Ithaca" narrator sees Bloom quite differently than the "Lotus Eaters" narrator did. In "Lotus Eaters" Bloom merely "walked cheerfully toward the mosque of the baths" (5.549) whereas in "Ithaca" he walks "with the light of inspiration shining in his countenance and bearing in his arms the secret race, graven in the language of prediction" (17. 339–41). In "Ithaca" Bloom's face is transfigured with light, like Moses's face when he came down for Mount Sinai with the Ten Commandments. Indeed the language here comes from the lofty speech about Moses in "Aeolus," placing Bloom in the company of Moses and Elijah. (Note the wonderful joke calling Bloom the ad canvasser an "advertising Elijah.") Bloom is transfigured here and associated with the two Old Testament figures who appear with Jesus at his Transfiguration.

So Elijah has come into the text, in the prediction of the Gold Cup race. The end of "Cyclops" tried to make Bloom into Elijah with its lofty rhetoric, but its language is hackneyed and clichéd and undercut by the final image: "And there came a voice out of heaven, calling: *Elijah! Elijah!* And he answered with a main cry: *Abba! Adonai* And they beheld Him, even Him, ben Bloom Elijah, amid clouds of angels ascend to the glory of the brightness at an angle of fortyfive degrees over Donohoe's in Little Green street like a shot off a shovel" (12.1914–18). Bloom's vigorous if inept defense of love in this episode is not enough in itself to elevate Bloom, and the poetic language, here in imitation of Old Testament language of the King James Bible, is insufficient to elevate him to the heavens. As Joyce said in that letter to Budgen, it takes the cold, bald style of "Ithaca" to accomplish the feat.

Mulligan's first act in "Telemachus," on the very first page of *Ulysses*, is to perform a mock Eucharist for the entertainment of the sleepy and displeased Stephen. This messenger mocks the very notion of God's becoming part of material creation; such is Joyce's way of introducing his highest theme into his text, for his ultimate aim was to bring Christ into his book. Even more pointedly, Mulligan sings a song of his own making that mocks the notion of Christ's Ascension:

> —*I'm the queerest young fellow that ever you heard.*
> *My mother's a jew, my father's a bird.*
> *With Joseph the joiner I cannot agree.*
> *So here's to disciples and Calvary. . . .*
> —*Goodbye, now, goodbye! Write down all I said*
> *And tell Tom, Dick and Harry I rose from the dead.*
> *What's bred in the bone can't fail me to fly*
> *And Olivet's breezy—Goodbye, now, goodbye!* (1.581–87, 593–99)

What's mocked in the opening episode is accomplished in "Ithaca," or at least Joyce hoped so if his letter to Budgen is of any account. Joyce labored in early episodes to present Bloom from within his consciousness as a man of unique and real personality, and we watch as he moves through his day in a graphically depicted locale. Joyce's attention to Bloom's body and personality are unequaled in all literature, and he continued to depict Bloom as a very real and unique character in "Ithaca," where we learn many new facts about him that make him idiosyncratic, including his height and weight. Weight is the measure of the force of gravity of an object, and Bloom last weighed himself "on the last feast of the Ascension, to wit, the twelfth day of May" (17.94–95). It is part of the great delight of reading *Ulysses* to witness such indirection: the coincidence of Bloom's finding out his weight on the feast of Ascension, which is the mystery of Christ rising against gravity, is exquisite. It is Joyce's oblique way of indicating his goal, of elevating this fully embodied character against gravity and heavenward.

And Stephen the artist is the one who has the vision. He sees in Bloom the traditional figure of hypostasis, the joining of the human and the divine, which is Christ. Booker wants to demonstrate Joyce's Rabelaisian side, saying that Joyce "consistently reject[s] Christ as an effective role model" (39), but how can a critic with Rabelais in mind miss this cold, bald statement of vision and how would he treat it if it were pointed out to him? (Schlossman, it must be said, noted this moment of vision but hardly made anything of it [45], as if seeing the Incarnation is not a major moment in a Catholic text.) As Brook Thomas has pointed out,[10] mistaken identities abound in *Ulysses*, and the anecdote about Mulcahy from the Coombe that Corny Kelleher recounts in "Hades" is especially enlightening about the possible absurdity in making such claims; and this could be another mistake. But not all claims of hidden identity must be false, and this identification of Bloom with Christ is not made by two drunken men but by a carefully drawn figure whose role in Joyce's fiction makes his vision harder to dismiss. It is Stephen the artist who sees this, and it is Bloom the good and decent man who bears the striking resemblance. When Bloom and Stephen go out to the garden to urinate, they perform a comic ritual that we are told commemorates the escape of the people of Israel from the slavery of Egypt. They have been liberated and look up to see "The heaventree of stars hung with humid nightblue fruit" (17.1039), which is an outburst of lyric poetry in an otherwise prosaic episode. Freed from their confinement to their material conditions, they raise their eyes and see with wonder the beauty of the stars, which play such a crucial role in Dante's *Comedia*, with each canticle ending with the word "*stele*," as Dante looks at the night sky with renewed and ever stronger vigor. After Stephen's departure we learn that Bloom feels "the cold of interstellar space, thousands of degrees below freezing point or the absolute zero of Fahrenheit, Centigrade, or Reaumur" (17.1246–47). He has indeed become like the stars at which they gaze.

Of course not literally. Or better, though he has achieved this apotheosis, he is still in the body and walking around his house. Bloom must finally make the homecoming that he has been deferring all day long, back to the bed of his adulterous wife. Having seen the Incarnation with and through Stephen, we now watch how Bloom treats Molly. He is remarkably calm and peaceful in his behavior. The narrator tells us that Bloom has passed from envy and jealousy to abnegation and equanimity (17. 2155). Bloom's greatest gesture of this day occurs when he encounters "new clean bedlinen, additional odours, the presence of a human form, female, hers, the imprint of a human form, male, not his, some crumbs, some flakes of potted meat, recooked, which he removed" (17.2123–35). He can brush the crumbs of Plumtree's potted meat that Molly and Blazes ate in his bed earlier that day, lie next to Molly, talk with her about his day, especially his meeting with Stephen, kiss her goodnight, and fall asleep: that is serenity. We know from early episodes how deeply he still loves Molly, and we know how deeply the prospect of her affair affected him throughout the day. But he is able to overcome what we might call petty emotions and still look at her with love. His reflections show extraordinary forbearance and resignation: "the futility of triumph or protest or vindication: the inanity of extolled virtue: the lethargy of nescient matter: the apathy of the stars" (17.2224–26). It is not that he does not care, it is that he can look on human affairs with the lofty indifference of the stars. As Dante revolves like a wheel around the Love that moves the sun and the other stars, as Dante is both temporal and timeless, so is Bloom. Still fully human, he can look at human existence with the lofty detachment of the eternal.

This is his great and heroic act of mercy and forgiveness. It does not matter at all whether or not Molly will wake up next morning and make him breakfast in bed; what is important here is Bloom's ability to treat his wife with such lofty charity. It is the mercy and love of a Christ who forgives an adulterous woman, but more, it is the divine mercy and love of a God who continually calls his people back to himself despite their adulteries and cruelties. Bloom exhibits, both for Stephen and for the reader who has learned from Stephen, the Incarnation.

This act of forgiveness and love and his openness to Molly's return to a loving relation with him constitute not only Bloom's great act of epic heroism—for what ordinary man could accomplish such mercy—but also Joyce's manner of establishing a new church at 7 Eccles. Eccles is a real street in Dublin, but it is also the root for the Greek word *ecclesia*, which is usually translated "church." Booker has portrayed Joyce as vehemently opposed both to the Catholic Church as it manifests itself in twentieth-century Ireland and to Christ himself as a role model for his characters. It is from this uncritical identity of Christ with the church he founded on a pun ("You are Peter and upon this rock I build my *ecclesia*") that Joyce and *Ulysses* must be rescued. For Joyce did see the church in his day as utterly corrupt and as one of the imperial forces oppressing Ireland, but he did not feel the same about Christ. Even Booker makes this distinction between Christianity as it operates in Ireland and Europe in Joyce's day and Christ, who, Booker implies, must be rescued from the ideology his church has fallen into, which promotes sadomasochistic fascination (28). Joyce wanted to rescue Christ from his Church and used the tradition of Christian writing sketched earlier in this book to establish a new, or a renewed, church at 7 Eccles. *Ulysses* has as one of its highest goals the reintroduction of Christian values into a culture that ironically considers itself Christian. It seeks to rescue Christ from a church that bears little resemblance to Christ or to this tradition of Christian writing.

Joyce is the culmination of this Christian tradition of writers who feature the Incarnation as the solution to the problems presented by the human body and its material conditions. His modernist depiction of Bloom as "the traditional figure of hypostasis" calls on the notion of such a tradition, and we can see the affinities between Joyce and the other writers. Like Augustine and Dante, Joyce opposed a disembodied Platonic conception of human existence and of our search for truth and fulfillment. Like them, Joyce turned to the Incarnation as the way to achieve a double vision that allows us to respect and even enjoy our life in the body while at the same time being able to raise ourselves upward toward a divine destiny. Joyce especially followed Dante, who slowly and gradually learned that his own life can be interpreted by the Christ event and that he can become one with the Incarnation, being both in time and out of time, occupying the "point of intersection of the timeless with time," as Eliot put it. Joyce's hero as a fully embodied man rises against gravity, against the laws of nature, as does Dante, who in *Paradiso* hears from Beatrice that such ascent is actually natural once our defects are purged and we act according to our pure and original nature. Bloom rises heavenward as the modernist manifestation of Christ's love and mercy for us to accept as the new center for a cultural regeneration.

Joyce's relation to Rabelais is especially important, for as Rabelais worked to make an ancient text—the Christian Bible, and especially the Gospels—seem new and interventionist in a culture that was becoming narrow and dogmatic, so Joyce used a Christian tradition to rescue the body from an official culture that saw progress as rational and directed by reason. Joyce had access to a Christian tradition that he could use to oppose a modernity that reinforced the mind/body split and elevated the mind to a position of control and mastery. Joyce used this ancient and medieval tradition to oppose an Enlightenment philosophy that wants to separate the mind from a body that it can control and direct toward rational projects. In *Ulysses,* Joyce made this ancient tradition seem new and startling (as did Rabelais), swept away the fraudulent, and exposed the conventional and clichéd as bankrupt and empty. Joyce had access to a tradition that can understand human nature as participating fully in the material world and the divine worlds, as fully part of the temporal and historical worlds and part of the timeless and eternal. *Ulysses* culminates this tradition and brings it into the modernist period, and it can function as a cornerstone of a modernist humanism. This great tradition allowed Joyce to oppose the extreme positions his own age made to seem necessary and irreconcilable: the disembodied rationalism of Cartesian enlightenment that makes transcendence seem facile and dangerous, or the reductionist theories of humanity championed by such powerful thinkers as Darwin and Freud that challenge the status of the conscious mind. With this great tradition, we do not have to choose one or the other of these extremes.

Joyce depicted Bloom as a fully embodied character who, with his full weight, manages to rise against gravity and ascend to become a cultural ideal of mercy, forgiveness, and love. Joyce did not depict the body to discredit Christianity, as Booker would have it, but to return his culture to a Christian ideal that seems strangely new and different in his hands, outside the culture of modernity and its Enlightenment values. Joyce had access to a tradition that allowed him to accomplish this goal, a tradition of Christian writing that makes the body central to its understanding of human nature and our destinies. His use of the body is not reductive or debunking, as it is for naturalist writers in fiction or for postmodern critics in theory. He had access to, and renewed, a tradition that allows the human body to counter the hollow Enlightenment understanding of man while still being able to elevate what has been reduced by skepticism and doubt.

Joyce's achievement answers the needs of those who wish to see Joyce as the great secular modernist who merely used an analogy to Christian doctrine as his way of placing an ideal of mercy and love back at the center after having, with good postmodern skepticism, swept the culture clean of all outdated and conventional values. At the same time, however, his achievement answers the needs of the more religiously minded who wish to see in this analogy to Christian doctrine something more literal and concrete. Either way, Joyce's *Ulysses* is the epitome of the modernist humanism I am advancing, sweeping away the corrupt detritus of an oppressive culture and then placing an ancient ideal back at its center, an ancient ideal he labored to renew and refashion for his time and his place. Avoiding the twin errors that stem from Enlightenment humanism, Joyce retrieved a middle way in his renewal of Christian humanism for the modern world.

2

A Most Unlikely Humanist

Wyndham Lewis and *The Revenge for Love*

Of the high modernists studied in this book, none is more unlikely to have developed a humanist philosophy than Wyndham Lewis, who not only applied the phrase "the Men of 1914" to himself and his peers but who delighted in the pose of iconoclastic enemy to his culture. His development of modernist humanism is the most surprising and for that reason perhaps the most instructive.

Paul Edwards, who provides a useful model for studying Lewis's work, comes close to my own position about modernist humanism in *Wyndham Lewis: Painter and Writer*. Setting up his paradigm for studying Lewis, Edwards says early in the book, "I take Modernism to be a continuation of Romanticism, by other means; it needs 'other means' because of materials and social changes that left the products of Romanticism looking unsatisfactory and inadequate" (4). In trying to restore the transcendent goals of the Romantics, however, modernism "discovers (sometimes in desperation) the conditions that are a presupposition of Post-modernism, which can be schematized as that stage where there are no grand narratives left." Edwards concludes, "If this is not, on the whole, what Modernists set out to discover, at least we can read what Post-modernism presupposes back into the characteristic products of Modernism." For Edwards, Lewis's paintings, criticism, and fiction can all be read as containing both the "fierce skepticism" that seeks "to undermine all grounds of value" and "another side" that "accepts absolutely the Romantic presupposition that value is real," that there is a "transcendent Absolute" (4–5). Edwards sees Lewis's work as moving between nihilism and romantic faith in transcendence.

It is not so surprising then that Edwards approaches *The Revenge for Love*, despite its highly political plot and setting, as a novel about "the problem of God" (444), and Lewis did seem to work to move beyond politics toward something transcendent in this work, which was finished in 1935 and published in 1937, a year after the beginning of the Spanish civil war, which the novel anticipated. In the middle of a decade of widespread political, social, and economic crisis, Wyndham Lewis wrote what most of his critics consider his first great novel, perhaps his only true novel, which at first and maybe even second glance seems indeed to be a thoroughly political novel in which competing ideologies are presented and debunked through an array of typical Lewis caricatures. But what distinguishes this novel from his earlier efforts in the genre is that his caricatures seem fuller and more complex while his plot seems more domestic and bourgeois. He seems much more interested in human beings in this novel than he had ever been before. Still blasting away at pretension as vigorously as ever, Lewis in *The Revenge for Love* also worked to move at least some of his characters toward the recognition of something transcendent and true. He created characters capable of removing themselves from the crisis in and of politics and basing their lives on a transcendent value for all human being, love.

Althusser and Antihumanism

The foundation of the modernist humanism that this study seeks to describe or invent is the concept of a transcendent human self or individual who subsists in a permanent and universal way beneath layers of constructed subjectivity, whose existence may be frustratingly difficult to detect but who nevertheless does exist in a subterranean fashion and can be reached through literary efforts designed explicitly to invoke feeling. The implications of Louis Althusser's critique of human subjectivity deserve to be taken seriously; his formulation is useful because his critique of humanism is the most rigorous and extreme of all postmodern critiques. *The Revenge for Love* seems uncannily to anticipate much of Althusser's thinking about ideology and the human subject, but the novel also implies that something may indeed exist outside ideology, or more properly, before ideology. That something is a human self who loves and is loved, a human self who by its nature feels love.

Althusser's thought underwent development, and it is impossible to say that any one formulation of the problems addressed here is "Althusser's thought." I rest my discussion on what is perhaps his best-known text, "Ideology and Ideological State Apparatuses" (published in 1970, translated into English in 1971), because it was written to clarify and correct certain contradictions and complexities that arose from some earlier attempts to describe the relation of what he called "ideology" to the individual/subject. As a reliable text for approaching these issues, this essay has had immense influence on our thinking about not just Marxism but the poststructural and postmodern as well.

Althusser thought of his position as antihumanist, as opposing humanism at its most fundamental and therefore most vulnerable point, the existence of a transcendental self outside culture, existing before and apart from history, society, language, and ideology. He adopted the basics of Jacques Derrida's position regarding human agency, transposing Derrida's claim that nothing is outside of language to nothing is outside of ideology. For Derrida we are "always already" exiled from presence; for Althusser we are "always already" subjects, born into ideology the way Derrida has us born into language and unable ever to arrive at a position that is not within ideology, that is not constructed by ideology and its apparatuses (ISAs). John Fiske makes this aspect of Althusser's position clear: according to Althusser, "we need to replace the idea of the individual with the idea of the subject. The individual is produced by nature, the subject by culture." Fiske offers a pithy summary of the implications of this replacement: "Althusser believes that we are all constituted as subjects-in-ideology by the ISAs, that the ideological norms naturalized in their practices constitute not only the sense of the world for us, but also our sense of ourselves, our sense of identity, and our sense of our relations to other people and to society in general. Thus we are each of us constituted as a subject in, and subject to, ideology. The subject, therefore, is a social construction, not a natural one" (307–8). What is rendered impossible by Althusser's propositions is the claim that there is a natural self outside or before ideology, the claim of the humanists that a transcendent human self exists independently of culture and at the core of our experiences. For Althusser humanism is simply another ideology imposed on and actively constructing human subjects.

Other Marxists theorists and critics have emphasized just this aspect of this essay as its most important contribution to postmodern Marxist critiques. Graham Lock notes the irony of "the self-recognition of the subject as a 'free' agent that 'works all by itself' but is at the same time necessarily ignorant of the mechanism that produces that self-recognition" (79). This is where Althusser's essay takes us, to recognize that the human subject thinks and feels himself to be free and independent and an agent in the world, while that awareness of the self as free and independent and capable of agency is the very illusion that ideology works so constantly and urgently to produce. Althusser and his followers emphasize the dynamic nature of ideology, its need to be working constantly in and through the material apparatuses the state makes available as it interpellates the individual and creates his subjectivity. "Among the effects produced by this essay, one has been decisive: the notion that the individual subject, the individual as origin of thought, speech, and action is not a given but is a product, neither the condition nor the foundation of ideology but its necessary effect" (93). The constructedness of the individual leads to the loss of the humanist faith in the agency of the individual, as authorizing his own thought and action. The denial of human agency in history leads to the conception of history as a process without a subject (Smith, 21–22). This is the basis of Althusser's antihumanism to which a modernist humanism must respond.

Wyndham Lewis's role in my conception of a modernist humanism is pivotal. Of all the modernists (with perhaps the exception of Joyce), Lewis shows the most awareness of the workings of ideology in the formation of attitudes, values, and identity. His novels often include depictions of individuals as mere puppets or mechanisms constructed according to national or political ideology, and his attitude toward his characters is such that someone as cautious as Charles Taylor refers to him as an antihumanist (461); yet Lewis is also the one who famously wrote, "The self is the only terra firma in a boiling and a shifting world" (*Time and Western Man,* 136). One can read his critique of what he calls the "time-philosophy" that damages the art of his contemporaries as his effort to advance the claims of a stable permanent self to be rescued from the temporal stream of consciousness that dissolves the self. As one critic puts it, citing another passage from *Time and Western Man* (132): "the individual is the result of a decision of what should and should not constitute 'my most essential ME'" (Corbett, 116). No modernist artist seems more aware of ideology and its powerful claims in constructing the subject; yet none seems more adamant in insisting on the existence of an essential human self and its potential for agency. This is the paradox of Lewis that shall inform this chapter.

Puppets and Natures

One of the most frequently noted aspects of Lewis's art in his novels is his tendency to create puppets rather than characters, figures whose behavior seems more like that of machines or beasts than that of free human beings. T. S. Eliot described this tendency in a review of one of Lewis's later novels, noting that Lewis had shown a "development in humanity" here that the earlier novels lacked: "In the first part of *The Childermass* one is too often, and too irritatingly reminded that Pulley and Satters belong to Mr. Lewis's puppet gallery. It is not that their creator *failed* to make them real—it is that he *denied* them more than a measure of reality. Just as one of them was about to behave like a human being, instead of a caricature (though a caricature that only Lewis could have drawn) the author would gibe a little twitch of the string (and how often, and how tiresomely, we are reminded that Pulley is a 'little' man) to put him in his place: 'if you are going to try to behave like human beings I'll slap you back in your puppet box'" (quoted in Schenker, 9). Eliot was careful to make sure that in no way could he be taken to imply that Lewis could not create "human beings," but that, apparently for no good reason, he chose not to. Robert Chapman has noted that Lewis approvingly quoted Johann Wolfgang von Goethe's distinction between puppets and natures in *The Art of Being Ruled,* where puppets behave mechanically and natures enjoy self-awareness and self-control (50). Chapman goes so far as to see the interplay between "natures" and "puppets" as one of the keys to approaching Lewis's plots (21). One question for this study is to understand why Lewis was so inclined and how, especially in *The Revenge for Love*, he labored to create at least one human being.

No novel can be studied in isolation from the history of the genre or from the philosophical and cultural contexts of its own time. By Lewis's time the development of the novel in general had become increasingly devoted to naturalistic depiction of humanity, with an emphasis on the individual feeling constrained within increasingly narrow parameters for understanding his behavior and affecting change in the plot of his life.[1] It would be too sweeping to say that characters in novels had become more and more puppetlike, but it would not be improper to note that characters in novels in the late nineteenth and early twentieth centuries increasingly thought of themselves as limited, paralyzed playthings of destiny or chance. And the plot of the novel had often become devoted to characters seeking to find a way out of a destiny that they feared or loathed, to break out of a pattern of repetitious acts that had come to seem too powerful too resist and frightening in its implications.

These tendencies may be seen in some of Lewis's predecessors writing novels in the English tradition. No English novelist developed characters inexorably doomed to pernicious fate more thoroughly than Thomas Hardy. Which is not to say that his characters are not well-drawn and complex. But no matter what they do, Hardy's protagonists are doomed to suffer at the hands of a mysterious destiny. The room for human will, for human agency, is severely limited and curtailed. Thomas Henchard in *The Mayor of Casterbridge* is perhaps the best example of this aspect of Hardy's characterization, for Henchard's whole life is dedicated to making sure that he has changed sufficiently in character and nature that he will never act the way he did in his youth when he sold his wife to a stranger. He commits himself to this project of transformation, and he exerts his will in a determined and steadfast manner that seems to ensure success. But we know better, for Hardy warns us that character is fate. In Hardy's universe one cannot change one's character, so one cannot change one's fate. No matter how strongly one wills, fate is stronger. Henchard ends up making a similar error in judgment that once again costs him his well-being and happiness. We are doomed to repeat.[2]

Perhaps Hardy is just an extreme case. After all, in his poetry he was fond of viewing human beings as "Time's Laughingstocks" and enjoyed writing "Satires of Circumstances." He chose to view human action from such a vantage point that human agency seems trivial and futile. But while Hardy may have been the most pessimistic of novelists in English at the turn of the century, he was not at all unique in his attitude. The problem of human volition and its power to affect change is ubiquitous. Joyce's *Dubliners*, a powerful set of naturalistic stories, begins with ominous words: "There was no hope for him this time." In the story for which this sentence serves as opening, the reference is merely to an aged lunatic priest who has suffered his third stroke and is about to die. But taken as an opening to the whole collection of stories, this sentence is meant to remind us of the inscription over the gates of hell in Dante's *Inferno:* "Abandon every hope ye that enter here." Human beings seen from the vantage of nature and naturalism have nothing to hope for, nothing to will toward. And characters in Joyce's stories range in self-awareness of the problem of paralysis, but the most acutely self-aware figures in the stories are no more successful at breaking out of their pathological patterns or transforming their lives than the densest among them. It might be argued that self-consciousness serves only to render the character more pathetic. The narrator of "Araby" looks back on his thwarted attempt to find romance in dear dirty Dublin with an adult's assessment of adolescent pathos: "Gazing up into the darkness I saw myself as a creature driven and derided by vanity; and my eyes burned with anguish and anger" (28). This self-awareness is not in any way hopeful but merely registers as exquisite suffering, his retrospective experience of vanity and futility. Much the same is true of the other self-conscious figures from *Dubliners;* Little Chandler and Mr. Duffy have little hope for change, despite the fact that they are aware of their predicament. Whether the character under Joyce's scrupulous scrutiny is a "helpless animal" (34) like Eveline or the simpleminded Maria; or whether it is Mr. Duffy, who can wax poetic and come up with fine phrases expressing his lonely despair. (He repeats a phrase he has fashioned as his comfort, "he felt that he had been outcast from life's feast" [113]). The characters who inhabit *Dubliners* are unable to exert their will and effect any change that allows them the hope for a satisfying escape from their circumstances.

Dubliners can stand as a monument for modernism in general, a text erected over the dead (recall the title and the theme of the last story in the sequence) that commemorates the lost hope that modernism feels compelled to address. In this regard then, Joyce began the twentieth century by developing a nineteenth-century technique and attitude toward humanity, a rigorous naturalism (or what Joyce in a letter called a "scrupulous meanness") that severely limits and contains the aspirations of the human being.

Another novelist who worked obsessively on this issue—and in the year 1900 finished his first great novel—is Joseph Conrad, who in *Lord Jim* also established for modernism a problem to be solved. It is largely Hardy's problem of repetition, which has philosophical affiliations to Nietzsche's notion of the eternal return but, more important, anticipates one of the fundamental features of mental pathology in Freudian psychoanalysis, the compulsion to repeat.

Conrad's story in *Lord Jim* is arranged according to perspective, not merely developing a sequence of actions by Jim but presenting a series of perspectives on Jim and his behavior. An omniscient narrator begins the novel, having four chapters to himself before the sudden entrance of Marlow, who tells the rest of the story. The omniscient narrator provides an initial perspective that, among other things, forces us to regard Marlow's views as partial and suspect; no matter how much he may earn our trust, Marlow is not "in the know" the way the initial voice is. Marlow then proceeds to give the reader many other points of view other than his own, primarily because he claims that he needs help in assessing Jim's case. There are the French lieutenant, Brierly, Stein, Jewel, and even Gentleman Brown, not to mention Jim. Conrad managed to make the novel about moral or ethical judgment in this manner of presentation.

What are we judging? Whether or not Jim atoned for his initial "crime" of jumping from the *Patna*. Conrad constructed a narrative that foregrounds the problem of free will and fate: is Jim fated to be someone who jumps, or can he change sufficiently to free himself from that destiny and enact a new plot for himself, as the loyal and reliable Tuan Jim? Paul Sheehan claims that Conrad created mechanized beings, people who come to operate as mechanically as the machines they have created (84). Can these machines become human again? Can the automatic responses of mechanized beings be radically altered and change occur?

Jim seems to think so. He is always looking for another chance and expresses gratitude to Marlow, whom he sees as a benefactor, for allowing him that opportunity. When Jim expresses his hope that he can start over again with "a clean slate," Marlow responds to himself, and to his audience, "A clean slate, did he say? As if the initial word of each our destiny were not graven in imperishable characters upon the face of a rock" (119). Marlow provides Jim with letters of recommendation that allow him to work again, but Marlow does not share Jim's faith that his protégé can start anew. When Marlow brings Jim to Stein after a series of failed "second chances," Marlow tells us that it was to get rid of Jim, who did not live up to the seaman's code when he jumped the *Patna* and who continues to run away from posts whenever anyone recognizes him from that infamous affair. By this behavior Jim proves to Marlow that he has not changed, and so Marlow turns to the enigmatic Stein to be rid of the burden of thinking about Jim.

Did Jim atone for his past through his heroic actions on Patusan, or is that behavior merely an extension of his earlier flaws, his imperishable character. Is one bound by fate to repeat, or can one find the will to effect a radical change? Conrad's novel is well-known for its ambiguity, and I do not intend to advance a definitive answer to this question. The question itself is important for this novel and for modernism. I think Jim is motivated to claim redemption and transformation, but not all would agree that his death does so. Certainly Jewel feels betrayed while Stein seems saddened and confused. Only Marlow might feel that Jim's death is good: at least he will not have Jim around any longer reminding him of the cowardice anyone might betray at any moment. Jim never escapes from his character, always trying to prove that he has or can change, and he would rather die than admit failure in this regard. Ironically, by trying so urgently to change, he betrays Jewel and the people he had sworn to protect, so perhaps he has "jumped" one more time.

Marlow actually seems to play a sinister role in *Lord Jim*, feeling so anxious about what he calls "a shadowy ideal of conduct" (270) that he manipulates Jim into feeling as if he had not already "proven" himself by all his heroic exploits in Patusan. A perverse confessor, Marlow wants Jim to continue to feel guilty and not absolved of his sins. Jewel guesses at Marlow's true feelings about Jim when she asks him to leave. Marlow plays upon Jim as if he were an instrument, as if he were a puppet. Jim's last glance is to Marlow, defiantly confronting his worst accuser and demanding acknowledgment of atonement.

Can a man change, or is he bound to live out a destiny based on his character? Is man free or determined, a nature or a puppet? Can we break free from mechanized being and become human, able to think and act freely? These are the questions that the novel at the turn of the century forced on modernism. The novel as a genre had come to focus on the placement of humanity within a natural and social world that limits the possibilities of agency, that may even deny the possibility of agency. The novel as a genre had become so self-conscious about the relation of the freedom of its characters to the design of its plot that by its very nature it came to question the possibilities of freedom. Sheehan uses the work of Frank Kermode[3] to discuss this aspect of narrative, as having a tendency toward tyranny over the individual: narrative is so plot driven, so end oriented, so driven by the exigencies of design, that there is little room left for freedom, for accident or surprise. The novel itself, especially as it developed toward the turn of the century, had raised serious questions about the human self that philosophy and social science had also raised. Like Joyce, Lewis responded to a mechanized culture.

Charles Taylor has traced the rise of a mechanistic view of the world in which the body becomes a machine, and he connects this view to the nineteenth-century rise of naturalism, where the body obeys natural laws that determine its goals and movements. Whether cast as animals or as machines, human beings were losing autonomy and agency. By the time Lewis started writing his novels, the freedom and independence of characters had been so severely questioned that it was easy for him to create figures resembling puppets more than characters, figures who dance at their creator's will and act in stiff and rigid ways implying a lack of free will and agency. The critics who deal with Lewis's early works of fiction, especially the often highly praised *Tarr*, emphasize how Lewis was comfortable in deploying his characters as almost allegorical figures presenting national or personality types. Paul Peppis advances a reading of this novel that seeks to demonstrate how in 1914 Lewis was "anti-individualist" (133–61). Peppis argues that Lewis, publishing *Tarr* serially in the *Egoist*, a journal founded to advance the thinking of Max Stirner and his thesis on the emancipated ego, was "challenging the Egoists' ideal of the autonomous ego at the heart of Individualism" (141). Peppis concludes that "*Tarr*'s characters end up grotesques trapped in a disjunctive and distorting narrative that scorns Individualism and its dreams of psychological, social, and aesthetic continuity and progress" (152).

This tendency to reduce the human being still informs *The Revenge for Love*, written twenty years later. Its opening pages extravagantly describe human beings in terms of the animal or the machine worlds. Don Alvaro takes note "that a dozen toads were engaged in a game of chance, but that, not being a naturalist, it was no business of his" (16). One prisoner is described in grotesque terms: "that squinting deathshead of a man in a crimson shirt, open at his throat to allow his Adam's-apple to jump up and down at will, as if it were some petted parasite domiciled in his gullet—bald except for a black patch over his left ear, like the last irregular tatter of a motheaten carpet—a week's blue piratic stubble to give his eating-hole a coloured border like a sink" (16). Objects in space are "grist for the mill of the sense" (19); memory is "recording machinery" (20); a girl's hips in motion are a "slowly trampling contraption" (21). Lewis's narrator even ventures a guess at the cause of this lack of humanity, as countries are "going rotten at the bottom and the top, where the nation ceased to be the nation—the inferior end abutting on the animal kingdom, the upper end merging in the international abstractness of men—where there was no longer either Spanish men or English men, but a gathering of individuals who were *nothing*" (17). Lewis loaded the opening of his novel with such phrases, which continue but in diminished number and urgency throughout the novel, to indicate that *The Revenge for Love* is a response to a crisis in humanity. Human agency is one of the central questions that the novel as a genre has come to propose, and it is at the heart of Lewis's greatest novel.

False Bottoms

If there is to be agency, it must be based on a self that is free and independent of culture, and this is precisely what *The Revenge for Love* places under investigation. Lewis participates in constructing a modernist humanism because in this novel he exposes ideology as a series of false bottoms and winds up with a sentiment-based sense of the human self as genuine and real.

Most critics who study Lewis and the development of his fictional art find *The Revenge for Love* his best novel, or at least recognize it as different and usually better from anything he had written up to that point. In his *Wyndham Lewis,* Kenner claimed that it is "a great novel," "at last the almost perfect articulation of a vision" (124–25). More recently Daniel Schenker has noted that it stands out from the rest of Lewis's novels and attributes it to the "other side of his savage indignation, a pastoralism that the harshness of satire deliberately obscures from view" (160). Though something does escape Lewis's satire, it is not so much pastoral as it is sentimental. Schenker feels that Lewis demonstrates sympathy for his characters in this novel and that it has "an intensely personal quality" (161). Valerie Parker has noted that the novel is unusual for the seriousness with which it takes love, which, "like art, . . . demands loyalty and dedication" (quoted by Schenker, 162). Timothy Materer, who does not fully appreciate this novel, has admitted that "Victor's art and Margot's love are not counterfeit values" (131). Edwards has claimed that this novel has been so widely accepted by the critics because of "Lewis's newly expressed 'humanity,' found in his concern for the fate of comparatively ordinary people" (443). The critic who put this most powerfully is Frederic Jameson, whose attitude toward Lewis and this novel differs greatly from my own. Noting the "unaccustomed emotional resonance" of *The Revenge for Love* and also the "general agreement" that it is "his finest and most moving" novel (145), Jameson attributed this distinction to a "structural permutation unique in Lewis's work: now for the first and last time, it is from the woman's, from the victim's, point of view that we are given to witness the deadly onslaught of the aggressive impulse" (145–46). There is more to it, however, than this "structural permutation"; the emotional depth of this novel, particularly regarding the character of Margot Savage, may be seen to represent a deep and subtle development in Lewis's own thinking and the purposes of art. To put it plainly, Lewis wrote a political novel that exposes the hollowness of ideology and moves deliberately toward a validation of love, the most traditional theme of the most traditional novel.

The working title for *The Revenge for Love* was "False Bottoms," and this phrase highlights one of the most prevalent figures in the novel. Many "false bottoms" are revealed, whether the literal false bottoms in the peasant girl's basket in the very first chapter and the motorcar Victor drives at the end of the novel, or the many figurative examples: the false bottom to Freddie Salmon's face, the false bottom that reveals hidden rooms at Sean O'Hara's party, and the forgeries of paintings or of Victor's signature. The dominance of this figure underscores the fundamental purpose of Lewis's political argument in this novel, to reveal ideology as a false front that is hiding something else or may be hiding the fact that there is nothing at the bottom of things. This is clearly indicated in the novel when Victor replies to Margot's urgent request that "we ought to get to the bottom of it" by saying, "You'll never get to the bottom of it, old scout! It *has* no bottom!" (282). The "postmodern" aspect of this modernist novel is its radical skepticism about any claims to have come to "the bottom of things," its sweeping away of fraudulent claims to arrive at some solid, immutable foundation. What is humanist about the novel is Lewis's decision, after all his polemics and energetic debunking of positions, to place love at the bottom, to place love *as* the bottom. Modernist humanism begins with love.

The novel opens with an important theme for modernist humanism, the question of the possibility of human freedom to will and to act. The warder of the Spanish jail explains to Percy Hardcaster that we are free only once in our lives: "when at last we gaze into the bottom of the heart of our beloved and find that it is false—like everything else in the world" (13). Everything in the world is false; that is the first note this novel strikes, and it reveals that the figure of "false bottoms" will largely be devoted to what we have come to call demystification. In this case we are free when we are no longer mystified by the bourgeois notion of love and are forced to recognize, in a way that seems nihilistic, that there is no bottom securing the words we use, no referent for the signifier "love." It is an ironic opening for this novel, for the reality of Margot's love for Victor, its genuine and absolute quality as an ideal for humanity, is the very issue under question. Here we are merely introduced to this large theme in a casual conversation between two cynical caballeros who are trying to outdo one another in skepticism. The second chapter brings us the second "false-bottom" in the book, the false bottom of the basket brought to Hardcaster by the peasant girl. Don Alvaro intercepts the girl and discovers its false bottom, under which is concealed a letter for the prisoner detailing the planned escape. There is a message under this false bottom, it is not empty like the first one, and its discovery by the warder dooms the escape attempt and leads to Percy's injury and the amputation of one of his legs. We are now alerted to the fact that every surface may indeed be a false front hiding something sinister, the most sinister of all being nothing.

In this way are we introduced to the theme of demystification in *The Revenge for Love*. Lewis anticipated the rigorous skepticism of the postmodern turn of mind and created an eponymous character who is on guard constantly to spot the fraudulent and to expose it when it suits his need. The most rigorous postmodern critic could not be more committed to the exposure of conventional thinking and received ideas than Lewis is in this novel. Giving Hardcaster his own (unused) first name, Percy, Lewis indicates how close to the author this attitude of debunking and demystification may be. As he waits with Serafin for the rendezvous that should free him from prison, Percy notes that "there was the beautiful night—a source of profound irritation to Percy, as was beauty upon all such occasions." Beauty, especially the beauty of nature, irritates him because it is blind to the causes of the social revolution he is committed to. He must be careful "not to be lulled into forgetfulness of social injustice" (46). It was a "lotus-eating Spanish-night," inducing lethargy and pleasure that dulls not the senses but the conscience. Hardcaster tries not to let himself be the dupe of any bourgeois ideology of nature or of art, but rather works to see through its dangers and pretenses in order to remain politically committed to the cause of social justice. There is already a fine irony in the fact that the "hard-boiled outcast" Hardcaster has already been duped by the warder in charge of a prison.

As he convalesces, Percy is attended to by a Catholic nun who treats him with kindness. "He spat on kind hearts as much as on coronets. Indeed, was it not the 'kind hearts' that kept the coronets on people's heads—and the mitres too!" (51). It does not take postmodern skepticism to see how bourgeois conscience and bourgeois charity—what Lewis calls "humanitarianism" on this page of his novel, as if to uncover the humanist base of such love—is complicit with despotic power of the princes and bishops of feudal times. Hardcaster unmasks this kind of charity as fraudulent, or at least complicit and dependent on an evil system. He does not doubt that she loves him; rather he doubts the goodness and purity of that love: "This Christian love gets me down—it's more than I can bear. . . . I don't *want* her love. It comes from a place I regard as putrescent. It is criminal love! . . . Someone is *robbed* every minute of the day in order to supply me with that kind of love" (51–52). "This Christian love" may not in itself be evil, but it plays a fundamental role in allowing evil to exist, in covering the evil of a system that is harsh and cruel. It must be exposed as complicit; it must be shown to be another false bottom.

Hardcaster is the character in the novel who is the most devoted to debunking, the most committed to the act of demystification. The theme of "false bottoms" is most closely associated with him because by following him we are learning to see through the various false fronts and fraudulent ideals of the dominant classes who want to confuse and befuddle the best men and women into merely trying to enjoy their lives and survive, and not to fight for social justice; into believing that they can live some pure and ideal life apart from political realities. Seen from his point of view, this is a political novel exposing the fraudulent ideals of capitalism and seeking to inspire proper political commitment. It is a "political novel" in the sense that it seems to be placing politics and political analysis as the dominant lens through which to evaluate the plot. When read in this way, the novel seems to be suggesting that the political is the proper way to view the world and to issue judgments.

One of the ways Lewis presents the political in this novel is to stage contests between different characters who vie for the title of most genuine communist. Hardcaster participates in three important scenes in different parts of the novel in which he engages with another politically oriented person in a debate about the true nature of communism, or, more precisely, who is the true communist. In a novel that doubts whether anything is foundational or if anything is "at the bottom" of things, these debates seem important in that those who are committed to politics are competing with one another to espouse the purest faith, the most genuine form of ideological commitment. One wonders if the most cynical is the most sincere. The first debate is between Percy and Virgilio in the hospital, and their disagreement centers on the problem of class. Hardcaster does not think that class can ever be abolished fully but that some higher class must always exist to administer the revolution and execute the justice it aims at: "But class, Virgilito, of *some* sort there always *must* be" (55). Virgilio protests that Hardcaster's position is contrary to standard communist rhetoric and ideology; in fact Percy does agree that class must be banished from the new communist society in principle, but he argues that it cannot be done in practice. Eventually Virgilio states that Hardcaster does "not have the communist mind" and that his "ideas of revolution are bourgeois. Administrative" (57–58). Virgilio does not find the expected hatred of the bourgeoisie in Hardcaster but instead detects contempt of the people, to which Hardcaster protests with some vehemence. Determining which character is the more genuine communist is outside the scope of this study, but tracing Percy's responses seems more interesting than examining his interlocutor's. Rather the fact that such debates are possible and do occur in this novel raises important questions. Does any ideology have a "true" expression against which all others are to be measured? Can an ideology that is based on demystification make claims to have a genuine and permanent form of belief? Because Percy is "a practical man" (his defense of his willingness to be flexible regarding any rigid notions of class to Virgilio), he seems to be willing to expose as false anyone and anything that gets in the way of his social revolution; in other words, he might be willing to accept that there is no "genuine" communist except the one who recognizes the practical goal of securing justice for the people. But is not that a value in itself, a telos that secures his positions and makes his debunkings purposeful? Must there not be, at the bottom of things, something in which one believes? And is it not for Hardcaster "the revolution"?

The political questioning of *The Revenge for Love* takes a postmodern turn in its radical skepticism toward any claim of truth or genuineness, but it also makes one wonder, as those who might want to ask the postmodern critic who applies such skepticism toward traditional values and meanings, if there is a position to which the debunker does wish to stake a claim, or if there is the never-ending process of debunking and demystification? I am not one of those critics, such as Richard Etlin, who wants to say that this is "proof" of the invalidity of the postmodern critique, or, even such as Tobin Siebers, who wants to claim that those committed to the postmodern exposure of the dogmatic and rigid have in turn become dogmatic and rigid in insisting on their method as true and valid and indisputable (though I respect Siebers's argument more than Etlin's). I recognize that the postmodern critic might follow the cautious road set out by Michel Foucault, who calls for us to suspend all continuities and unities, not expel them. We suspend them all, doubt them all, because we must agree with Derridean language theory that no ground can halt the play of meaning and so we must respect the differential nature of language. We must demystify and debunk, but then we can build back again, this time on the delicate ground that we have chosen, as a "fiction" that we will not believe in but will use to organize discrete parts into local unties in a strategy of rebuilding toward something more just and more equitable. Lewis seems to have recognized, through Hardcaster, that demystification cannot be an end in itself but must itself have an end it serves. The "principles" of communist ideology are less important for Hardcaster than the revolution that will secure a portion of justice for the proletariat.

There are two more scenes of this sort in the novel, which serve to underscore this aspect of Hardcaster's ideology and which can also be used to chart the "progress" of this character through the book. The second debate is with Gillian (Jill) Phipps after they had become lovers. When he realizes Jill has believed the stories that have been circulating about him, how at the hands of the nuns in the hospital he had salt rubbed in his wounds and other tortures, he begins to instruct her about the nature of communist politics. He explains the importance of "atrocity propaganda" in inciting the people to oppose the system, which is cruel but not in such blatant and obvious ways. Jill feels humbled by his instruction: "Here was the *ultra-professional* point of view, in all its unattractive starkness. She saw that at once. She was unquestionably in the presence of the real thing—which was of course thrilling. Or it should be so. She saw before her a communist, and (in the words of the poet) *she felt small*" (189). Note that for Jill, Percy has come across as "the real thing." But her need to feel genuine returns, and she begins to press back, wondering how communism can be a true ideology if it is founded on lies and propaganda. She persists in questioning the lack of heroism in Percy's brand of communism, which prompts Hardcaster to say, "But you do get worked up about heroes! . . . I thought you were a communist" (192). He explains that heroes are "capitalist dope," but that makes communism seem dull and uninteresting to Jill. She is able to rouse herself to call Hardcaster a fascist, which rouses him to a long and compelling debunking of Jill's position. "You're in the game for the fun of it, like most people of the moneyed class, and you want it to be *all* fun and excitement. The little peep behind the scenes you got from me debunked your little romance of revolution" (195). He is once again able to humble her ("Gillian *felt small*" is repeated on the next page after his lecture), but she rebounds and asserts herself twice: once by having Jack Cruze beat him; and second, when she says to her husband, Tristram (Tristy) Phipps, "It is we so-called 'intellectuals' of the upper-classes, who are the only real communists" (208). It is important for Jill to insist that she is the real communist. Her ability and her need to feel this way suggest how effective ideology is in constructing feelings of certainty.

Debunking can be dangerous, as Hardcaster learns all too well at the hands of Jack. Jill's romantic view of the heroic communist struggle is matched against Hardcaster's "harder," more realistic attitude of countering lies with lies, even as he says, "We communists prefer to see things *as they are*" (192). Do we have any way of judging who is the most sincere, or who is the most genuine? In a novel that abounds in false bottoms, forgeries and counterfeits, the answer might well be no.

Hardcaster has one more encounter with a fellow ideologue in which there is a contest of this sort. This last debate occurs near the end of the novel, when Percy is back in Spain overseeing the bootlegging mission that Victor is on, and at such a juncture the encounter represents one final chance for us to assess his legitimacy as a communist. In this encounter, with Mateu, he seems to come off less well than he has with either Virgilio or with Gillian. Mateu calls Hardcaster "at bottom an individualist." At this he flings "up his hands, in token of surrender. 'I withdraw. I withdraw'" (305). This is the charge that Percy seems unable, maybe even unwilling, to counter, and his acceptance of this designation marks a radical change from the intentions of Tarr as Peppis has described them. Something has happened to Hardcaster by this point in the novel to make him withdraw from the world of political intrigue and communist agitation into the inner world of the individual self.

Jack and Jill

The Revenge for Love turns from the political to the personal in its focus, and the figure on whom the novel so turns is Jack Cruze. Lewis took care to introduce Jack into the novel, comparing him to Shakespeare's Jack Falstaff and to an eighteenth-century "sport." Both comparisons are instructive. Falstaff is such a powerful figure of play and misrule that he comes to dominant a stage otherwise peopled by kings and princes and rebels. Shakespeare's Jack is a man of the body, a man who lives for pleasure and for fun. He stands for the personal to the exclusion of any serious consideration of one's obligation to the public world of shared values. Prince Hal learns from Falstaff important lessons about being a prince, but Hal must ultimately reject Jack. As Hal learns from Falstaff, we must learn from Jack Cruze some lessons about the place of the body and its pleasures and needs in the political world. Such claims of the body and desire challenge the ideology of politically committed characters and even expose their political commitments as less powerful than these "lower" claims. Both Jacks are out of place in the world of political commitment and intrigue, and both Jacks disrupt what otherwise would be much simpler plots about the politics of their respective eras. Jack Cruze is a disruptive figure who brings the claims of the personal into Lewis's novel.

The other comparison is no less instructive. We are told that Jack Cruze "hailed from an eighteenth-century Wiltshire village, brought up among horses, dogs and cows—with a soft download wall overhead, remarkable for a white nag picked out in chalk, and a long valley of water-meadows, complete with hawkweed, stretching away to the woods of a Georgian park, dating from the great building time when squires had become small parish kings, upon the extinction of the Stuart monarchy" (93). We are soon told that "he was behaving in a quite eighteenth-century fashion all over the township" (94). Lewis has pulled Jack Cruze out of an eighteenth-century novel and placed him in the middle of all the politically obsessed figures of this 1930s political novel. The setting and description of his behavior may remind the reader of Tom Jones in particular, that rollicking lad who lives in just such a setting. (People say of Jack Cruze, "There's a bright lad, my word!") Lewis wants us to think of Jack as a figure from a "traditional" novel who does not feel he has to apologize for being concerned with the private affairs of ordinary people, as a figure from the beginnings of the genre that—by the time Lewis was writing—must work strenuously to carve a space for the private and ordinary in a world of politics and ideology. Jack is so at home in his countryside setting that he belongs "more to the natural order than to the human order"; he is not "in time" the way these other figures are aware of the goings-on of the day, not squarely placed in a particular place and at a particular time (say 1930s Spain) but in a timeless order of nature. This "nature" is not the Darwinian nature that limits human freedom as much as it is the world of ordinary pursuits in a rural or pastoral setting, the one in which the eighteenth-century novel allows us to watch men and women pursue their domestic agendas without the disruption of history or politics. Jack brings *The Revenge of Love* back to the novel's origins in order to help Lewis earn the right to assert the importance and privilege of the personal and ordinary in Margot and Victor.

Lewis may be seen as resisting the political in favor of the personal. Lewis is a wonderful test case for this because he was, along with Pound, the most politically committed of the modernists in this study, and he seems to have intuited the need to resist the dominance of the political as a way of understanding human life. With the advent of Jack Cruze in his novel, Lewis begins a debate that might well be as much about literary history and literature as it is about politics. The novel—with its history of documenting and depicting ordinary human life in the most personal circumstances—is every bit as valid a way of explaining our behavior as the most incisive political critique may accomplish. He brings his political novel into contact with a traditional novel, and it will be a contest to see which emerges as the most valid.

Tristram Phipps brings Jack into the novel's plot, but it is Jill who makes Jack's role evident: "With Jill and him it was something at first sight. It was not *love*. I don't know what it was, but it was there. Maybe it was love" (103). Their response to one another is visceral, unconscious, and perhaps even natural, but the narrator does not know what to call it. This is an interesting and important moment in the text. The narrator says first that it is not love but then, almost immediately, changes his mind and says that maybe it is. The key to reading this passage might be the italics that present the first use of the word love here: it was not love in its noble and romantic manifestation, but maybe it bears some relation to that concept, as "love" does to "*love*." Their relationship allows for a different kind of debate than the kind Percy has with Jill, for in her relation with Jack she is the more articulate person who does the educating. She sees Jack as a "man of property" who wants to do some "prospecting on her" and to "take possession" of her body. She explains to him that even the self is a private possession that must be given up as we all become part of one big self. But the scene in which this explanation occurs seems more flirtatious than didactic, as Jill teases Jack and encourages his advances. Jack is afraid of her rational tongue, and she "started him looking at himself," making him feel as if a "pale cast of something abstract . . . fallen upon this pagan soul" (184). It is typical of Lewis in this book to have competing ideologies seem weapons capable of inflicting influence, even if the person wielding that particular sword is going to eventually lose the competition. It is part of the agonistics of this book that ideologies compete, and Jack is momentarily intimidated by Jill. But her more "natural" response to him—that is, her flirting—is something he also notices, and it leads to his own eventual "success" with Jill.

One sees the influence of Jack on this novel in a scene in which he is not even present. When Jill is with Percy, she engages in what Lewis calls a "Jackish dialogue"—picking up on sexual innuendo and being keen to flirt. She feels "herself beneath the spell of Jack, and his irrepressible *joie de vivre*." As she continues to flirt with Percy, the narrator tells us "she involuntarily persisted, Jacking away without restraint." Jack's influence is so strong that he has affected her manner of speaking and relating, and Percy himself feels "he had been drawn into the Jack-business in spite of himself" (187–88). Once Jack enters the novel, the interest in politics becomes divided as other claims, those of the body, are announced and take charge of the action. Both Jill and Percy would like to seem above such concerns, but they have yielded to Jack's powerful influence.

This is the beginning of the scene in which Hardcaster educates Jill and exposes her romance of communism. As we revisit this scene, we might see another influence at work as Jill feels betrayed by Percy and becomes angry with him. It is not just for debunking her fairy tale; it is for having confused her about her own desire. As she begins to press back against his teaching and reassert her own version of communism as genuine, Jill also tells Percy that she "was kissing an idea. Not a fat little bricklayer fellow." Her sexual desire has become confused with her politics. When Percy counters that she should keep her kisses for her boyfriends, she startles the reader (and perhaps herself) with this telling line: "Jack Cruze is a better man than you are!" (194). Not a better communist, not a better ideologue, but a better *man!* She has, for this moment at any rate, left the world of politics and entered the world of desire. She has exchanged the public for the private. She has entered the world of the traditional bourgeois English novel in which sexual desire is prominent and politics plays a minor, usually background, role. She eventually chooses to be with "the better man" as her partner, leaving Tristy for Jack. Even though the rumor is out that Tristy left her over a difference in politics (225), such a proposition is seen in the novel as absurd and exposes politics as something relatively trivial in force and power when forced to stand against desire.

The novel in England from its inception was a genre devoted to the depiction of ordinary people pursuing ordinary fates. Its plot was most often propelled by sexual desire and domestic goals. This is not to say that other factors that could be considered political are ignored or unimportant. Economic, legal, and political issues are often present in the story of desire, as financial obstacles must be met and overcome, or inheritance law makes the heroine's plight more complex, or stories of imperialism make the innocence of gentrified English society seem fraught with moral tensions. But these are more often than not "background" issues that provide the plot complexities and character motivations of the foregrounded plot of desire and domesticity. E. M. Forster's *Howards End* might offer an instructive illustration of how the traditional bourgeois novel fares in the context of modernism in the arts. This novel may be read as the end of the traditional novel, which brings the plot of desire and domesticity into the world of imperialist finances and politics. In many ways the novel bears the same fundamental plot as Jane Austen's *Sense and Sensibility,* which submerges the political and foregrounds the personal. In Forster's novel Margaret is the sensible sister and Helen the sensitive one, but part of Margaret's sense is that the leisured and easy life she and her siblings are enjoying is based on the work of people such as the Wilcoxes, who make their money in and through imperialistic concerns. Helen disdains the Wilcoxes, but Margaret has a grudging respect for them and comes even to love Henry Wilcox, despite his many flaws. Through Margaret we are made aware of the dirty nature of the money that people in her crowd take for granted, and we can appreciate the plot of her trying to "connect" her kind of life with its source in imperialism. What was always hovering in the "background" of the English novel finally emerges into its foreground, at least for a brief appearance.

One of the things Forster seems to self-consciously show us is that the novel will repress the political whenever it can and will try to assert—as his narrator does when speaking of Margaret's successful emergence as the savior—that "the inner life had paid" (236). The novel ends back on a eighteenth-century country estate with new life and reconciliation all around. So what if Leonard Bast has died, and Charles Wilcox is in prison, and Henry Wilcox seems a shell of a man: the magic of Howards End has triumphed over politics. But there is an ominous note at the end when Helen (of all people) has to remind Margaret (in a moment of role reversal) that "London's creeping" and that "Life's going to be melted down all over the world" (268). The victory of the personal over the public, of the inner life over that of politics, is partial and temporary. The novel as a genre wants to stubbornly celebrate the personal, and Forster managed to do so still, even if it is only with two cheers.

One of the attributes of modernism in the arts, especially painting, is the reversal of background and foreground, or, more properly speaking in terms of cubist technique, the refusal to make such distinction at all and present all aspects of a scene or event on one plane, with neither foreground nor background. Lewis, as a painter whose vorticist art looks much like cubism to an untrained eye, would have understood this well, and he applied that kind of technique to his novel, where the political plane and the personal plane meet and compete for dominance. Jack Cruze brings the elemental world of sexual desire into *The Revenge for Love,* and the claims of that world confuse Jill (whose section of the novel is called "Gillian Communist," as if that is her chief attribute), as she is attracted to Jack and eventually chooses him over the politically oriented figures, including her husband. It is in the scene immediately after Percy's lecture on communism that Jill's confusion takes place, as Jack Cruze and Percy Hardcaster square off. Lewis makes these two figures mirror images of one another: "The two stock figures, of such Saxon sameness, of breadth and of pigment, confronted one another, pausing to measure the five foot eight of proletarian massiveness opposite each, a dull thick match, tissue for tissue, in a sort of Box and Cox melodrama" (197). The ideologue and the elemental man of passion look alike but stand for very different allegiances. And Jill chooses Jack over Percy and sets him to beat the amputee savagely. Jack's beating of Percy is brutal, and it signals the eruption of the plane of desire onto the plane of the political. Desire wins, easily and brutally. That Percy is already greatly handicapped before this fight not only underscores the viciousness of the elemental and sexual; it may indicate that the deck has been loaded against him all the time.

Jill has told Percy that "Jack Cruze is a better man than you are"; and when she sees Jack she says to him, "I'm glad you've come, Jack! You're just the man I want" (194, 197). It seems significant that Lewis has had Jill use "humanistic" language—Jack is just the *man* she wants—as if what interests her is not political credentials but the qualities of a man *as a man*. The elemental rises into the book abruptly and violently through the figure of Jack and forces us to see the two planes in conflict.

The Art of Counterfeiting

Just as it does with the personal and the political, *The Revenge for Love* also features an extended meditation on the role of art in the world of politics, as it considers which of the two can be thought superior to the other in determining human being and human nature. While in the novel the art of painting seems bankrupt and incapable of asserting its humanistic privilege in defining humanity, Lewis arranged the polemic in such a way as to indicate that literature, and the novel in particular, is the art form that can rise above politics and reassert humanistic claims for art in general. It is hardly a coincidence that, in the work most often hailed as his first or greatest novel, Lewis made the novel itself the bearer of a methodology capable of founding a modernist humanism.

Painting is the art form that receives most of the attention in *The Revenge of Love,* and it is generally regarded by most of the characters in the novel as impotent and futile in asserting any privilege or priority above the political. During a political discussion at Tristy and Jill's, the argument is advanced that capitalists no longer support art and so "help show themselves up. Art covered their beastly nakedness for them once. It's not covering them *now*. The fools have killed it. They don't even know their own dirty business" (104). To see art in this way is not to grant it any privileged place in determining human identity but to see it as complicit in aiding a corrupt and degrading system in its claim to enjoy some "humanist" principles, whereas these principles were only a covering, something hiding the truth about the workings of capitalism. How far is this from the demystification of postmodern critics, who want to tear away from our eyes the veil that art has woven to please us, to distract us, to offer beauty in place of rigorous analysis of the ills we ought to fight? Alan Sinfield put it very cogently when he wrote, "We can build nasty suburbs, offices and shops if we list and preserve 'monuments to the human spirit.' One makes space for the other" (29). Humanist art is complicit with the antihuman system that uses it as a covering, as a sop to the conscience that can be eased with some beauty and sham transcendence. Humanist art makes space for dehumanizing practices, and it is imperative for the politically minded critic to expose this complicity. This is the position that Lewis seems to be describing through the artists in this novel, a stance that might be called Lewis's "postmodern" critique of art and aesthetics.

The most extended conversation about art and politics occurs at Sean O'Hara's party, inspired by a color print of a painting by Pablo Picasso. Already this is a complex scene, as the artists and ideologues at the party are debating art and using a mechanical reproduction as their referent. The relation of the mechanical reproduction to the original has been amply studied, starting with Walter Benjamin, whose critique is contemporaneous with Lewis's novel.[4] The debate is already at a remove from the conditions of the painting's origin, and the print at which they gaze is already within the capitalist system of mass production and profit making. So when at the beginning of this conversation someone claims, "It is bourgeois art all the same. Its values are capitalist" (145), one might hesitate to question whether they are discussing the print, which is certainly bourgeois and capitalistic, or the thing that the print stands for, the original painting by Picasso? This issue is not irrelevant to this novel, because the only way for gifted artists to make a living in this novel is to work at a counterfeiting factory. So the work of art is already under question, especially its value.

Tristy overtly challenges the art critic Pete that Picasso's work is not capitalist, even though silently he feels certain that the ideological art critic must be right. "And yet he was compelled to sustain an opposite opinion to all that he *knew* to be true, for the reason that there was another conscience, namely that of that pitiable thing, the artist" (147). Despite the power of the ideologue's position, Tristy wants to assert that the privilege of the artist to be independent of the historical and political context in which he paints and to provide from that independence an alternative conscience. But Tristy, as both an artist and an ideologue, is caught in a dilemma: he knows the proper Marxist critique and cannot reject it. Victor is the artist who more boldly wants to "leave everyone out except Picasso." When Pete wants to "get back to the fundamental thesis of the Marxian dialectic," Victor says, "Why drag old Marx in? What's Marx got to do with it? . . . Marx wasn't a painter" (148). Nothing should stand in the way between the observer and the work of art, no ideology and no system. But something is already in the way, the print and the reputation of the name "Picasso" and their distance from the original and its aura. But Victor wants to understand

Picasso's painting as a painting, not as a symptom or as an aesthetic production of a vile system. Pete's rejoinder is quite in keeping with recent critiques of art that we call new historicist: "You *can't* regard painting as suspended in the ether, attached to nothing in heaven or on earth. That's art for art's sake. You can't do that" (148). The power of the ideologues' position makes Victor's effort to remain outside politics seem naive and weak. Victor wants art to have its own independent value, not that given it by the capitalist who can make profit from mechanical reproduction nor that given it by the Marxist ideologue who wants to minimize its power as merely symptomatic. He stands for a position that seems hopelessly outdated and unable to refute the political arguments.

Victor is part of the main plot of this novel, and his seeming naïveté is matched by the daring of my own claims that the love between Victor and Margot may be viewed independently from politics and as the only genuine thing in the novel, the only genuine thing in the world. Lewis includes the postmodern critique of art and of the self not to cast them out entirely but to get rid of much that is sloppy and sentimental about the humanist claims as he works to restore the foundation for humanism: that an art form can define the nature of the self, and the basis of the human self is something called love.

Victor is in no way a successful artist, either by reputation (as Tristy is) or by sales, so eventually he tries his hand at counterfeiting original paintings at Freddie Salmon's counterfeiting factory. Salmon had his doubts about Victor, as he "recognized that Stamp's heart was not in his work" (229). That one's "heart" must be in one's work seems an odd idea in a counterfeiting factory, where the artist is merely copying what the original artist painted, presumably from his own heart-felt emotions. One's heart ought not be in the act of counterfeiting, for in the act of counterfeiting one does not feel what the artist felt; one should not even try to feel anything at all and simply imitate what "the original" painting looks like. The irony may be a way of indicating that Victor, by thinking that art is about genuine emotion, is the one who is false to the true nature of art. We are very near the proposition that all art is counterfeit, that there is nothing original and genuine in art. This point is made in the novel by the man who is considered a "genuine" artist, Tristy, who "was predisposed to believe that Van Gogh must have been a determined and inveterate 'faker'—a confirmed muscler-in, coiner and cribber, of other people's art, and most prone to help himself to all he could lay his hands on." He "was dreamily elated at the thought that Van Gogh had burgled the capitalist art-citadel back in the bourgeois Eighties of the last century, and had spat on the notion of property that resides in that unregenerate principle that only Rembrandt should paint Rembrandts, and only Van Gogh a Van Gogh" (235). So while Victor is counterfeiting a Van Gogh self-portrait (dressed up like Van Gogh, trying to feel what Van

Gogh felt), we are positioned to see that he is merely faking a fake, copying a copy, or counterfeiting a counterfeit. Victor is too idealist and too humanist to see it this way and struggles to "become Van Gogh" in order to make his counterfeit somewhat valid, but Tristy is pleased with the notion that what Victor is doing in the counterfeit factory is no different from what the Rembrandts and Van Goghs were doing when they painted their "original" "masterpieces."

Victor cannot do this work and makes a bold gesture when he puts his foot through the canvas of his counterfeit Van Gogh. This is Victor's signature to this counterfeit (as the narrator tells us, "*Victor Stamp—his mark*"), and as such it indicates that he will stamp through the counterfeit and assert his own unique personality in a world of counterfeits. With his departure, we are told, this "particular underworld of art—this particular false-bottom to the dream of beauty—having rid itself of this discordant particle, settled down to unruffled itself and get down to business-as-usual" (242). Lewis has brought us to a position quite similar to the postmodern critique of aesthetics and beauty, as merely a covering for a fraudulent system and without any transcendent or genuine value of their own. Only Victor wants to maintain this dream of beauty. Only Victor retains his faith in the original and the authentic.

Freedom and Love in the Novel

What Lewis accomplished in *The Revenge for Love* is the novelistic and modernist equivalent of a postmodern critique of idealist aesthetics and humanism, bringing the reader to a position that may be fairly characterized as radically skeptical (if not cynical) regarding any claims of transcendence and authenticity. This is certainly a strong tendency of this novel, but it would be wrong to see it as its only note or even its dominant one. For this radical skepticism serves another purpose, to debunk any loose or sloppy claim of transcendence in order to set up a plot that may indeed rise above this skepticism.

The plot in question is the main plot detailing the relationship between Victor Stamp and his partner, Margaret Savage. They are marginal to the politics of the novel, and they are brought into this world almost against their will. It is their love that the novel tests, it is their claim to have some genuine relationship that the postmodern critique of modernist humanism must challenge before validating. It is Lewis's own eponymous representative, Percy Hardcaster, the most hardboiled and cynical figure in the novel, who accompanies the couple to their end and makes the final judgment on them.

At this point it is important to make a distinction between being outside the political and rising above the political. The former is the naive dream of formalism, that art can be independent of politics and exist in its own right for its own purposes; the latter recognizes that all art, as all life, lies within the political but also allows for the possibility that art can rise above the merely political and achieve something higher, something transcendent. Lewis was careful to lay a political foundation and set political parameters, but he came to focus on Victor and Margaret as they struggle to enact a more personal, a more "humanist" plot. It is not possible to say that they are outside politics; everything in the novel has forced them to lie entirely within the political. But the political is not all-encompassing, is not all-determining. They manage to rise above the political and achieve something we have long called love.

The novel introduces the ideal of love in a complex way that, once we disentangle some of the implications of Lewis's presentation, is quite instructive. On the very first page, Percy and his captor are discussing freedom, and Don Alvaro asserts that the only time in our lives that we are free is "when we gaze into the bottom of the heart of our beloved and find that it is false—like everything else in the world" (13). As Joyce opened *Ulysses* with the arch debunker mocking the very things the novel will be taking seriously, Lewis opened his defense of love with the most radical statement of doubt concerning its validity. Don Alvaro's interlocutor is not someone who is going to take up the defense of love, not at this point in the novel at least; Percy is still not ready to take up its defense much later in the course of action when, after he had been beaten savagely by Jack Cruze, he says to Tristy that he bore that suffering "All for nothing, as you say. . . . All for love!" (251). The same man who debunked the Christian love of the nun who nursed him is still insisting, quite near the end of the novel, that love is nothing, that love is a word that has no transcendental signified, that it refers to and so is nothing at all. Not defending the validity of love, his response to Don Alvaro is to challenge his claim of freedom: *"All things are lawful for me, but not all things are expedient."* Percy is self-consciously quoting Saint Paul, and even cites his source, an epistle to the Corinthians. Percy wants to claim that he is in a position of radical freedom, able to do whatever is useful for the revolution, his freedom limited only by expediency. He wants to claim the same position of radical freedom that Saint Paul achieved through his conversion.

Is Percy Hardcaster a closet Christian? Of course he is not. But the letter he cites is the same one in which Paul goes on to define love, in its thirteenth chapter, the most famous and perhaps most moving definition of love in the Western literary tradition. The debate between Don Alvaro and Percy Hardcaster connects freedom and love, and the citation from first Corinthians allows us to move perhaps from the cited passage about freedom to the better-known passage about love. We must separate Hardcaster's meaning in quoting Paul from Lewis's purpose. Hardcaster wants to counter his warder's comment on the lack of freedom in life, while Lewis wanted his readers to see that the comment may also be a veiled response to Don Alvaro's denial of love as possibly genuine. In this indirect way, the problem of the validity of love is brought into *The Revenge for Love* on its very first page.

Paul Edwards has labored to show that in *Time and Western Man* Lewis rejected all "attempts to locate a humanly satisfying value system in nature" as "a sham" and that he suggested clearly that human values must be sustained by something transcendent (311–12). Edwards's attitude to *The Revenge for Love* is that it pushes the reader toward the brink of nihilism only to indicate that there may be something beyond it, something of transcendent nature that can ground human values (451). That something is Margot's love for Victor; this ordinary bourgeois love is made to suggest a more supernaturally based Christian love. As Charles Taylor commented, to refute the nihilism of Nietzsche one needs agape (516). That is what Lewis discovered in this novel, that on the other side of nihilism is agape.

It is worth noting that Hardcaster makes a claim for freedom, as if he has developed or discovered a self that is free to act in ways that it sets forth. It is a claim to agency by a man who seems cynical about such claims on the part of others. In his last debate about communism, with the partisan Mateu, Mateu calls Hardscaster "at bottom an individualist!" (305). Hardcaster's response is important: "Percy flung his hands above his head, in token of surrender. 'I withdraw—I withdraw!'" He does not dispute this claim, as he did in his other debates, and he "withdraws"—a word that is loaded when used in conjunction with the individual self, into which one typically "withdraws" for safety and stability from hostile environments. Percy Hardcaster, the hardboiled outcast who both opens and closes the book, has been safeguarding a humanist self all along.

So the opening of *The Revenge for Love* is setting up the main plot by first establishing Percy's role as its cynical reader. The theme of love, so obliquely brought into the novel in its opening but loudly trumpeted by its title, is quickly announced as soon as Margot enters its pages. She had been crying, "saying to herself that love was in vain, that love could do nothing, that the gods had a hatred for love; that love, in short, was unlucky! What could love do against events?" (69). Margot has developed a morbid philosophy concerning love, that external events were against it, that the gods who rule destiny and fate were plotting constantly against any manifestation of it in human life. She felt certain that if she were not in Victor's life, fate would have dealt more kindly with him: "She was the cause of all the ill-luck that came his way. It was because *she* was there that no pleasant thing ever happened. It was *the revenge for love!* This, on the part of fate, was the revenge for love" (70). The events of the world that she calls fate and destiny and that we would call politics are opposed to their love. But this does not mean that she is going to stop loving Victor; it is her love that makes him special: "Victor would always be, whatever happened to her, *the man who had been loved*, in the way she had done (it was *the way* that she had loved that was at the bottom of the matter)" (70). Her love is so intense, so genuine, that it gives Victor his identity, and it is her manner of loving that is "at the bottom of the matter." In a book with so many false bottoms, we have for the first time the proposition that Margot's love might be at the bottom, the foundation for a modernist humanism. In fact this novel can be read as Lewis's complex attempt to sweep away so much that is false and fraudulent and to place at the bottom of things, as the foundation of a renewed humanism, the emotion of love.

Lewis presents Margot and Victor's relationship with a sensitivity that most critics of the novel have noticed and recognized as unusual for Lewis. Kenner claimed, "Hanging onto the border of non-entity, Margot remains precariously real. Her reality, indeed, is the key to the meaning of the book, and the Lewis prose, addressed for the first time to the presentation of such a figure, respects her egg-shell autonomy" (125). Edwards has seen the character of Margot as the weakness of the novel, "conceived by Lewis too much on Dickensian lines" (443). Dickensian sentimentality is just the effect Lewis was aiming at. The relationship between Margot and Victor is depicted with concrete attention to their mutual consideration and solicitude. When Victor says he feels rotten, she tries to talk him into better feelings. And though Victor has violent moods and can be quite excessively emotive, she is able to calm him down and bring him to a better mood (see 75–77). Victor reflects on his relationship with Margot in terms that seem quite ordinary and sincere: "Not to let down another creature, who had brought her life over and cast in her lot with yours, what sort of fool's dream was that? But maybe it was a question of good luck, if nothing more: just as you would not willingly betray the trustfulness of a bird that makes its nest against your window. A rugged unrevolutionary principle, founded on sentiment, not intellect. But Victor Stamp was prone to accept it, because of the simple life that was his natal background. It was the pact of nature; but with the human factor it became more. Was it not the poetry of the social compact? Here was one of the elemental things in life" (79). The love relation between two human beings is a compact of nature, with the human factor added on: natural and humane. It is one of the elemental things in life, simple and true. It was not revolutionary, not part of the intellectual movement that was going to free us from bourgeois relationships and open up the world to something higher and better. This is quite ordinary and bourgeois, founded (as Lewis had Victor say with utter clarity) not on intellect but on sentiment. Victor is aware of how "backward" such a principle would sound to the ears of his politically active friends and associates, but that does not move him to reject this natural, human bond.

The modernist humanism I want to describe is, up to a point at least, founded squarely and primarily on sentiment. The intellect is responsible for the scorching critique of the fraudulent, but once the false bottoms have been revealed, what is left "at the bottom of things" is this sentiment, the mutual feeling of love. Beyond politics, above ideology, is the human capacity for love.

This love is at risk throughout the book. At Sean O'Hara's party, Margot feels threatened by the people who surround her:

> As she listened to their voices—big, baying, upper-class voices, with top-dog notes, both high and low—shouting out boldly in haughty brazen privileged tones what they thought, as only the Freeman is allowed to—the subject of their discourse invariably the commonplaces of open conspiracy and unabashed sedition—*coups d'etat* and gunpowder plots—she felt a sinking of the heart. It seemed to spell, for her private existence, that of Victor and her, nothing short of lunatic menace, of arrogant futility. They were not so much "human persons," as she described it to herself, as big portentous wax-dolls, mysteriously doped with some impenetrable nonsense, out of a Caligari's drug-cabinet, and wound up with wicked fingers to jerk in a threatening way—their mouths backfiring every other second, to spit out manufactured hatred, as their eyeballs moved. (153)

Clearly Margot is able to describe her uneasiness in the very same terms that critics have used to describe Lewis's usual characterizations in his novels, that they are puppets jerked around by a malevolent puppeteer speaking manufactured hatreds. There is nothing real here; yet these eerie wax dolls threaten Margot's private existence. Jameson recognized that there is a contest here between the sham ideologues who threaten Margot's reality, a contest about which is most real (148). Even Jameson acknowledged that Lewis took more pains to make Margot real than he did with any other character in this or any other novel (146). This "realistic" character feels threatened by the politically constructed puppets, grasping instinctively that they pose a menace to her existence with Victor. The political ideologues mouthing their ready-made phrases threaten the genuine feelings of love that Margot lives for.

She also notes that their language is fraudulent: "It all seemed to register nothing—or just nonsense. They recited to each other, with the foolish conceit of children, lessons out of textbooks—out of textbooks concocted for them by professors with thick tongues in the treacherous cheeks, with a homicidal pedantry, in the jargon of a false science—such as might have been established by a defrocked priest of International Finance, for the amusement of an insane orphanage" (153–54). There is *nothing* under this language; it is just nonsense devised by an intellectual elite that intends harm toward its students as they learn to mouth its sayings by rote. The language of ideology is both threatening and false to Margot's ears. What is ironic is that Margot herself is an avid reader, and the narrator of the novel takes pains to tell us that her personality has been to some degree constructed by the literature she reads. Which brings us to a question and a problem: if all value and identity are constructed by rhetoric, can we talk of something being true or genuine in this novel? If all value and identity are constructed by language and ideology, is any one's personality or character more genuine than anyone else's?

The skeptic's answer is that there is no "truth" to the human personality and so all forms of consciousness are constructed by language and ideology. We might be able to counter this by suggesting that it matters what you read; it matters what you use to construct yourself. Such an answer allows us some room for autonomy even within the Althusserian box: the self may indeed be constructed, but we can at least choose the material for the construction. It is Margot who uses what we call "literature" to construct her character, while most of the characters she feels opposed to use politics. She recalls with fondness her early days with Victor, almost wishing she could "experience the romantic courtship of 'the hermit girl,' as she had nicknamed herself, all over again. Victor was so happy then! It was for Victor's sake that she desired to go back and retrace her steps: to sacrifice once more, upon the altar of Australian passion, 'the hermit girl' of her a little enervated fabrication—the clever virgin-soul to whose immaculate conception Virginia Woolf had so decisively contributed" (214). Margot seems quite aware that she fabricated a self to be courted by Victor, aware of the fact that she used her reading to make this construction of the "hermit girl" to be sacrificed on the altar of passion. Through Margot, Lewis presented the possibility that literature may have its own political use, as material for fashioning a self capable of resisting the sway of the political.

But Lewis was not a sentimentalist about literature, at least not this easily and naively. Later in the novel, near its climax, we again follow Margot as she prepares to construct a new character from her reading, something more heroic being required as she faces a looming crisis. Reading John Ruskin as she walks out in nature, she comes across a line that makes her pause: "Are Shakespeare and Aeschylus, Dante and Homer merely dressing dolls for us?" Which causes her to wonder, "was *she* a doll?" (277). She becomes more self-conscious about the formation of her character than she has already shown herself to be, more aware that she was allowing these "great works" and "great writers" to dress her up as a doll controlled by their plots, a puppet whose actions are laid out before her. Margot has been studying to become a character out of a book, a heroine out of Shakespeare. But this chapter ends with a gesture that clearly is meant to suggest something important to the reader: as she leaves the scene of nature to return to Victor, she leaves the book behind. Literary models are rejected. She ventures out nakedly, without the aid of her beloved books, to pursue love and its destiny.

Margot's studied affectations are certainly part of her character, but they are not what she brings to the ending of the novel. What Margot's reading has accomplished for the thematics of this novel is to raise the question of literary forms as part of the art world under suspicion in *The Revenge for Love*. We may smirk at her efforts to construct a heroic model for herself, and Mateu's critique of Margot zeroes in on just that aspect of her character. But she leaves literature behind to follow Victor on his mission, going out to meet their destiny armed only with the power of love. She leaves behind the counterfeit self she has tried to construct out of her romantic curriculum and prepares herself for "the revenge for love" that she anxiously intuits as her fate. Literary art may be as counterfeit and empty as painterly art.

This all seems to add up to recognition on Lewis's part that art is by its nature a fake and a fraud. Except—we must assert with some effort to get back to the obvious—that we are reading and Lewis is writing a novel. Is the novel the form of art most to be trusted? Is it, as Sheehan claims, the genre most closely associated with humanism and so the one genre to be taken seriously in trying to make claims for a renewed humanism? Jack Cruze has brought the traditional novel with its themes and plots into a modernist novel whose themes are overtly political and whose techniques seem akin to painterly abstraction. Jack has brought the theme and plot of personal desire abruptly and powerfully into this novel, and his role is largely to expose the emptiness of political posturing and the primacy of desire in human life. And it is the theme and plot of the traditional bourgeois novel that describes the relationship of Victor and Margot. She may have left Ruskin back in nature and refused to be a character from a Shakespearean play, but she rushes back into the plot as a character in a novel, this novel we are reading. It is the novel that propels the action now; it is the novel that thinks about human nature and its foundation in feeling.

I am talking as if the genre of the novel is an agent that makes decisions and advances propositions, and I do so to underscore what I think is happening in *The Revenge for Love*, which many commentators consider Lewis's first genuine novel, his first narrative in which the characters seem more than puppets and achieve what Lewis, following Goethe, liked to call natures. It is his first attempt to subordinate politics and history to the personal and the ordinary. The puppets he constructed earlier served his political needs, but we have been watching how this explicitly political novel has been made much more complex by the intrusion of the traditional novel's theme of desire and the depiction of a character with the "reality" of Margot. We have watched the "brutal invasion of the external plane by the internal plane" (288), language that could easily describe a cubist or vorticist painting's contest of planes offering competing perspectives. In *The Revenge for Love* Lewis was writing something different from his previous novels, taking from those earlier texts the political novel and complicating it by having it collide with a traditional, bourgeois novel. In *Modernism and the Fate of Individuality*, Michael Levenson argues that this collision occurs in Lewis's work as early as in *Tarr*, but not with the result of eventually privileging the traditional novel over the political novel. And bringing the traditional bourgeois novel into the political novel forces certain things to happen. Paul Sheehan's sense of the novel form begins with his meditation on the principles advanced in Frank Kermode's *The Sense of an Ending*. Kermode was acutely aware of the genre's potential to become what Sheehan has called "tyrannical" in pushing events toward a plot that humanizes time. The novel as a genre had certain demands, and it is the novel as a genre that brought Lewis toward his modernist humanism.

Sheehan's claim about the novel as the genre most closely associated with humanism is rooted in his sense that the protagonist of a novel is experiencing an education about the possibilities of human potential. It is the novel as bildungsroman[5] that most deserves the claim to be "humanist" in Sheehan's formulation. In these terms the protagonist of *The Revenge for Love* is Percy Hardcaster. Recall that Percy is the cynical reader of the love story, but that description needs some extension. As he follows Victor and Margot, he is learning something about the human potential for love. He is sent by Abershaw and O'Hara to oversee Victor's expedition in Spain, and as he literally follows the couple, he is forced to expand his thinking. The first stage of this late education into humanism occurs when Margot tries to intervene in the gunrunning affair. She is anxious that Percy is duping Victor and makes a plea to Percy that Victor be spared as much danger as possible. Percy objects to Margot's claim that she loves Victor, not by denying that fact but by trying to rouse her ire against "the system that dooms him to perpetual unemployment" (293). Her concerns are purely personal, objecting to their forgery of Victor's signature as their use of "a person's name without their permission"; she objects to his person and personality being used by these ideologues, and Percy tries to counter these personal objections by appeals to abstract ideology that purport to aim at the securing of some justice for people such as Victor. Percy talks about the cause, and then he adds, "I know what *your* Cause is—or *who* it is" (296). His cause is political and abstract, hers personal and concrete.

That Percy learns from this encounter is not immediately evident. In fact this dialogue ends with Percy's reassurance to himself that Victor wants to continue to be used. But when Percy and Mateu discuss Margot, what begins as a meeting of the minds concerning Margot's "bourgeois affectations" gradually diverges until we see a pointed opposition between the two communists. When Mateu says, "Victor is just a violent fad of hers!," the narrator tells us, "Contemptuous conviction flashed in Percy's eyes." Percy really believes in something here, and that something is Margot's love: "She loves him very much. It is a passion. A great passion" (305). As an argument ensues between them about whether her love is genuine or just a fad and fabrication, Percy insists on its being authentic and powerful. In the course of their conversation, Percy betrays himself to Mateu when he starts expressing concern over Victor and whether or not he is being used. "That has got me worried, Mat. I had better tell you." To which Mateu responds: "You are easy to worry." When Mateu expresses indifference regarding Victor's fate ("'What of it,'" he asks dismissively), Percy is vehement: "'What of it?' Percy got rather red in the face. 'I shouldn't like old Vic to get in a jam! I'm not so hard-boiled as to stand by and allow that.'" When Mateu continues to show no concern and seems on the verge of indignation, Percy slips into the language of bourgeois relationships of the traditional novel he is now entering: "Whatever he is, he's my friend. You get that?" Mateu is now the "genuine" ideologue: "Your *friend?* What is that?" (307). That Margot loves and that Percy has a friend are not consistent with the ideological positions hardboiled communists ought to be taking, and Mateu catches Percy's lapse into bourgeois sentimentality. Unlike critics who would agree that this is a lapse, I will argue that, for Lewis in this novel, this is an advance for Percy, a gain in human feeling. Mateu's accusation takes on more significance now: Percy is "at bottom an individualist!" Underneath all the false bottoms that have been exposed lies the individual human self: Mateu's accusation is a positive formulation, the basis for Lewis's version of a modernist humanism.

There has been important scholarly work on the notion of a "modernist self" (Dennis Brown's study) and on "the fate of individuality" in modernism. The second phrase comes from Michael Levenson's 1991 study of the place of the individual self in the experimental writing of the modernists. Levenson has rescued from relative obscurity the work of Max Stirner and assigned him a prominent place in modernism, as a once-neglected thinker whose *The Ego and His Own* was published in forty-nine editions in England between 1900 and 1929 and whose thinking led to the forming of the influential journal the *New Freewoman* and who inspired the change of its name to the *Egoist*. In his *Genealogy of Modernism* Levenson described various attitudes toward the self, neatly dividing modernism into two camps, one that seeks the communal and one that seeks the individual. While Paul Peppis has demonstrated that Lewis may have started out as an "anti-individualist," Lewis most certainly belongs in this latter camp, having claimed in *Time and Western Man* that "the only terra firma in a boiling and shifting world is, after all, our 'self.' That must cohere if we're to act in any way other than as mirror-images or as lowest organisms, sponges or worms" (136). The self is what makes us human, above nature and higher than other life forms. Percy Hardcaster has entered fully into possession of a self that is capable of learning, and what he is learning is the place of love and friendship in human experience as more valuable than the political cause he has been formerly devoted to. Percy even acts on this new knowledge when he allows himself to be arrested as a way to help Victor and Margot escape and return to safety (312–13). He sacrifices his freedom for the sake of his friends; no greater love hath man.

Percy has learned to love by observing Margot, who is, we learn finally, "at the bottom of this adventure!" (326). In a novel of false bottoms, we have discovered two sure foundations: Percy is at bottom an individualist, and Margot's love is the bottom of the plot. The last paragraph of the novel brings us to the fullest extension of Lewis's modernist humanism:

> But meanwhile a strained and hollow voice, part of a sham-culture outfit, but tender and halting, as if dismayed at the sound of its own bitter words, was talking in his ears, in a reproachful singsong. It was denouncing him out of the past, where alone it was able to articulate; it was singling him out as a man who led people into mortal danger, people who were dear beyond expression to the possessor of the passionate, the artificial, the unreal, yet penetrating voice, and crying to him now to give back, she implored him, the young man, Absalom, whose life he had had in his keeping, and who had somehow, unaccountably, been lost, out of the world and out of Time! He saw a precipice. And the eyes in the mask of THE INJURED PARTY dilated in a spasm of astonished self-pity. And down the front of the mask rolled a sudden tear, which fell upon the dirty floor of the prison. (336)

Margot has become a voice haunting Percy Hardcaster, a voice reproaching him for his reckless disregard for love and for lovers. The voice comes from the past, from a bourgeois past that still thinks in terms of a human voice as the embodiment of a human tradition that can form a conscience that reproaches and upbraids. His recognition of his guilt in regard to Victor leads him to a moment of genuine emotion, as the mask he has tried to wear over his human face dilates in spasm, a spasm of self-pity. He feels sorry for himself, for the self that he has condemned to loneliness and that will not know the kind of love Victor knows from Margot. The tear that comes from his eye is sudden, an unexpected eruption of something genuine from this hardboiled character. In *Men without Art*,

Lewis asserted that we can choose "to *humanize* ourselves, or to *dehumanize* ourselves" (232), and this novel ends with a humanizing tear. Even Jameson, who wanted to read this book skeptically, was forced to admit that "on the closing page of *The Revenge for Love*, before our astonished eyes, there hangs and gleams forever the realest tear in all literature" (177). This formulation is powerful, especially as it highlights the tear as Lewis's great literary achievement in the novel: to bring this cynical ideologue through an education that allows him to experience friendship, guilt, and love (if only in its absence) is Lewis's great accomplishment here, and it is his contribution to what I am calling a modernist humanism.

3

Conflicting Humanisms

The Development of *The Cantos of Ezra Pound*

Despite protestations to the contrary, most critics of *The Cantos of Ezra Pound* treat the poem as a uniform text, making claims about the entire poem based on a section or sequence and ignoring the rather obvious fact that the poem is a "work in progress" stretching over forty years in the making and undergoing continual shifts in focus, purpose, and technique. In *Pound's Epic Ambition* I followed the deployment of Pound's wanderer as his way of providing something constant in an inconstant poem, a stable figure around which the poet can maintain some degree of continuity while at the same time announcing his new aims and intentions sequence by sequence. The first part of Pound's poem—up to Canto LXXI—can be read as an embodiment of a humanism based on Enlightenment values and beliefs, but then, from *The Pisan Cantos* through *Rock-Drill* and *Thrones*, events caused Pound to make a serious reassessment of his poem that led him to a modernist humanism.

Pound's project is especially important in my attempt to describe a modernist humanism because *The Cantos* as a whole can be, and often has been, taken as the single most egregious example of what is wrong with modernism. If any text in English by a major literary figure can be seen as complicit in constructing the cultural values that led to Auschwitz, it is this poem by this poet, and any attempt to ignore this possible complicity would be an irresponsible critical act. But it is equally negligent to assume that the poem never makes any adjustments in its attitudes and techniques, that Pound was incapable of reassessing his project and determining how to shift its bases and focuses. Indeed, from Pisa onward, Pound worked to reevaluate his project, and our observation of this process of self-correction allows us to learn not only what was wrong with modernity but how this most troubling poet could salvage his project from the ruins of fascism by developing his own version of a modernist humanism.

The Cantos is a notoriously difficult poem to categorize or classify, though it may be called an epic, which—leaning on Pound's own definition of the genre—is "a long poem containing history" or "a long poem including history." What the former definition emphasizes is the need to find a shape, a form capable of holding the heterogeneous material of history together. What the latter emphasizes is the need for inclusion, to open up for poetry its proper domain to include materials formerly excluded. What both definitions share is a call for poetry to confront something called "history," and it seems quite apparent that for Pound poetry must try to intervene in cultural and historical affairs. Michael Coyle has claimed that "Pound worked continuously to expand poetry's 'proper' domain" (2) and that "Pound's determination to recover what he took to be the ancient centrality of poetry had led him to create a broadly heterogeneous poem that included the various discourses in which cultural and political power was most immediately manifest" (102). For Pound, poetry must become capable of intervening in contemporary social and political issues. Sinfield's characterization of modernism as a kind of literature that seeks to evade the temporal is defied by *The Cantos*, especially in the boldest and most fatal moment in the poem, the poet's decision to include Mussolini as the current manifestation of the epic hero, an extraordinary blurring of the boundaries of literature and politics, of the aesthetic and the historical. It is extraordinary because the poem's success or failure is now tied to the success or failure of a man whose political future is very much open to the fortunes of events. Pound opened his poem to contemporary politics in an unprecedented way in an effort to make his poem capable of intervening in current events, attempting to mold and shape them.

What is remarkable about this "interventionist poetics" of *The Cantos* is that it seems to arise from the very same kind of dissatisfaction that inspired and gave rise to the postmodern critique of modernism. Paul Morrison, no friendly critic of Pound, has noted that in the 1930s Pound did not want to describe an unattainable ideal divorced from reality but rather something to be achieved through active engagement with political realities of the time and place. Morrison cites Pound's *Jefferson and/or Mussolini* on this point: "The Duke of Xq was in the cabinet and brought in a law which the boss said was tyrannous and oppressive, oppressive to the working man. So the boss rewrote it a week or so later; not, I believe, as a law for an ideal republic situated in an platonic paradise but as an arrangement possible in Italy in the years VIII or IX of the Era Fascista" (*Jefferson and/or Mussolini*, 57, cited in Morrison, 37). In fact Pound's dissatisfaction with such "idealism" led him to want to write a literary text that the postmodern turn of mind might seek to write. Yet *The Cantos* is the modernist text most often castigated by the postmodern critique as an example of what is wrong with modernism. What is wrong with *The Cantos*, however, is what is wrong with modernity and not with modernism in literature, and the postmodern critique itself may be liable to the same errors that Pound makes in his poem. Furthermore, from Pisa onward, with his practical hopes for an earthly paradise devastated, Pound reviewed and revised his poem and came to write a modernist humanism.

The Cantos as Enlightenment Project

At this point it is worth recalling the distinction between Enlightenment or rationalist humanism on the one hand and a modernist humanism akin to the humanism of the early modern writers on the other. In calling the first part of *The Cantos* an Enlightenment project, I want to align it with Enlightenment confidence in the mastery of our rational powers to engineer a better social world.

One of Pound's fundamental aims of *The Cantos* was to educate, to provide for a limited readership what he called in *Guide to Kulchur* "The New Learning." In fact, Coyle informs us, "The New Learning" was the original title for *Guide to Kulchur*, a pedagogically oriented text (145), calling to mind the revolution in education effected by the early modern humanists of the fifteenth and early sixteenth centuries. In this project Pound seems to have been aware that he was occupying a position regarding his culture analogous to that of the early modern humanists, many of whom were primarily pedagogues and primarily interested in providing the basis for a sound education for the elite, who had to face radically new conditions and so needed such a foundation to assure that the best of the past was neither lost nor uncritically accepted as rigid and dogmatic knowledge:

> Despite appearances I am not trying to condense the encyclopedia into 200 pages. I am trying at best to provide the average reader with a few tools for dealing with the heteroclite mass of undigested information hurled at him daily and monthly and set to entangle his feet in volumes of reference.
>
> Certain ground we have gained and lost since Rabelais' time or since Montaigne browsed over "all human knowledge." (*Guide to Kulchur*, 23)

These words constitute the opening of the second chapter of *Guide to Kulchur*, which Pound titled "The New Learning Part One." His language needs to be analyzed carefully, for some of the phrases anticipate some of the poem's greatest challenges. Pound was aware of the new conditions for the dissemination and circulation of "undigested information," which we must distinguish from "knowledge" and which is "hurled" at the reader in quantities hitherto unknown. Philip Furia has noted the analogy between the conditions facing the early modern humanists and those facing Pound: "If he could transmit—in 'documentary' poetry, in haranguing prose, and, finally, over the radio, the lost documents from our past, he could help to transform his age just as medieval

Europe was reborn when a flood of long-lost classical documents was channeled through the new technology of printing" (4). Pound seems to have been keenly aware that his culture faced the same fundamental challenge regarding information as did the early modern period. As in the days of Rabelais and Montaigne, when the printing press and the spread of the university made information more readily available for more people, so in Pound's day the development of the new media for the presentation of information, newspapers and monthly magazines and especially the radio (which was complicit in Pound's own personal tragedy), led to rapid advance in the sheer amount of information people had to digest.

The word "heteroclite," which Pound used late in his career to explain the failure of *The Cantos* to "make it all cohere," is also a loaded term intended to suggest that the information refuses to be unified on any single ground or plane but rather exists in discrete units that can at best be unified in small clusters but not in any total way. Foucault used this term in *The Archaeology of Knowledge* for just this point,[1] and its use in *Guide to Kulchur* indicates Pound's awareness of the enormous difficulty of bringing all this information together in any meaningful way so that the "information" can become "knowledge." *Guide to Kulchur* and *The Cantos* attempt to provide the reader with a way of approaching the heteroclite mass of information so that he or she can retain control over it and assign it meaning. Both texts provide the reader with a new way of presenting information, in apparently loose and unconnected fashion, that demands of the reader the effort of organizing and connecting the information into wholes and perhaps even to discover how to totalize the information. Pound's way of writing history in his poem—at least in its first phase, up to Canto LXXI—prompts the reader to seek to unify and totalize. In fact one chapter of *Guide to Kulchur* is titled "Totalitarian," an unabashed acknowledgment of his ambition to "contain" history in a way that can explain everything in a "master narrative." *The Cantos* is a poem that seeks not only to present important and often neglected information but also to educate the reader in the very process of learning from the discrete facts important knowledge. The first chapter of *Guide to Kulchur* is called "Digest of the Analects," and its basic point is that Confucius did not try to know everything but to "reduce it all to one principle" (15). The undigested information is digested and made into a knowledge that nourishes. How not to be lost amid a sea of facts but to be able to steer with assurance and conviction based on some fundamental position or principle: this is Pound's "New Learning," and it is (in his estimation) perhaps the first attempt to remake learning since the early modern humanists did so.

This description of Pound's texts features his faith in knowledge and learning, and as such connects to a different aspect of the early modern humanists than is described in the introduction or in the chapter on Joyce's Christian humanist tradition. This is the kind of humanism that will be maintained and even refueled in the Enlightenment, in its emphasis on reason and the rational self. Pound even connected Pierre Bayle—a French encyclopedists with whom Pound wanted to associate Jefferson and Adams and the beginning of America—to Rabelais, as if the attitude toward learning and toward humanism remained constant from the early modern period through the Enlightenment (*Selected Prose*, 148, 154). Pound's pedagogical project is of the Enlightenment, as one can see in the title of a journalistic essay he wrote in the mid-1930s, "History and Ignorance" (*Selected Prose*, 267), or in a line such as this from "A Visiting Card" (1942): "Without history one is lost in the dark, and the essential data of modern history cannot enlighten us unless they are traced back at least to the foundation of the Sienese bank" (*Selected Prose*, 308). This essay was written in Italian and this phrase was certainly intended to suggest the opening of Dante's *Comedia*. Dante's "dark wood," which was a place of sinfulness, has become in Pound's hands a place of ignorance, and if lost documents can be discovered and circulated, there will be enlightenment. Pound repeated this understanding of Dante's poem in the opening of a 1944 essay, also written in Italian, called "An Introduction to the Economic Nature of the United States": "For forty years I have schooled myself . . . to write an epic poem which begins 'in the Dark Forest' crosses the Purgatory of human error, and ends in the light" (*Selected Prose*, 167). At this point in his career, purgatory is about error and not about sin, about the human intellect alone and not about the more complex being called man, with mind and body that may indeed drag one down to hell. The first movement of *The Cantos* is written as an Enlightenment project, based in a deep confidence in reason and in a rational self able to sort out the heteroclite mass and master it. Events in the world—the fall of Italian Fascism, the death of Mussolini, and Pound's own arrest as a traitor—led Pound to reassess this confidence and to write a new kind of history from Pisa onward.

Pound's infatuation with Mussolini and Italian Fascism (which seems to be the proper order of priorities for Pound) may also be explained by following Pound's adherence to an Enlightenment model of knowledge and mastery. He had developed a method of writing history in his poem that allowed him, almost as if he were following the instructions of Foucault, to invent a new kind of historiography, one that sweeps away the old continuities and allows the man reaching for cultural authority and power to place his own values and ideals in the space he has cleared away with his postmodern and skeptical critique of received knowledge. Using the model I advanced in my preface, Pound swept away the clichéd and conventional knowledge of his day, sweeping his house clean but filling it with a demon that took over his project, the demon of totalitarian politics. I use the term "demon" to connect back to Christ's parable about the possessed man who sweeps his home clean only to have seven other demons move in, making his last condition worse than the first. The term also calls to mind Robert Casillo's *The Genealogy of Demons,* a facile and strained attempt to paint Pound as a vicious anti-Semite from his youth, a study that refuses to pay attention to any temporal development of views or attitudes on Pound's part. Following Leon Surette's *Pound in Purgatory* and not Casillo's study, I argue that Pound's "demons" of fascism and anti-Semitism arose as part of his commitment to Enlightenment principles and that Pound's descent into the viciousness of anti-Semitic thinking reflects Adorno's point, that modernity moves toward the death camps.

From Sigismundo to Mussolini: The Development of Pound's Fascist Hero

Lawrence Rainey, especially in his important contribution to Pound studies, *Ezra Pound and the Monument to Culture,* has argued that Pound's scrupulous study of the documents surrounding the history of Sigismundo Malatesta and his Tempio not only led to the composition of those four early cantos, but that Pound's writing of the Malatesta Cantos "crystallized the design of the larger poem for him" (4). Through Rainey, we learn of the development of the cult of Sigismundo, beginning in 1860 with Jacob Burckhardt, who placed Sigismundo at the conclusion of a chapter called "The Furtherers of Humanism," thus implying that Sigismundo indeed could be seen as the epitome of what humanism represented. Burckhardt's romantic interpretation of Sigismundo was repeated in 1874 by John Addington Symonds and in 1882 by the French art historian Charles Yriarte. Pound's main source for his initial understanding of Malatesta's greatness was the work of Antonio Beltramelli, whose 1912 book *The Temple of Love* developed the romantic, Nietzschean understanding of Sigismundo's heroic role in the early modern period. This same Beltramelli also wrote the first biography of Mussolini, published in 1922 and called *The New Man,* a title meant to connect Mussolini back to the Renaissance ideal of the whole man that Sigismundo epitomized. Rainey's diligence in detailing Pound's research for these pivotal early cantos puts us in a position to appreciate how Pound's understanding of the early modern period is shaped by contemporary views and contemporary events. Pound's humanism was of the Enlightenment version, and he looked back to Malatesta from an Enlightenment perspective and from a present featuring Mussolini's actions in Italy. Rainey's essay in *A Poem Containing History,* encourages us to see Pound's writing of the Malatesta Cantos in the context of Mussolini's march on Rome in 1922. Indeed Pound's understanding of Malatesta was shaped not only by a romantic tradition inaugurated by Burckhardt, Nietzsche's one-time colleague at Basel, but also by the heroic example of Mussolini in Pound's contemporary scene. The present informed how he viewed the past, much more than the other way around.

This is an important point because Pound's understanding of the early modern period may be seen as having been shaped by his needs in writing what is clearly and deeply an Enlightenment project, by his Enlightenment beliefs in the individual, in will, and in the possibility of one man directing the course of history. Pound's project, in short, was shaped by his need to discover a contemporary hero. That is not to say that from the first moment he encountered Malatesta, Pound saw the figure of Mussolini for his poem. As Rainey has said, however, by 1932 the analogy between Malatesta and Mussolini "would strike Pound as the central axis for the shape of his magnum opus and his understanding of its place in the modern world" (74). Pound's humanism, despite the fact that it originated in a study of Malatesta, a figure from the early modern period, is really Enlightenment humanism, one based on supreme confidence in the ability of reason to master history and nature. Pound provided an instructive example of how an eighteenth-century, Enlightenment project based on rationality and will can move us frighteningly near the death camps. As Tim Redman has said several times, Pound had an "eighteenth century conception of politics" (107). "His political philosophy . . . is close to an eighteenth-century ideal and praxis. Political movements, in this view, come into being through the understanding, will, and direction of individual men" (112). As Pound figured it, the concept of heroic action is an Enlightenment concept, an offshoot of the Cartesian view that the rational mind is autonomous and can master the body and the world of nature.

The first half of *The Cantos,* up to Canto LXXI, may thus be described as a cohesive unit written as part of an Enlightenment project of educating an elite readership about the principles necessary for economic reform and the creation of economic justice. Pound saw ignorance as the chief problem facing him, and as he faced this problem, he became slowly but surely convinced that the ignorance was not natural but deliberate: "Ignorance of these tricks [various policies of the bankers designed to prevent monetary reform and economic justice] is not a natural phenomenon; it is brought about artificially. It has been fostered by the silence of the press, in Italy as much as anywhere else. What is more, it has been patiently and carefully built up" ("Gold and Work," *Selected Prose,* 339). "The enemy is ignorance (our own)" (*Selected Prose,* 344). Commenting on similar moments from Pound's prose, Redman asserts, "The points here are typical Pound. Wrong action results from ignorance, not evil. When ignorance is corrected by education, right action will ensue" (238). Pound had enormous confidence in reason, which is capable of seeing the truth about such things, and in education, which is capable of showing others and leading them to act in accordance with sound economic principles capable of securing economic justice. This confidence is a version of idealism, as if the mind and the rational intellect are split from the body and its material circumstances, can diagnose calmly and surely the ills of society, and then proceed to direct a new course of events that will make the material conditions of society just.

One can also already see how this confidence in reason and the enlightened intellect can lead, fairly quickly and surely in Pound's case, to conspiracy thinking and anti-Semitism. Pound was convinced that "ignorance is not a natural phenomenon" but rather something deliberately aimed at by the usurers who want to maintain their monopoly over monetary policy. He believed that the newspapers were particularly to blame in maintaining this ignorance: "A very great and slimy ignorance persists. American concerns hire the lowest grade of journalists to obscure the public mind" ("What is Money For," *Selected Prose*, 301). Pound's aim was to counter this deliberate ignorance by revising and rewriting American history.

Which is what *Eleven New Cantos* (1934), Cantos XXXI–XLI, seeks to do. Philip Furia's study, *Pound's Cantos Declassified,* is based on the conviction that what "Pound believed he . . . was fighting was the 'historical black-out,' a universal conspiracy to destroy, suppress, and subvert vital documents" (1). Furia has used Pound's metaphor from the Jefferson Cantos (XXXI–XXXIII), canals and canalizers, to describe what these cantos were aiming at, opening up the channels of communication and providing new documents to flow in circulation (50–53). This may remind one of the Hell Cantos (XIV–XV), where the sinners are those who block distribution of knowledge and of wealth, creating the squalid conditions of the modern world in their deliberate perpetuation of ignorance. In 1937 Pound wrote that he had many problems with the American university system, but two problems rose above the rest: "one with the modus of teaching history omitting the significant documents, and second the mode of teaching literature and/or 'American literature,' omitting the most significant documents" ("The Jefferson-Adams Letters as a Shrine and a Monument," *Selected Prose,* 147). The letters exchanged between Thomas Jefferson and John Adams in their retirements and toward the ends of the lives were for Pound especially precious in shedding light on the battles being waged against the evils of a fraudulent banking system led by Alexander Hamilton, so these letters are featured prominently in these cantos, along with phrases from other important early American figures, John Quincy Adams and Martin Van Buren especially. "The struggle between the financial interests and the people was continued in the battle between Jefferson and Hamilton, and still more openly when the people were led by Jackson and Van Buren. The decade between 1830 and 1840 has practically disappeared from the school-books" ("Gold and Work," *Selected Prose*, 338). *The Cantos* at this point is primary a pedagogical text, supplying missing facts and more importantly a method: "And, I reiterate, until America at least makes the intelligence of her founders available in print, we may expect all forms of idiocy, as usual, in that mind-swamp" (*Guide to Kulchur*, 246). One of the main theses of *Guide to Kulchur*, in fact, is that usury blocks circulation of knowledge and seeks to promote ignorance, while the poet's own efforts are opposed to this conspiracy and seek to shed light on economic issues: "We have in our time two parties: the infamous, which tries to sabotage economic knowledge; the intelligent, which demands full light on the issue of coin, paper means of immediate exchange, and of credit" (*Guide to Kulchur*, 271). "We know that history as it was written the day before yesterday is unwittingly partial; full of fatal lacunae; and that it tells next to nothing of causes. . . . We know that there is one enemy, ever-busy obscuring our terms, ever muddling and muddying terminology, ever trotting out minor issues to obscure the main and the basic, ever prattling of short range causation for the sake of, or with the result of, obscuring the vital truth" (*Guide to Kulchur*, 31). Those who obstruct circulation of documents and of knowledge contained therein, leading to the swamp and slime of ignorance versus those who know the truth and seek to shed light: that is how simple the state of affairs was for Pound in the mid-1930s through the early 1940s, and his language and metaphors are all indicative of the Enlightenment and its faith in the intellect to enlighten the curious and the intelligent.

But the deeper purpose of *Eleven New Cantos* is to introduce Mussolini into the poem, which constitutes the boldest and most fatal act in the entire poem. As Redman has suggested, Pound had fallen into the Enlightenment attitude toward politics, of seeing political events unfolding under the direction of great men: what America had at its founding—namely the good fortune to have great men such as Jefferson and Adams directing its affairs—Italy had at the present time in Mussolini. And Pound, aware of the world's growing objections, wanted to cast Mussolini as the heir of Enlightenment and American principles. In *ABC of Economics*, written in 1933, in a section called "Dictatorship as a Sign of Intelligence," Pound wrote: "The phrase 'intelligence' is more interesting. Mussolini as intelligent man is more interesting than Mussolini the Big Stick. The Duce's aphorisms and perceptions can be studied apart from his means of getting them into action" (*Selected Prose*, 261). Mussolini understood economics and took means to get his ideas into action, and Pound wanted to separate understanding from action in order to underscore Mussolini's intellect here. But, as this citation already indicates, it is another central feature of Enlightenment thinking that truly dominates Pound's writing on Mussolini and Fascism, and that is will. In fact he calls his own brand of Italian Fascism a "volitionist economics." In a section of his *ABC of Reading* called "On Volition," Pound anticipated, "It will be objected that I am trying to base a system on will, not intellect. . . . No economic system is worth a hoot without 'good will.' No intellectual system of economics will function unless people are prepared to act on their understanding" (*Selected Prose*, 238). This is why Pound laid such emphasis on the *directio voluntatis*, the "direction of the will," when discussing Mussolini in the book he called his *Monarchia, Jefferson and/or Mussolini:* "There is . . . the opportunism of the artist, who has definite aim and creates out of the materials present. The greater the artist the more permanent his creation. And this is a matter of WILL. It is also a matter of the DIRECTION OF THE WILL" (15–16). Redman has studied this aspect of *Jefferson and/or Mussolini*, concluding that Pound's enthusiasm was more for Mussolini as a great man than for Italian Fascism itself (see especially 105–6, 117–18). Pound's enthusiasm was for strong men, men with the will to order that he claimed Mussolini was displaying at the present moment. One man can rise above material and cultural circumstances in order see the problems clearly and their solutions as well, and then can impose his will upon events to secure an increasingly large portion of justice for a particular place at a particular time: such is Pound's cultivation of the epic hero for his poem, and such is the essence of his politics. The rational mind that can see the problems and the autonomous will that can move people and events toward a new goal, these are at the heart of eighteenth-century humanism, founded upon Cartesian faith in rationality and the autonomous subject; these lead to modernity, and in Pound's case, to the support of a brutal quasi-totalitarian regime. As Redman has said, "The eighteenth-century rationalist character of Pound's political thought is at the root of his problem" (116).

It is not just that Pound wanted to place Mussolini in the context of eighteenth-century America, it is that he was writing a poem that is based on Enlightenment confidence in the rational mind and autonomous will. That is why the epic may be outdated for the twentieth century, because the way to depict historical problems and their potential resolutions can no longer be based on hope for a single man to rise above his time and place, impose his will on a recalcitrant material world, and move it toward the enlightened goal of justice he has seen. Alec Marsh wants to see Pound's fascism as rooted in an outdated agrarian ideology that was dealt its crushing blow in 1896, when William Jennings Bryan was defeated by the imperialist William McKinley. Marsh calls Pound's fascism "a belated case of American populism" (1–7). It is true that Pound's Mussolini, like Jefferson and his descendants up to Bryan, sees the land as the source of all cultural value. Mussolini is praised in Canto XLI for having drained the marshes, so that more people can eat and drink and build homes in the newly reclaimed land. It is true, as Redman has reported, that Pound's dissatisfaction with Marx is that he failed to see that money is not just a way of measuring labor but of what human labor does with nature (52). This adds to my conviction that Pound's Mussolini functions as an epic hero, able to restore an outmoded set of values to the twentieth century. That is what Pound implied when he asked, "*Do the driving ideas of Jefferson, Quincy Adams, Van Buren, or whoever else there is in the creditable pages of our history,* FUNCTION *actually in the America of this decade to the extent that they function in Italy under the Duce*" (*Jefferson and/or Mussolini*, 104). *Eleven New Cantos* is arranged so that it begins with Jefferson and ends with Mussolini, bringing the man of the moment into the poem, making a politician's success or failure part of the poem Pound was writing.

This is a radical moment for the poem, unlike any other moment in any other work of literature: to allow the fortunes of a contemporary politician, whose future is very much open, to direct the poem's future and become the basis for the poem's success or failure. Pound's *Eleven New Cantos* intervenes in his social and cultural present, asking Americans to consider the example of Mussolini as they try to work out of their own present economic crisis. Pound did not fly to the timeless and the ideal, as critics such as Sinfield accuse modernist artists of doing. Instead Pound made his work of art very much open to and even contingent on the social and political realities of the day. Indeed Pound seems to fit neatly Roger Griffin's definition of "programmatic modernism," "in which the rejection of Modernity expresses itself as a mission to change society, to inaugurate a new epoch, to start time anew" (62). While Sinfield wants to castigate modernism in literature for being too detached from the world of politics, Griffin can critique Pound for his excessive commitment to the political.

One of the main contributions of Griffin's important study of modernity and modernism is the distinction between what he has called "programmatic" modernism and "epiphanic" modernism, the latter focusing on "the cultivation of special moments..., a purely inner, spiritual kind with no revolutionary, epoch-making designs on 'creating a new world'" (62). This allows Griffin to criticize all modernist literature as either too committed to politics or too detached, whereas the modernist humanism I am describing is able to establish a bridge to connect the special moments of transcendence (Griffin uses Eliot as the epitome of epiphanic modernism [63], while the phrase itself derives from Joyce) with a commitment to the body, to material culture, and to politics. Both kinds of modernism identified by Griffin are products of the Enlightenment severing of mind and body, spirit and the material world; programmatic modernism is based on confidence in reason to master the body and the material world, whereas epiphanic modernism is based on confidence that the mind or spirit can easily unloose itself from the body and material world and achieve union with the timeless. Both are extreme, and modernist humanism reconciles the two extremes.

Up through the cantos written before World War II, Pound offered a program of study that he thought could indeed be epoch making. He offered new documents in his poem, hoping that they would become part of a new understanding of America's past; he then connected that newly fashioned past to Mussolini, who is the fulfillment in the present age of early American greatness. Pound had discovered in Malatesta an image of the new man of the Renaissance who goes against the decadent currents of his age to build a monument to beauty and love; the Tempio became for Pound "a rebellious critique of the very culture that engendered it" (Rainey, 127). So Pound's accidental discovery of Malatesta as the Renaissance whole man led to his discovery of Mussolini as the epic hero capable of bringing the modern world to justice. Pound misread the early modern humanists and confused them with the encyclopedists of the Enlightenment, and in such misreading he indulged in a hero worship that is more modern than modernist and contaminates both his poem and himself.

The Return of the Demons: Pound's Anti-Semitism and Modernity

The cantos that Pound wrote through 1939—that is up to Canto LXXI—are by and large and for the most part intended to instruct America about the economic crime of usury and the way this evil system was met in the past and was being met in Mussolini's Fascist Italy in the present. There are other, more traditionally "poetic," elements to these cantos, and the different kinds of discourses make this poem the epitome of experimental poetry in the twentieth century, especially in how Pound enlarged the proper domain for what poetry can be and what a poem can include or contain. But, as a glance at Pound's other activities during these years makes clear, his main focus and deepest purpose were to instruct; hence the number of primers he wrote, some with the phrase *ABC* in their titles, indicating the effort to explain difficult material in simple forms as part of a pedagogical project. So clearly did he see the "truth" of economic matters that he made a visit back to the United States in 1939 in order to meet President Franklin D. Roosevelt and advance the relationships with some congressmen and senators that he had developed in exile. Redman has reported that Pound was working toward, and hoping for, a political appointment back in Washington, perhaps in a William Borah administration (see 169–70 especially).

Pound had come to such position of certainty and mastery largely through the process of writing a revisionist history of the West, particularly of America, in his poem. He had seen through the conventional knowledge offered by schoolbooks and the official press, sweeping them away as part of a deliberate intention to place misleading and fraudulent ideas into circulation. His demystification of the status quo is similar to the kind of deconstruction we learned through Derrida and the early poststructuralists, sweeping away conventional truths and received knowledge as merely constructed by powerful groups who control the circulation of information. According to Redman, one of the cardinal moments in Pound's development of his economic positions occurred during the World War I, when the British government removed the pound from the gold standard only to restore it in the postwar years. Suddenly people were aware of the arbitrary nature of money (52), that it has no transcendental signified to ground its meaning and value but is open to manipulation by those with financial power. Seeing that this lack of grounding has the potential to make money inherently fraudulent, Pound tried valiantly to make nature, especially land, the source of value, its ground or origin or center. His repeated assertion that Marx did not understand the nature of money rests on Marx's definition of money as the measure of labor, whereas Pound insisted that money is the measure of labor and nature. Pound seems to have been aware that if one leaves value or meaning without a transcendental signified, one leaves the culture open to domination by those who want to perpetuate fraud at the expense of the good of the nation. He hastened to convince himself that just economics does indeed have a bottom, a ground, in nature and natural increase. He had to do battle against the forces that want to depart from this natural base, who want to deny the natural and exert their own arbitrary power.

Pound swept his house clean, and—afraid of the emptiness—he filled the void with an outdated agrarian ideology and the heroic image of Mussolini as a man of action who would restore land as the source of value for the West. In his anxiety at having seen through the fraud of usury, he hastened to bring into his center a demon worse than that which he saw through.

We already saw how the Enlightenment project is prone to conspiracy thinking, as was the agrarian ideology of the populist movement that Bryan represented and brought to its last great gasp in 1896 (see for instance Hofstadter, 62). Pound could not help but see that the ignorance about money was deliberate. His logic seems to have run like this: if he could see through the mists and swamp of ignorance, so could anyone; if one man could reach enlightenment, then so could everyone of reasonable intelligence; and if reasonably intelligent men do not express the truth, it is either that they were brainwashed or part of a conspiracy to keep the light from shining. And once there is a conspiracy about such matters of light and darkness, truth and fraud, it is but a small step toward anti-Semitism, the conspiracy theory of choice in the West in the late nineteenth and early twentieth centuries.

This is why Leon Surette's *Pound in Purgatory: From Economic Radicalism to Anti-Semitism* is so important. Surette has labored to "date" Pound's anti-Semitism through a careful reading of Pound's poetry, prose, and letters, and his study demonstrates quite conclusively that Pound became anti-Semitic between 1934 and 1936, concluding "that Pound's anti-Semitism was driven by his paranoid belief in a Jewish conspiracy rather than by simple racism or even an antipathy for Hebraic religion and culture. . . . The finding that Pound's anti-Semitism has a conspiracy theory provenance in no way excuses it. On the contrary, it reveals it as an intellectual failure rather than as some mental tic or emotional aberration" (6–7). Surette's position lends support to my thesis that Pound was driven to such extremes more by his intellect than by his character or emotions. Surette has distinguished his conclusions from Robert Casillo's strained and partial analysis, which seeks to explain Pound's anti-Semitism as the result of "prejudices imbibed in his youth," as Surette puts it (7). Casillo failed to date Pound's rhetoric and positions and almost always used examples from Pound's infamous radio broadcasts to prove his point. Surette's study places Pound's vicious and extreme anti-Semitism in a temporal context that does much to show us the possible dangers of the Enlightenment project.

Of course not everyone who believes in the rational mind and the autonomous will becomes paranoid and anti-Semitic; nevertheless the logic is there, and Pound's development of an intellectual hatred of Jews and of a paranoid belief in a worldwide conspiracy against civilization is one possible fruit of such Enlightenment convictions. In 1933, just before what Surette sees as the beginning of Pound's fall into anti-Semitism, Pound explained that what motivated him was intellectual rage: "Hatred can be bred in the mind, it need not of necessity rise from the 'heart.' Head-born hate is possibly the most virulent" (*Selected Prose*, 228–29). Going on to explain "that economic order is possible and that the way to a commonly decent economic order is known," Pound explained that, despite the fact that he himself has grown fat under the existing order, he has "blood-lust because of what he has seen done to, or attempted against, the arts in my time" (*Selected Prose*, 229). By 1934 Pound had met Mussolini and had written *Jefferson and/or Mussolini* and *Eleven New Cantos*, signaling a shift in foci from writing about the arts to writing more about economics and politics. By the time the war broke out in 1939, he was seeing himself as an historian. As he thought that he saw the truth clearly, he set out to explain it to as wide an audience as he could; as he saw little acceptance of his ideas, his frustration grew; as his frustration grew, his belief in a conspiracy against the truth grew, until he became a rabid anti-Semite, born of intellectual hatred and, as he foresaw, far worse than the suburban prejudice he so famously confessed to Allen Ginsburg late in his life.

It is superficially paradoxical (but only superficially so) to note that at the very same time Pound was expressing virulent anti-Semitism, he was also becoming more of an idealist and dreamer. In 1944, toward the end of his time as a radio propagandist—during which he had become prone to the ugliest kind of anti-Semitic rhetoric—Pound wrote these words in "The Way of Utopia," the opening section of "Gold and Work": "On the 10th of September last, as I walked down the Via Salaria and into the Republic of Utopia, a quiet country lying eighty years east of Fara Sabina. Noticing the cheerful disposition of the inhabitants, I enquired the cause of their contentment, and I was told that it was due both to their laws and to the teaching they received from their earliest schooldays" (*Selected Prose*, 336). A belief in utopia can go hand in hand with anti-Semitism, especially if one lacks the skepticism and irony of a Thomas More. Pound's dreaming of a utopian republic lacks the playfulness of More's and also the subtle irony of More's implied critique of such rational plans. For though More certainly used Hythloday's narrative of Utopia to critique contemporary European conduct and values, he also made Utopia too rigid and severe in its application of rational modes of conduct, and at times the Utopians seem every bit as brutal and coercive as the Europeans seem inept and greedy. More's irony is nowhere better on display than at the end of his text, where a character named More (who is not the spokesman for Utopia but rather one of Hythloday's interlocutors) informs the reader that he considers many of the Utopian practices quite "absurd," especially "the basis of their whole system, that is, their communal living and their moneyless economy" (84). My own reading of this text is that of all the things Hythloday presents, these are the most important and least absurd, the features of Utopia most seriously advanced as a critique of the European status quo, so the character named More, in his inability to accept them, shows himself to be an unreliable judge. The more objectionable parts of Hythloday's Utopia are its rational laws governing the family, the practice of euthanasia, the need for permission to move about freely, and other aspects of a coercive regime based on rational measures. These go unquestioned by "More," while the most impressive aspects are mocked. More the writer invented a world that is different from his present in order to begin dialogue and open up debate, whereas Pound saw his utopian dreams as a Platonic ideal that should be imposed on the world; and Mussolini was the man who could realize this dream.

The Plight of "The Hero" in the Twentieth Century

The hero is either an Enlightenment concept, or a bourgeois concept, or an imperialist concept, the adjective chosen depending on which aspect of modernity you wish to critique and debunk. But it appears certain that the traditional concept of hero, and the concept that informs the first part of *The Cantos*, deserves to be analyzed and demystified. Pound's concept of heroism is clearly a result of his Enlightenment values, and his form of hero worship was dangerous and outdated. Joyce's version of the hero as developed in Bloom differs dramatically from Pound's and provides an instructive comparison.

Pound's version of the hero challenges, and is challenged by, the kind of critique of the self and agency provided by Althusser, for Pound's hero can rise above his culture and see and act freely, independent of the culture that defines and constructs most of us. In short the Enlightenment hero can transcend his culture. The hero, as Joyce deployed that category in *Ulysses*, is ultimately able to achieve this transcendence and freedom as well. Both the modernist humanism based on early modern antecedents and the Enlightenment humanism of someone like Etlin do share the belief that ultimately a transcendent self can be discovered and can act freely and independently. And this achievement is in itself heroic. Dante's *Purgatorio*, the only section of the *Comedia* that Dante himself called epic, provides the model for the individual who undergoes a penitential process that results in transcendence, a purgatorial itinerary that frees the individual of the stains and marks his culture has placed on him. And this is the difference between the two versions of "hero" under examination here; Pound's Enlightenment version glories in powerful men who will themselves over and above their cultures, as Malatesta and Mussolini did, while the hero in the Christian humanist tradition must humble himself to undergo a process of purgation that can peal away the effects of his culture and bring him to an original purity. Joyce devised stylistic journey for Bloom that allows us to see him moving ever away from cultural construction and ever toward a condition of freedom. When Bloom and Stephen perform their playful ritual of leaving Bloom's house to go out to the garden to relieve themselves, it is described as "the exodus from the house of bondage to the wilderness of inhabitation" (17.1021–22); accompanying them is the "intonation *secreto*" of the "commemorative psalm," number 113, "*In exitu Israel de Egypto: domus Jacob de populo barbaro*" (17. 1029–31). Joyce understood before Singleton that this psalm is the key to Dante's entire poem, which Dante used in his letter to Can Grande to explain his allegorical method of writing and which the penitent souls in *Purgatorio* sing as they approach the island that will be the place of their painful purgation of sinfulness. Dante's higher purpose was to write about the individual soul's experience of moving away from the slavery to sin (figured in Israel's bondage in Egypt) and its moving toward the freedom of wandering in the desert. Joyce took Bloom on a purgatorial journey that climaxes in his ability to be free of his culture's effects and live according to a different set of principles than the rest of the Dubliners.

The individual suffers in order to purge the negative effects of being-in-history, and reaches, by himself and for himself, a freedom to love: that is the kind of heroism Joyce indulges in, and its difference from Pound's is clear and distinct. The humility of the Christian paradigm stands in stark contrast from the Nietzschean exuberance and arrogance of Pound's heroes.

The Fall of Fascism: Humility and Learning to Love

The fall of the fascist state, the death of Mussolini, and Pound's own arrest as a traitor to his nation occasioned Pound's quite radical reassessment of his poem, in which he reevaluated some of his fundamental concepts and purposes. Paul Morrison has noted the reassessment well but casts it in negative language meant to dismiss Pound's achievement in these cantos: "The lyric interlude [the entire Pisan sequence] heralds the collapse of the poem that contains it. The late romanticism to which Pound was heir tended to reduce poetry to what *Hugh Selwyn Mauberley* calls the status of 'friend and comforter.' If poetry bears any relation to the historical, it is on the order of the compensatory or redemptive. Jürgen Habermas characterizes bourgeois art as 'the refuge for a satisfaction, even if only virtual, of those needs that have become, as it were, illegal in the material life process of . . . society.' Art consoles for what history fails to provide" (19). What Morrison has noticed is that the poem before Pisa was not satisfied with being a refuge where the individual could indulge in feeling, but sought instead to intervene in the actual world of politics in order to help move the world closer to a happier condition in which people would have actual and not virtual satisfaction. In Pisa, Pound had to adjust his aims because of the failure of Mussolini and the Fascist state. Morrison has rightly noted that the poem now has a "smaller" purpose, but it is not as wistful and impotent as his remarks, and those of Habermas, would have us think. The poem is smaller only if one thinks consolation and redemption are unworthy aims. It is quite confusing: Sinfield and Habermas want a literary culture that has public influence, but the one poet who most exhibits the desire to do so is the most reviled; then when he reassesses his poem, he is reviled for forgoing the proper ambition of poetry. It is worth pausing here to express some wonder at how the political has become the only genuine kind of engagement with reality and how issues that are personal or religious (consolation or redemption) seem secondary and pale. Watching the development of *The Cantos* may indeed teach us not to ask from poetry what we ask from politicians and not to use terms from the one field glibly in scathing critiques of the other. Forced to reassess his faith in Mussolini to bring about social justice, not to mention his faith in himself as a man in control of his own utterance, Pound began the process of writing a poem that fits into the paradigm of modernist humanism.

The Pisan Cantos begin with a lament occasioned by the death of Mussolini, which puts an abrupt halt to his attempt to build the ideal city: "The enormous tragedy of the dream in the peasant's bent shoulders" (Canto LXXIV, 445). For Pound the death of Mussolini makes his poem a tragedy, no longer an epic. The great man could not rise above all circumstance and impose his will on a recalcitrant world after all; he hit an obstacle that showed the limitations of human greatness and human ambition. Pound moved away from worshipping the kind of hero that Mussolini embodied because the material and historical circumstances of the world order proved to be too powerful for even such a man to affect and alter. Pound had a Greek sense of tragedy, as he finally recognized that even the greatest of men must fail in the face of the enormously complex causes of modern social and cultural ills. The failure to realize the dream of justice, which would have lifted up the peasant's bent shoulders, is seen most tragically in their continued and maybe even perpetual oppression. That Pound felt as if his world has come to end we see in the lines he addresses to T. S. Eliot: "yet say this to the Possum: a bang, not a whimper, / with a bang not with a whimper, / To build the city of Dioce whose terraces are the colour of stars." Mussolini was not a hollow man but a man of great strength and will, so the effort to build the city of God on earth could only end with a bang, with the powerful opposition of the Allied forces that defeated the Axis nations. History and its forces are too large and too mighty for even the great man to overcome. Such a hero must be rejected for the poem.

The Pisan sequence has as its purpose the construction of a new kind of hero, and a new candidate for the job was the imprisoned and disgraced poet himself. One of the things *The Cantos* had lacked up to this point was any sense of humility or irony on the part of the poet. In fact we have hardly seen Pound the man in this most personal of poems, personal in that the views and opinions and attitudes are so idiosyncratic and personally felt. He does make an appearance in Canto III, as a young man with few resources or prospects who nonetheless can attain a visionary state and see "Gods float in the azure air, / Bright gods and Tuscan, back before dew was shed" (11); in Canto XXII, when he recounts meeting the economist John Maynard Keynes in the presence of C. H. Douglas and feeling exasperated at Keynes's inane responses to his queries; and in Canto XLVI, when he presents himself with some humor (a sorely lacking aspect of the poem) as the "fuzzy bloke" with "legs no pants ever wd. fit," who understands Douglas's ideas and can restate them in clearer and more direct formulations and who, later in the same canto, is "on the case" against usury, presenting evidence to an imaginary law court. These three scattered representations share the trait of depicting him as the man of genius who sees through it all, who sees better and more clearly than the rest of us. In Pisa, however, Pound presented himself on almost every page as an old man (almost sixty) imprisoned in a cage in the Detention Training Center outside of Pisa. There is clear continuity between the two main divisions of *The Cantos*. The Pisan sequence continues many of Pound's earlier points about history and continues teaching, in fact, but the dominant presence of the poet's own bodily predicament already alters the kind of poem this is. His mere physical presence looming so large throughout *The Pisan Cantos*, not to mention the threatening circumstances in which he finds himself, brings a measure of humility and irony to a poem whose root flaw was their absence.

The introduction of Pound's physical presence into this sequence encouraged the poet to recognize what he always tried to bracket off: the problems associated with the body, its limitations, and its complex needs and desires. One might counter that Pound indeed paid attention to the body in its sexual desire and in his arcane sexual theories that smack of paganism and Eleusis, and such is indeed the case. But his poem was so idealist in its faith in the intellect to cure social ills that the body and sexuality are relegated to subordinate places, as images of what a healthy society would look like and what the few great men in the world have been able to attain on their own and through the exertion of their will. Pound's neopaganism celebrates figures such as Malatesta, who were able to assert their sensuality against the attacks of their ecclesiastic cultures. As Redman has concluded, "Pound was deficient in his conception of evil" (117), a deficiency that led him, "the Confucian, the Dantean, and the rational man," to seek the explanation of social ills in errors and in ignorance and not in sinfulness or evil. I am not sure how Redman reconciles Pound's emphasis on rationality and error with Dante, who certainly valued reason but had the most comprehensive and exquisite sense of sin of any writer ever to have written in the West. But after Pisa, Pound did come to a recognition of the place of sin; as he said in a note written in 1972, the year of his death, "RE usury: I was out of focus, taking a symptom for a cause. The cause is AVARICE" (*Selected Prose*, 3). This is an important reassessment: he had seen the problem of bad economics as purely intellectual without a moral dimension; now he saw usury as a symptom of one of the deadly sins. The human body, its complex needs and desires, and our capacity for sinfulness were not part of his focus when the poem was written as an Enlightenment project, but he began the process of correcting the poem's focus, merely by bringing his own body and his own personal experiences into the poem. The body that can be incarcerated and made to suffer as punishment brings the poem a radically new focus on sin and suffering.

Conflicting Humanisms   143

That Pound suffered during his internment is obvious, and he made it a part of the poem by frequently referring to the camp and his place within it. The most poignant expression of personal anguish is, like all such utterances in the sequence, short and controlled: "but that a man should live in that further terror, and live / the loneliness of death came upon me / (at 3 P.M., for an instant)" (Canto LXXXII, 526–27). The experience of suffering and of the threat of execution (he was anxiously paying attention to the fates of other radio propagandists) brought a dimension of vulnerability and fragility to a poem that has been dominated by self-assurance and arrogance. In his controlled and measured way, Pound even registered some degree of doubt about whether his actions had brought him to a place of hellish punishment or purgatorial penance. He referred to himself often as "No man," the name Odysseus gives himself when confined by the Cyclops, and this identification brings in issues of naming and identity for the sequence. Odysseus pretends to a humility he does not have and is forced to undergo humiliation back in Ithaca before he can return to his former princely identity. Pound begins a long sequence as "No man," claiming that the ideal city he had been dreaming of is "now in the mind indestructible," and then he includes lines that pose a problem: "at sunset / ch'intenerisce / a sinstra la Torre / seen thru a pair of breeches" (Canto LXXIV, 431). The first Italian phrase comes from the opening of the eighth canto of Dante's *Purgatorio,* as Dante tells of "the hour that turns back the longing of seafarers and *melts* their heart"; the second Italian phrase calls attention to a tower that Pound could see between a soldier's legs, implying that Pound sees this tower while lying down in his cage, a humble position indeed. Later in the same canto, Pound identifies the tower he "sees": "To the left of la bella Torre   the tower of Ugolino / In the tower to the left of the tower / Chewed his son's head / and the only people who did anything of interest were H., M. and / Froebnius der Geheimrat" (436).

Is he in purgatory, cleansing himself through his suffering, or is he in hell, punished as a traitor as Ugolino was? The first image allows us to feel that Pound is softening at the hour of sunset and recalling his past in a way that will eventually purge him. But the latter image allows us to consider Pound one of the treacherous, especially as he still thinks that only Hitler and Mussolini, along with the unobjectionable Frobenius, have done anything of interest. In canto 33 of *Inferno,* Dante allows Ugolino to tell of the horrible experience he endured with his children locked in a tower, watching each of his sons die of hunger before succumbing to the temptation to eat them. It is the most heart-wrenching story in the *Inferno,* designed to cause the reader to feel pity for Ugolino. But Dante also reminds us that Ugolino was a traitor, and he is justly punished for his treason in one of the deepest places in hell. We might feel similarly about Pound. By including this reference to Ugolino's tower, Pound raises the question, despite the fact that he is suffering, might he not be a traitor who is similarly being punished justly? Is he frozen in hell under this punishment, or is he undergoing a purgation that will allow him to soften, change and move to paradise?[2]

Canto LXXIV ends with images assuring us that Pound has come up "out of hell, the pit" and so is waiting to plunge into Lethe, the river at the top of Mount Purgatory in Dante's poem, which wipes away memory of one's past. But Pound is not ready for that immersion yet, having much to purge and set straight, so at the canto's end he identifies himself as one of those "who have passed over Lethe" (449). He has work to do in these cantos before he can indulge in forgetfulness. When he finally does allow himself to taste of the bitterness of Lethe, he utters what can only be taken as a confession, similar to what Beatrice extracts from Dante on the top of Mount Purgatory:

When the raft broke and the waters went over me,

> Immaculata, Introibo
> > for those who drink of the bitterness
> Perpetua, Agatha, Anastasia,
> > saeculorum

> repos donnez à cils
> > senza termine funge   Immaculata Regina
> > Les larmes que j'ai creées m'inondent
> Tard, très tard je t'ai connue, la Tristesse,
> I have been as hard as youth sixty years. (Canto LXXX, 513)

Reluctant to taste these bitter waters, he is forced to when his raft breaks, an image of loss of control, crucial in his reassessment of the nature of heroic action. No longer the master man directing his strong will on events, the hero is overwhelmed by events and must take the risk of being drowned. But instead of drowning, he emerges from this immersion clean and ready to begin his Mass, his ritual of making himself capable of prophecy: he is immaculate. "Introibo" is the first word in the Roman Catholic Mass (and also the first words out of Buck Mulligan's mouth, an irony that probably escaped Pound here). Pound is now able to confess, and his confession is in a foreign tongue, allowing him some distance perhaps from the pain of the utterance. But the river he has tasted is of his own tears, and he admits that he has been too hard, too cold, as young men are wont. He has known sadness too late, but he is embracing it now and allowing it to soften and change him.

The sadness he has been forced to embrace bears new and unexpected fruit. Never surrendering the role of teacher or his faith in pedagogy as a worthy endeavor, he continues some of his teaching about monetary reform and notes something he recalls from his study of Aristotle about youth and age, which he now seems to appreciate and understand:

> But in Russia they bungled and did not apparently
> grasp the idea of work-certificate
> and started the N.E.P. with disaster
> and the immolation of men to machinery
>   and the canal work and gt/ mortality
> and went in for dumping in order to trouble the waters
>   in the usurers' hell-a-dice
> all of which leads to the death-cells
> each in the name of his god
> or longevity because as Aristotle says
> philosophy is not for young men
> their *Katholou* can not be sufficiently derived from
>   their *hekasta*
> their generalities cannot be born from a sufficient phalanx
>   of particulars. (Canto LXXIV, 441)

Aristotle advised only men of experience to attempt philosophy, because one needs many concrete examples and particulars in order for valid ideas to form. As Pound has already expressed in his confession about his own failings, young men are hard, and he needed to be softened through suffering. But part of that hardness, apparently, is also to rush to form ideas that are not yet legitimate, and perhaps again Pound indicates that only now, at age sixty and under such discipline, can he really lay claim to understanding. But more important than this is the inclusion of a phrase from the Hebrew prophet Micah, "each in the name of his god," that Pound repeats seven times in the Pisan sequence, finally citing the source for the phrase on the very last page of these cantos, a deferral of information that only serves to heighten its importance. He cites it again, in a slightly different context but still alongside Aristotle, a couple of pages later:

> but this air brought her ashore a la marina
> with the great shell borne on the seawaves
>   nautilis biancastra
> By no means an orderly Dantescan rising
> but as the winds veer . . .

> "in the name of its god" "Spiritus veni"
> adveni / not to a schema
> "is not for the young" said Arry, stagirite.
> (Canto LXXIV, 443–44)

This time the phrase from Micah and the warning from Aristotle are part of a section in which Pound sees Aphrodite coming ashore on a white shell, as Botticelli has painted it for us. Canto I ends with a glimpse of Aphrodite on the waters, whom the poet sees after he sails "outward and away" from his culture and returns to a mythic consciousness capable of seeing "the gods float in the azure air." But only now, with old age approaching and the experience of suffering accepted, is seeing this pagan goddess of love truly understood, and that is where Micah and other Hebrew prophets come in.

The line from Micah comes from a part of this prophet's book dealing with the restoration of the just city by the God of Israel:

> Many nations shall come and say, "Come, let us climb to the mount of the Lord, to the God of the house of Jacob, that he may instruct us in his ways, that we may walk in his paths." For from Zion shall go forth instruction, and the word of the Lord from Jerusalem. He shall judge between many nations; they shall beat their swords into ploughshares, and the spears into pruning hooks; one nation shall not raise the sword against another, nor shall they train for war again. Every man shall sit under his own vine or under his own fig tree, undisturbed; for the mouth of the Lord of hosts has spoken. For all the peoples walk *each in the name of its god*, but we shall walk in the name of the Lord, our God forever and ever. On that day, says the Lord, I will gather the lame, and I will assemble the outcasts, and those whom I have afflicted. I will make of the lame a remnant, and of those driven far off a strong nation; and the Lord shall be king over them on Mount Zion, from now on forever. (Micah 4. 2–7).

We should recall that in the Detention Training Center, Pound was denied access to books, and among the few he had in his possession was a Bible. It is a testament to his ingenuity that he could find in a text that he was predisposed to vilify, especially the Hebrew scriptures, a line that seems to express a tolerance for polytheism, "each in the name of its god." But the relation of Pound's polytheism to the God of Israel is more complex. As we see when we read this line in context, there will come a day, perhaps at the end of time, when the Lord comes to establish justice. All the peoples of the earth will come, each in the name of his or her god, to Mount Zion, and there hear the truth from the one Lord, the God of the house of Jacob. Pound comes in the name of his god,

Aphrodite, and is now open to hear from the God of the Hebrews. As a young man Pound could not have listened to such a God, but in his suffering and in his old age he has achieved a humility that allows him to turn and be open to instruction from the God he has rejected in his enthusiasm for pagan gods and goddesses.

This is an extraordinary turn for Pound and the poem. He does not renounce his delight in pagan gods and goddesses, but he no longer refuses to listen to the God of the Old and New Testaments regarding justice and truth. Pound is ready to see himself as enacting a Christian model of confession and conversion, and these cantos constitute his Mass (another book he had was a small missal that explained the parts of the Roman Catholic Mass), his ritual that renders him pure and able to be the prophet of the ideal city. It requires tremendous humility for Pound to turn to the Hebrew prophets for this instruction, especially when we consider the venom he spewed in his radio broadcasts concerning Jews and their various beliefs and practices. The phrase from Micah opens the door, so to speak, for other moments from the Hebrew prophets to enter the poem. In "A Visiting Card," written 1942, at the height of his anti-Semitic outpourings, Pound asserted, "Not a jot or a tittle of the Hebraic alphabet can pass into the text without danger of contaminating it" (*Selected Prose*, 320). Ironically, in finding this phrase from Micah and the other Old Testament texts he used with some regularity, he allowed his poem to be taken over by their presence. In Pisa, Pound's neopaganism became subordinate to a Hebrew-Christian sensibility.

As Lawrence Rainey has asserted, Pound's paganism was one of the sources for his great enthusiasm for the Tempio; Malatesta was remaking a Christian church into a pagan temple of love. The tradition that Burckhardt began and Beltramelli culminated emphasized this aspect of Malatesta's efforts, and Pound believed that it was the main reason for ecclesiastical opposition to Malatesta and his legend. The Tempio is a "monument to neopaganism" and to the "new man of the post-Christian era" (Rainey, 204). Rainey has characterized Pound's religion as a "secular spirituality" "charged with shades of vitalism and aestheticism, sensuality and voluntarism" (209). All that is true for Pound and *The Cantos* before Pisa, and this is one of the problems with failing to see the possibility of some radical breaks in the poem's bases. While Pound did not renounce his "neopaganism," the kind of religion he had been espousing became tainted by his hero worship of Mussolini, and for him to continue his poem, he needed to reevaluate his religious positions. Thinking he had been beyond Christian humility and worshipping the vitalism of the new man in Malatesta and Mussolini, Pound learned that such secular spirituality ends disastrously and that Christian humility may produce an identity capable of a different kind of greatness.

Pound turned to the Hebrew prophets because the new identity he wanted to establish for himself is that of prophet of the ideal city, the visionary who records the dream of social justice that Mussolini tried to achieve but failed to deliver. Canto LXXIV contains many references to these prophets, the main point summed up in this line: "to redeem Zion with justice / sd/ Isaiah" (449). This longer passage contains several such references:

> and the greatest is charity
> to be found among those who have not observed
> regulations
> not of course that we advocate—
> yet petty larceny
> in a regime based on grand larceny
> might rank as conformity nient' altro
> with justice shall be redeemed
> who putteth not out his money on interest
> "in meteyard in weight or in measure"
> XIX Leviticus or
> First Thessalonians 4, 11. (Canto LXXIV, 434)

Pound finds in Hebrew scriptures calls for social and economic justice that allow him to align his own ideas with Old Testament prophecy. The call in Leviticus for just measures must have been particularly pleasing to him, because his own view of money was based on the simple notion that it is not a thing but a measure, and he cites it several times. (In Canto LXXVI he tells those who have castigated the Jews, "and there is no need for the Xtns to pretend that / they wrote Leviticus / chapter XIX in particular / with justice Zion" [454].) He also includes Saint Paul in the passage above, first in his statement that the greatest of the virtues is charity and then from the first letter of Paul to the Thessalonians, in which Paul counsels the members of the church there to live quietly and work with their own hands. Love—not eros but agape—is about to become the base of the poem. These lines lead soon to his assertion that he has not given up on "the empire, nor the temples plural / nor the constitution nor yet the city of Dioce / each one in his god's name" (434–35), after which he calls for Aphrodite's shrine to be rebuilt by Terracina. He embraces the Hebrew prophets while still able to maintain—thanks to the appropriated line from Micah that he has made his own—his neopagan values.

Pound has left his hero worship of Mussolini—that story is now a tragedy and not part of an epic—and has turned his efforts to remaking himself as the hero of the poem, as a man who has survived the debacle of the fascist state and who, through suffering and humility, can emerge as the prophet of the ideal city, recording it for posterity. Mussolini has become "poor old Benito" (Canto LXXX, 495), while the poet is "a lone ant from a broken ant-hill / from the wreckage of Europe, ego scriptor" (Canto LXXVI, 458). Mussolini is reduced to a pathetic figure, while a more modest and humble heroism is attached to the writer who survives the wreckage. We must remember in reading this sequence that Pound had every reason to believe that this could be the last poetry he would ever write, and so he labored to fashion a new identity for himself, not "No man" but the prophet who calls upon fallen humanity to continue to hope for, and work for, social justice. Critics have wanted to see in this sequence Pound's abject apology for his former behavior, and when they fail to see it, they then complain that he is still asserting faith in Mussolini and fascism. What these critics miss is that Pound does confess to hardness and excess while still maintaining steadfast belief in the economic policies he had advocated, as well as a stubborn faith in the dream of the ideal city. His suffering has brought him to a position of humility that he hopes will allow him to become the prophet of this city.

The change in Pound's orientation to the self is nowhere signaled more boldly or more clearly than at the beginning of Canto LXXX, an important canto containing his immersion in the bitter waters of Lethe and his emergence, purified and renewed, as the prophet of the ideal city: "Amo ergo sum, and in just that proportion" (493). He rewrites Descartes' famous dictum: not "I think, therefore I am"; but "I love, therefore I am." So important is this revision that, "when Pound could order his own stationery in 1946, printed as a crescent at the top was this statement: 'JAYME DONC JE SUIS' ('I love, therefore I am')" (Nadel, 170). Pound exchanged rationality as the basis of the human self for love, and such is the shift from an Enlightenment humanism to a modernist humanism. He learned that love, what may be considered a universal human emotion and experience, is the foundation of a self that can transcend history and be the basis for prophetic utterance. The Pisan sequence is different from the rest of *The Cantos* also in the indulgence on the poet's part in personal memories, often of famous literary figures such as Joyce, Yeats, Eliot, and Ford Madox Ford; but also memories that are strictly personal to Pound himself. These constitute an effort on his part to build up this self through memory of beloved images from the past that have carved their traces in his mind: "nothing matters but the quality / of the affection— / in the end—that has carved the trace in the mind / dove sta memora" (Canto LXXVI, 457). In the end all that matters is love as it is retained "where memory lives," as he translated the Italian phrase from Guido Cavalcanti's "Canzone d'Amore" back in Canto XXXVI. A self founded on love is being constructed in these cantos. As Pound experiences the pain of forced incarceration and faces the terrifying prospect of execution as a traitor, this self is being built up:

> What thou lovest well remains,
> $\qquad\qquad$ the rest is dross
> What thou lov'st well shall not be reft from thee
> What thou lov'st well is thy true heritage
> Whose world, or mine or theirs
> $\qquad\qquad$ or is it of none?
> First came the seen, then thus the palpable
> $\qquad$ Elysium, though it were in the halls of hell,
> What thou lov'st well is thy true heritage
> What thou lov'st well shall not be reft from thee.
> (Canto LXXXI, 520–21)

Among the best-known lines in *The Pisan Cantos,* these are also crucial in aiding our understanding of what Pound accomplished in the sequence. Memory, which is the source of personal identity, is here associated with gathering beloved images and forming one's own heritage, the sense of a tradition of love on which the self can be founded and act. Having relinquished the rational mind as the source of selfhood by replacing Descartes "cogito" with his own "amo ergo sum," Pound has moved from an Enlightenment project to one more in line with the early modern humanists and more in line with the modernist projects of Lewis and Joyce. The fall of the fascist state and Pound's consequent suffering have led him to a modernist humanism.

Overwhelmed by History, Saved by Love: The Late Cantos as Modernist Humanism

The late cantos—*Rock-Drill, Thrones,* and *Drafts and Fragments*—constitute Pound's late but successful achievement of a modernist humanism. If in Pisa he exchanged one form of heroism for another and worked to construct his own self as the prophetic hero of the poem, in the later cantos, perhaps because of furthering chastening while incarcerated at St. Elizabeths or more simply because he now had time free from terror to develop the implications of his conversion, he portrayed a self that is not in any way master of circumstance but is instead overwhelmed by the history he seeks to understand. Despite this sense of the immensity of history, Pound managed to write fragments that lay claim to visionary status.

By "history" I mean the historical sense that Foucault, based on his reading of Nietzsche, described in his seminal essay "Nietzsche, Genealogy, History": "the true historical sense confirms our existence among countless lost events, without a landmark or a point of reference" (155). This essay makes a distinction between traditional historiography and what the author calls "genealogy" after Nietzsche and elsewhere "archaeology." The key difference in the two approaches to the study of history is that what Foucault advocates is based on the suspension of all continuities and linearities, on the disruption of any and all lines of connection that purport to "explain" how a certain event cam to occur. Traditional history follows an organic model, claiming to find a pure origin, the "seed" that then leads to an inevitable sequence of events, culminating in the "fruit," the event at the "telos" that one wanted to explain from its causes. What is wrong with this model is that all it does is give the event in question a sense of inevitability, the sense that once that seed was planted it just had to grow until that bit of fruit was produced. Such an attitude toward history is dangerous because it assists the status quo in making the present seem as if it is inevitable and in implying that no other course of events could have been possible. It is counterrevolutionary and discourages hope for change in the world. Instead of this approach, Foucault wanted to initiate a new kind of historical examination, one that at first does the "negative work" of suspending all notions that diversify the theme of continuity. "Once these immediate forms of continuity are suspended, an entire field is set free. A vast field, but one that can be defined nonetheless: this field is made up of the totality of all effective statements (whether spoken or written), in their dispersion as events and in the occurrence that is proper to them (Foucault, *The Archaeology of Knowledge*, 21, 26–27). Liberating "effective statements" from their place in a continuous chain of event leading to event breaks up the old explanations but poses a new problem: without continuities or lines of causation, the accumulation of effective statements must lead, for a long period at any rate, to a sensation of chaos. Without the lines of causation providing narrative design and a sense of order, these liberated events have no landmark or point of reference that gives them a stable place or a stable significance. Without the traditional categories that explained the past, a "vast field" is set free. To study history as an archaeologist, one must experience feeling lost amid a sea of texts. This is the risk to be confronted and taken.

Rock-Drill and *Thrones,* the cantos Pound wrote while confined to St. Elizabeths in the 1950s, often depict a sense of utter chaos, as single lines refer to different texts, in a dizzying and apparently random accumulation of "effective statements." Canto XCV, the last of the *Rock-Drill* sequence, epitomizes this method of "containing history":

> Mist weights down the wild thyme plants.
>   "In favour of the whole people." "They repeat"
>   said Delcroix
> Van Buren unsmearing Talleyrand,
>   Adams to Rush before that, in 1811
> And there were guilds in Byzantium.

> "Not political," Dante says, a
> "compagnevole animale"
> Even if some do coagulate into cities. (643)

One can find many such passages in these late cantos, and their first effect is to bewilder and bedazzle. Pound was still writing history, still writing "a long poem containing history," but the container has burst and the fragments of effective statements spill over, overwhelming the poet and threatening to drown him in this sea of texts. In fact, *Rock-Drill* ends and *Thrones* begins with a scene from *The Odyssey* in which Odysseus almost drowns:

> That the wave crashed, whirling the raft, then
> Tearing the oar from his hand,
>   broke mast and yard-arm
> And he was drawn down under wave,
>   The wind tossing,
> Notus, Boreas,
>   as it were thistle-down.
> Then Leucothea had pity,
>   "mortal once
> Who now is a sea god. . . ." (Canto XCV, 647)

Pound began *The Cantos* as Odysseus, in full control of his destination and with confidence in his destiny. Here that sense of mastery is strikingly absent. He used this image of the raft breaking and the waters covering him back in Pisa, in the climactic Canto LXXX, where he finally is immersed in the bitter waters of Lethe and is purified by his confession. That is a loss of mastery and control too, and he uses the same image, at much more length and in prominent positions, in these late cantos. Trying to gather discrete fragments of effective statements together so they can form a whole, the poet-historian is overwhelmed and loses control, his raft whirling and breaking and he himself drawn under the waves to drown. These are images of a loss of control and mastery, and as such announce a radically different orientation toward his project. Earlier he strove to be the master of history, understanding the past and connecting it to the present and even hoping to direct the future; now, history has become so complex that he cannot maintain control and becomes almost lost in the effort to assemble some fragments into a unity. And what saves him is love. Leucothea saves Odysseus by giving him her magic cloth, which becomes in Pound's poem her bikini: the sight of her naked beauty is what saves the drowning poet-historian and allows him to reach land, from the safety of which he will begin the process of assembling the fragments all over again. That is why *Thrones* begins with the same moment from *The Odyssey,* to underscore the continual and perpetual effort to making some order out of the confusion of historical statements. Leucothea has often been associated with Sheri Martinelli, a model and amateur artist who was a frequent visitor of Pound's at St. Elizabeths. This figure of youthful beauty and sensual love is what saves Pound from utter collapse and allows him to continue his efforts.

What Pound was doing in these late cantos was trying to gather a number of discrete "effective statements" and form them into a unity, into a pattern or an idea of justice. I use the term "idea" in its root and Platonic sense of form or pattern, from the Greek "eidos." Pound's poem has always been about justice, in the earlier cantos about trying to achieve it in the actual and in these later cantos about having a moment of vision in which one can glimpse the ideal of just law or just action. Pound is trying to suggest Platonic forms or ideals by gathering enough particulars that can, when they are seen together, form a cluster of statements about justice. Pound had discovered Richard of St. Victor and the distinction he drew between "three modes of thought, cogitation, meditation and contemplation. In the first the mind flits aimlessly about the object, in the second it circles about it in a methodical manner, in the third it is unified with the object" (*Guide to Kulchur,* 77). In the late cantos, Pound associates Richard with Dante: "Dante, out of St Victor (Richardus)" (Canto LXXXV, 566); "'Cogitatio, meditatio, contemplatio' / Wrote Richardus, and Dante read him / Centrum circuli" (Canto LXXXVII, 590). Pound noted this connection back in 1942 in "A Visiting Card": "And I have to thank Dante for having drawn out attention to a treatise of Richard of St. Victor *De Contemplatione* in which the words *cogitatio, meditatio,* and *contemplatio* are defined" (*Selected Prose,* 33). In *Paradiso,* Dante refers to Richard as one "who in contemplation was more than man" (10.132). The ability to gather discrete fragments of just acts and just laws together and think about them—that is, contemplate them—until one is unified with the ideal of justice, that is the highest goal of these cantos. In that achievement we become "more than human," we transcend the human condition. Following Richard's method, we can rise upward toward our highest status, still human but rising toward the divine. This is Pound's modernist humanism.

The poem that began as attempting to intervene in the world has become one that seeks the attainment of vision, the attainment through contemplation of transcendence. In one of the *Drafts and Fragments* Pound recognizes the error of the early cantos:

> again is all "paradiso"
>   a nice quiet paradise
>   over the shambles,

>   and some climbing
>   before take-off,
>   to "see again,"
>   the verb is "see," not "walk on." (Canto CXVI, 796)

This shift in the verb, from walking on to seeing, signals a shift from the Enlightenment project of directing the world to the creation of an earthly paradise, to a project more in line with what I have been calling a modernist humanism, as the individual self is rescued from the historical process that threatens toward crushing or drowning him to achieve moments of personal transcendence. *The Cantos* is no longer an example of programmatic modernism, but one would be mistaken to claim that it has become epiphanic, at least in the way Griffin sets up the dichotomy. For Pound's effort to achieve transcendence is still rooted in the material and political facts of his culture. His epiphanies are rooted in historical knowledge.

Pound's use of images from *Paradiso* increases dramatically in these late cantos, and he wrote lines of his own that seem designed to echo or reflect Dante's great poem of heaven. From Pisa onward Pound's poem has changed from one that seeks to master history to one that seeks to construct a human self capable of surviving the complex and monstrous events of the historical process and capable of achieving personal fulfillment in an ideal realm, for Pound, the eidos of justice. In Pisa he underwent a purgation that allowed him to project himself as prophet of the ideal city, but now, on review, even that is too arrogant and unearned; he merely wants to survive and achieve, for himself and for the few readers who might take up the challenge, a personal satisfaction of joining with the ideal of justice, even if only for a few scattered moments. The images he uses for paradise always suggest that it is fragmented, momentary, and scattered, and not something attained once and for all.

Pound emphasized this aspect of his paradise in these cantos:

>   Le Paradis n'est pas artificiel
>   but is jagged,
>   For a flash,
>   for an hour.
>   Then agony,
>   then an hour,
>   then agony,
>   Hilary stumbles, but the Divine Mind is abundant,
>   unceasing. (Canto XCII, 620)

The state of transcendence, the attainment, through *contemplatio,* of unity with the ideal of divine justice, can only be achieved for moments here and then,

Conflicting Humanisms 155

and, for Pound at any rate, the rest is agony. Pound's agony may well be attributed to several sources, not the least being the pain of his incarceration, the public humiliation he was forced to endure, and also perhaps the prick of conscience for having expressed views that, in hindsight, even he must have found objectionable, if not downright vile. But Pound's way of indicating this last is, in keeping with his character and style, oblique:

>   not arrogant from habit,
>   But furious from perception,
>   Sibylla,
> From under the rubble heap
>   m'elevasti
> From the dulled edge beyond pain,
>   m'elevasti
> Out of Erebus, the deep-lying
>   From the wind under the earth,
>   m'elevasti
> From the dulled air and the dust,
>   m'elevasti
> By the great flight,
>   m'elevasti
>   Isis Kuanon
> From the cusp of the moon,
>   m'elevasti. (Canto XC, 606)

Pound used the phrase "m'elevasti" from the first canto of *Paradiso,* where Dante marvels that he is being raised through the heavens while still in the body, that he is "passing beyond humanity" (the Italian is "trasumanar," transhumanized) while still in the human condition. In his pain and depression, still furious from having seen so clearly what ails the world, Pound nonetheless attains moments of being raised above himself and lifted into the heavens, into the third heaven, in fact, as he tells us at the end of Canto XCI and on the second page of Canto XCII, the heaven ruled by Venus. That he is aware of his errors is clear when he repeats his confession from Pisa, now in the context of paradisal light:

> Piccarda,
>   compassion,
> By the wing'd head,
>   by the caduceus,
>   compassion;
> By the horns of Isis-Luna,
>   compassion.

> The black panther lies under his rose-tree.
> J'ai eu pitié des autres.
>   Pas assez! Pas assez!
> For me nothing. But that the child
>   walk in peace in her basilica,
> The light there almost solid. (Canto XCIII, 628)

He is aware of the great virtue in compassion, and he repeats his admission that he did not manifest this quality enough in his younger, harder days. His confession is now linked to a simple assertion of his visionary achievement, that he has seen "the light there almost solid."

Those are the kind of images that Dante uses throughout his *Paradiso,* especially in its upper reaches, and that Pound created in the late cantos. For instance: "Light & the flowing crystal / never gin in cut glass had such clarity / That Drake saw the splendour and wreckage / in that clarity / Gods moving in crystal" (Canto XCI, 611). The following lines are quite Dantesque:

> Over harm
> Over hate
>   overflooding, light over light . . .
> the light flowing, whelming the stars.
>   In the barge of Ra-Set
> On a river of crystal. (Canto XCI, 613)

There are many images of such light in *Paradiso,* and this one especially recalls the river of light that Dante sees in his thirtieth canto. It is a testimony to Pound's honesty in these cantos that this last image precedes the ugliest, most venomous moment in all of *The Cantos,* one that would be quite in keeping with the rhetoric in the radio broadcasts:

> *Democracies electing their sewage*
> *Till there is no clear thought about holiness*
> *A dung flow from 1913*
> *And, in this, their kikery functioned, Marx, Freud*
>   *And the american beaneries*
> *Filth under filth.* (613–14)

The italics, it should be noted, are Pound's, and as such they function to ensure that such lines be noticed and emphasized in any reading of these poems. I am confident that, while Pound might indeed feel this way about the degradation of the holiness, he uses and highlights the vile rhetoric that he used on the radio (and never before or after let into the poem in such direct and brutal a manner) to juxtapose the rage he can still feel about the betrayal of holiness by the forces of usury with the delight and joy of having reached paradisal bliss. It is one and the same man who experiences both, and who is to say that the one experience can be had without the other. There are expressions of great rage in Dante's *Paradiso* too, most notably the thundering anger of Saint Peter at the degradation of the church. Pound goes further than Dante in this, for his anger is not righteous indignation as Saint Peter's most surely is, but vile and reflective of great evil. Heavenly joy can keep company with the vilest rage.

In these late cantos, Pound continued to make *The Cantos* highly personal, in order to emphasize that the man who has, like Dante, transcended the conditions of history is still very much within those conditions and suffering from that fact. His use of Dante, however, is different here than it was in the earlier cantos, and this difference is nowhere more evident in Canto XXXVIII, in *Eleven New Cantos*, in the sequence that brought Mussolini into the poem. There Pound explained the "A+B Theorem" as Major Douglas had taught him, after which the poet exclaims: "and the light became so bright and so blindin' / in this layer of paradise / that the mind of man was bewildered" (Canto XXXVIII, 190). The poet is so thoroughly engaged in his Enlightenment project that even Dante's heavenly light has become the mere light of the intellect comprehending some complex economic equation. In the late cantos, still obsessed with historical matters and still teaching about money and the economic ills resulting from the uncontrolled banking practices of fraudulent usury, Pound uses Dante's light not to signal his intellectual comprehension and mastery of such matters but rather to show his being lifted up, through *contemplatio*, into the third sphere of heaven, the part of heaven ruled by love.

The end of Canto XC quotes a line from Richard of St. Victor that is close to Dante's view of the relation of love and vision: "UBI AMOR IBI OCULUS EST" (609), "where love is, there is the eye." As she guides him through the spheres of heaven, Beatrice explains to Dante that love comes from perfect vision: "If I glow on thee with the flame of love beyond all that is seen on earth so that I overcome the power of thine eyes, do not marvel, for it comes from perfect vision" (*Paradiso*, 5.1–5). Pound quotes the opening words of these lines in Canto XCIII, "e ti fiammeggio," beginning a passage with many Dantesque lines. Later in *Paradiso*, Beatrice explains, "the state of blessedness rests on the act of vision, not on that of love, which follows after" (28.109–11). Dante's sequence, one that Pound accepts and follows, is thus: Once we see, we can love; when we love, we can reach beatitude. Proper seeing leads to love. Having achieved visionary status through *contemplatio*, Pound is finally ready to conclude the theme of love for his poem.

From the very first canto, which ends with the appearance of Aphrodite, the poem has been about love. Pound had always been under the sway of the goddess of love, wishing for her statue to be replaced by Terracina as a signal to the world that a neopaganism could be reinstated and would renew ancient values. In Pisa he imagines her coming ashore in the manner Botticelli made famous, and it is in the name of this goddess that he drew near to Mount Zion to receive his prophetic mission while incarcerated in Pisa. In the late and last cantos, Pound wants us to understand that, like Saint Paul, he has entered, while still in the body, the third sphere of heaven, where "the fair Cyprian rays forth mad love" (*Paradiso,* 8.2–3). It is a constant in his poem that love must be renewed if the world is to attain justice and joy.

Pound opens Canto LXXXIX with lines that bring together several strands of his poem:

>   To know the histories
>   to know good from evil
>   And know whom to trust.
>   Ching Hao.
>   Chi crescerà
>   (Paradiso). (590)

Pound tried to "know the histories" and "good from evil," and certainly one of the main goals for Pound, as it was for Dante, was to earn the readers' trust in the poet's language and authority. But Pound adds to this a phrase from *Paradiso,* "Chi crescerà," "Lo, one *who will increase* our loves" (5.105). This line is an important one in establishing the very different laws that operate in heaven than on earth. In nature, the more there are to share, the less each person can enjoy, but not so with love and not so in heaven, where the coming of another person to the sphere increases the amount of love there is for each to enjoy. By having tried to master history, even though he finally admits he did not and could not accomplish his goal, he has been raised up to the heavens, increasing the love to be shared. He has not denied the validity of his project entirely, for if it could not result in mastery of the historical process, at least (at least!) it can yield transcendence.

Pound uses the navigational metaphor from *The Odyssey* to indicate that he no longer expects to be able to master history. Rather, in the effort to form the ideal of justice, he embraces the risk of drowning but hopes to be saved by love. A long passage in Canto XCIII develops the new hope that is Pound's paradise:

>   nuova vita
>   e ti fiammeggio

Conflicting Humanisms 159

> Such light is in sea-caves
> e la bella Ciprigna
> where copper throws back its flame
> from pinned eyes, the flames rise to fade
> in green air.
> A foot-print? alcun vestigio? . . .
> A butcher's block for biographers,
> quidity!
> Have they heard of it?
> "Oh you," as Dante says
> "in the dinghy astern there." (630–31)

There are six clear references to Dante's *Paradiso* here, plus one to *Purgatorio* and one to *Vita Nuova;* later on the same page occurs the second citation of "chi crescerà." As such, this is almost a Dantesque collage, and one can use the various references to tell a little story. A new life ("nuova vita") begins when one's "pinned eyes" are freed to see the flame of love ("ti fiammeggio") and enter the third heaven of Venus, "the fair Cyprian," "la bella Ciprigna." Liberated thus to see the heavenly lights and, following that perfect vision, now able to love most truly, one has been empowered to follow the traces ("alcun vestigio") that love leaves behind. The word "quidity," which Pound wonders if people have even heard of, is used twice by Dante, both times in association with faith in things unseen (*Paradiso*, 20.92 and 24. 66, this last being where Dante declares that the quidity of faith is the evidence of things unseen). Those of us following these poems of heaven may not have seen these things yet but are asked to believe in them. Finally those few are hailed ("Oh you in the dinghy astern there") who are able to follow Dante's ship, which singing makes its way (see the opening of the second canto of *Paradiso*), reading a poem that promises to leads us to transcendence.

This last line Pound repeats as the very last line of *Thrones,* and as such it occupies an important place in the poem. With its navigational metaphor, it connects up to the scene from *The Odyssey* that Pound uses in the late cantos to indicate the experience of being overwhelmed by history, saved by love. Writing, and reading, paradise is very difficult and even dangerous, as we are constantly threatened with losing control and mastery over our very selves in the process. But those of us who follow closely, watching the traces left by the poet on his journey, can achieve along with him, not mastery of the historical process but personal transcendence. The exchange of one kind of humanism for another, from Enlightenment humanism to a modernist humanism, may seem a diminishment to some critics who call for literature to became politically engaged and to intervene in the culture from which it emerges, but Pound's vigorous engagement and effort to intervene led to his endorsement of Mussolini's fascist state and the poet's descent into the ugliness of anti-Semitism. His reassessment of his poem in Pisa led him to write sequences that salvage the poem from the ruins of modernity as he finally embraces a modernist humanism.

4

"In the fullness of time"
Eliot's Christian Humanism

Lewis, Joyce, and Pound each came to an understanding of human being that requires a base in love, more precisely in a Christian conception of love. Joyce in particular grounded his resolution of pressing modern issues in the Christian mystery of the Incarnation. T. S. Eliot's contribution to this study as a whole lies in his clear and full use of the Christian doctrine of Incarnation to resolve the problem of human existence within time. Of the modernists in this study, he was the most explicitly religious and worked deliberately and steadily to construct an understanding of human being that requires a religious base. In fact his understanding of human being as developed in his poetry bears striking resemblance to that of the early modern Christian humanists.

In 1935, around the time he was writing *Burnt Norton*, Eliot expressed some considerable anxiety about being called a "religious poet": "'*religious poetry*' is a variety of *minor* poetry: the religious poet is not a poet who is treating the whole subject matter of poetry in a religious spirit, but a poet who is dealing with a confined part of his subject matter" ("Religion and Literature," *Selected Essays*, 345). Eliot was not considering himself a "religious poet" but rather a poet who deals with human life and experience "in a religious spirit." Eliot's distinction allows us to study his poetry for its religious spirit without letting that focus diminish Eliot's ambition and achievement, and it might also bring us to a new way to appreciate that ambition and achievement. For Eliot was able to develop and describe a religious dimension to human life drawn from purely poetic insights and from purely poetic practice. He was able to make the poetry appear first and foundational to his examination, with the religious dimension seeming to grow from a lyrical base. Eliot presented himself as an experimental modernist poet who—as he devised a verse capable of describing and understanding our fragmentary lives in time—discovered a religious dimension that resolved his pressing concerns.

The great poet with a religious sensibility (such as Eliot) treats "the whole subject matter of poetry in a religious spirit." One of the subjects that certainly obsessed Eliot—and other modernists as well—is the problem of time, especially as time is understood in the early twentieth century as a continual flux with no fixed point or stable anchor. Any writer who wants to locate a sure and permanent ground within such a medium of experience is radically open to failure, essentially and deeply likely to be swept away in a never-ceasing flow and lost in a wholly human world of temporality. Eliot offered his fullest resolution of this problem in *Four Quartets*, which provides a poetic solution to the religious anxiety generated by the time philosophy that Henri Bergson renewed for the twentieth century and that Wyndham Lewis described as overwhelming and corrupting the art of the greatest modernist writers. While he expressly used theological terms in *Four Quartets* and while the poem can be called a poem of faith, Eliot based the religious resolution on an almost wholly poetic sensibility. It is as a poet that Eliot arrived at the mystery of the Incarnation; indeed one might say that it is as an experimental modernist poet that Eliot arrived at his theological understanding of the Incarnation as the "point of intersection of the timeless with time."

The Waste Land, Language, and Transcendence

The thesis of this chapter is that Eliot developed a poetry capable of leading to an apprehension, or at least description, of some cardinal Christian truths. *The Waste Land* is important to this thesis because a central feature of this poem is its exploration of the role of language in the quest for the divine, in our longing for transcendence. It is a poem about silence, nonsense, prayer, and God's voice.

The Waste Land is a poem first about silence. What I consider the central moment in "The Burial of the Dead" records a moment of silence: "I was neither / Living nor dead, and I knew nothing, / Looking into the heart of light, the silence" (39–41).[1] This silence stands out quite poignantly from all the other noise of the section. In fact "The Burial of the Dead" is the noisiest section of a pretty noisy poem, making this central silence quite distinct and emphatic. We have known for a long time now that Eliot referred in the manuscript to the first two sections of *The Waste Land* as "He do the police in different voices," a comic title that highlights one of the poem's central features, Eliot's playing with different voices. "The Burial of the Dead" is indeed a cacophony of voices mixed together in no apparent order with no apparent organizing principle: we jump from one distinct voice to another without narrative transition or stylistic glue. The only organizing principle he allowed in this section is the title, "The Burial of the Dead": the various voices are all responding, each in his or her distinctive way, to the problem of time as seen in its linear progression toward decay and death. The first voice is somber and depressed, dreading springtime as a cruel reminder of his movement toward death as the rest of nature undergoes renewal. The second voice, who identifies herself as Marie, is anxiously restless (notice the grammatically unnecessary commas that break up her speech into breathless fragments), as she tries to ward off fear of death by trotting around Europe in her leisured life, hoping for freedom in the right topography ("In the mountains, there you feel free"), and staying up late at night reading because she is insomniac. The third voice sounds like an Old Testament prophet, who at least has the advantage of being capable of showing us what it is exactly that we fear: "I will show you fear in a handful of dust." This figure may stand out from most of the others in this section, as his voice sounds more authoritative; and he stands in sharp contrast to Madame Sosostris, "famous clairvoyante," who instead of asking us to confront our fears helps us find a way to avoid them—in fact, she explicitly warns us, "Fear death by water." It is no mere irony that the reader will soon confront a section with that very title, as if to suggest that, try as we may, we come to that fate eventually and inevitably. The fortune-teller of the modern world stands in stark contrast to the Hebrew prophet, as she helps us avoid bad things—in this case death by water—while he exposes the half-submerged reality of human being by revealing what it is that troubles us most deeply. The prophet's commission is to reveal the truth to humanity, not to help us defer the inevitable by telling us to avoid a sea voyage.

The tone of Eliot's presentation of Madame Sosostris tells us not to take her counsel seriously. For instance we learn that she has a bad cold, but she is still the wisest woman in Europe, as if the one might cancel out the other and we need the reassurance. The name "Mrs. Equitone"[2] sounds like something out of a Monty Python sketch, and Madame Sosostris wants someone to tell Mrs. Equitone that Madame Sosostris will bring the horoscope herself. "One must be so careful these days," she says, as if she is engaging in something either dangerous or difficult. Eliot was always deft at giving us a sly wink, but there is something serious going on here beyond the ironic contrast Madame Sosostris provides to the Ezekiel voice. As she opens her tarot deck, she notes two things that she does not see: "this card, / Which is blank, is something that he carries on his back, / Which I am forbidden to see. I do not find / The Hanged Man." What she is forbidden to see might just be the cross and the Hanged Man might just be Christ, and the fortune-teller, who receives payment for helping us avoid suffering and death, is blind to the potential resolution available to all those voicing their fears of death. What attracted Eliot to Christianity is that it is not a religion that offers ways around suffering and death but a religion that places suffering at the center of the human condition. Even God, as a man in the Incarnation, has suffered through to the experience of death. The Hebrew prophet wants to force us to confront our fear as he prepares for the Christ event, but in the modern world, the wisest woman is blind to this event and—more akin to Marie than anyone else perhaps—wants to flee from it.

Eliot brought "The Burial of the Dead" near its close with a haunting Dantesque vision of humanity as a group of automatons flowing up and down London streets as they make their way to work by nine o'clock. Undoubtedly Eliot presented his morbid understanding of modern humanity as most like the neutrals in Dante's *Inferno*, where they are described as without passion, without desire, without energy: "so many, / I had not thought death had undone so many." Eliot learned from Dante, who in turn may have learned from Augustine, that the same energy that drives us toward sin can drive us also to blessedness, if only we can control and direct it properly. Eliot's respect for Charles-Pierre Baudelaire,[3] who begins and ends the final section of "The Burial of the Dead," centers on what he saw as Baudelaire's honest and independent examination of sin and damnation, an examination of suffering that implies the possibility of beatitude. Those in the modern world, like Dante's neutrals, are incapable of either damnation or beatitude, being neither bad nor good but lukewarm and indifferent. This too may be a response to a fear of death, seeking comfort in a numbed state of being that Eliot first explored in "The Love Song of J. Alfred Prufrock," published in *Poetry* magazine in 1915, and that opens *The Waste Land* so famously, in the voice that prefers "a little life with dried tubers" to the passionate renewal associated with April.

In his notes on *The Waste Land*, Eliot identified another allusion to Dante in these last lines of "The Burial of the Dead": "Sighs, short and infrequent, were exhaled." This refers to the sound made by those in Limbo, the souls of those, such as the virtuous heathen, who did not know Christ and so suffer "grief without torments." The best we can hope for in a world without Christ is a morbid grief that cannot find rest or satisfaction. The poem ends with nothing in which we can hope, nothing that seems a positive experience—except perhaps the silence at the center of "The Burial of the Dead."

This potentially central voice recounts an evening with a woman who calls herself "the hyacinth girl," and we can infer a little soap opera from his brief reminiscence. She is speaking out loud to him, I presume, and reminding him of an evening that occurred a year ago, plaintively reproving the man for some recent neglect by reminding him of an earlier happiness. But his memory of that evening is quite different from hers: he recalls an experience that may have little or nothing to do with her, an experience of feeling neither living nor dead, unable to see or speak or know. All this is quite negative, until we hear that this odd state was induced by an experience of "Looking into the heart of light, the silence." The liaison with the hyacinth girl gets pushed into the background as a trivial affair along side this experience of a light beyond knowing, beyond seeing, beyond hearing. The snippets from Wagner's *Tristan und Isolde* that introduce and conclude the "hyacinth girl" section lament the failure of Isolde to arrive from beyond the sea to comfort the dying Tristan. As such, it is a general lament at the failure of erotic love to resolve the problem of death that the poem features as central to our unhappiness.[4] There is no Isolde to comfort us as we lie dying, and even if she were there, she might be as silly as the hyacinth girl.

My reading of the scene may seem unduly harsh to the young woman. Dominic Manganiello advances a more positive reading of their relationship, where the hyacinth girl is the man's Beatrice, leading him toward the transcendent experience of "the heart of light."[5] The point of "A Game of Chess" is to underscore the failure of human erotic love to resolve the problems of *The Waste Land*. Whether it is in an upper-class drawing room or a working-class pub, the love between men and women is presented as incapable of bringing happiness, no less satisfaction. One might say that the world has become a wasteland largely because of the loss of a higher love, because love has become smaller and more narrow as it became merely human. If there is to be a more positive evaluation of eros, it comes in "The Fire Sermon."

To insist on my negative reading of the relationship of the hyacinth girl and the speaker would be a mere quibble, however, for the main point about this passage of "The Burial of the Dead" is that the man claims to have had an ineffable experience of divine love, of the *heart* of light that is beyond all our sensory and cognitive abilities. We know Eliot was fascinated by Conrad's *Heart of Darkness*, having "the horror! the horror!" as the epigraph in drafts of *The Waste Land* and using the figure of Kurtz again later as epigraph for "The Hollow Men." But the most important citation of Conrad's story might be this one, where Eliot turned the phrase around and has the speaker record a visionary experience of the "heart of light." Eliot's world would be very much like Conrad's if it were not for this experience. Without the possibility of transcendence, Kurtz's words—"the horror, the horror"—would be Eliot's too. We would not be capable of anything positive or of upward moving, if it were not for this experience, "Looking into the heart of light, the silence."

We can find this convergence of silence, light, and transcendence in the upper reaches of Dante's *Paradiso*. As Dante moves steadily higher through the various spheres of heaven, he is forced to note how often he cannot find the proper words—or any words, for that matter—to convey the experience of beatitude. In her book on Joyce and Dante, Lucia Boldrini has detailed how Dante pushes language to its limits as he tries to convey as much as he can the experience of transcendence that is ultimately ineffable. In a 1966 essay, George Steiner expressed the problem of language when faced with the burden of depicting experiences beyond language: "It is decisively the fact that language does have its frontiers, that it borders on three other modes of statement—light, music, and silence—which gives proof of a transcendent presence in the fabric of the world. It is just because we can go no further, because speech so marvelously fails us, that we experience the certitude of divine meaning surpassing and enfolding ours. What lies beyond man's word is eloquent of God. That is the joyously defeated recognition expressed in the poems of St. John of the Cross and of the mystic tradition" (*Language and Silence*, 39). This is the one moment in "The Burial of the Dead," and maybe within *The Waste Land* as a whole, that we can classify as mystical, as reaching beyond language. This is the one positive moment in an otherwise morbid section devoted to death and our various responses to it, and Eliot could find no language for it.

With this silence at the center of its first section, *The Waste Land* develops into a poem about nonsense and prayer. Indeed "The Fire Sermon" can be read as a complex struggle merely to pray. In order to bring us to a position where even just a broken prayer can be spoken, Eliot felt the need to historicize desire. "The Fire Sermon" opens with a complex mingling of phrases from present-day England and the late Renaissance. A tag from Spenser's "Prothalamion" interrupts Eliot's depiction of the emptiness of modern London, and it also introduces a more sustained use of Andrew Marvell's "To His Coy Mistress," in which Eliot develops the contrast between a modern world with little or no passion (as with Dante's neutrals) and a more healthy culture where desire was expressed with joy and a certain innocence: "Sweet Thames, run softly till I end my song, / Sweet Thames, runs softly, for I speak not loud or long. / But at my back in a cold blast I hear / The rattle of the bones, and chuckle spread from ear to ear." The gentle and quiet grace of Spenser's lines from his marriage poem are in stark contrast to Eliot's macabre version of lines from Marvell's seduction poem, as the celebration of eros has turned eerie and grim. Marvell's elegant lines—"But at my back I always hear / Time's winged chariot hurrying near"—are transformed into something almost grotesque. There's no denying that Marvell was expressing an anxiety about time, but Eliot's version makes time sinister and maybe even horrifying. Eliot uses Marvell again just a few lines later: "But at my back from time to time I hear / The sound of horns and motors, which shall bring / Sweeney to Mrs. Porter in the spring. / O the moon shone bright on Mrs. Porter / And on her daughter / They wash their feet in soda water." Here, Marvell's lines join with John Day's from his *Parliament of Bees*, whose lines celebrate the bringing Actaeon to Diana, and these Renaissance lyrics turn into a bawdy and vulgar ballad from the Great War. I think that the point of this conflation, which structures most of "The Fire Sermon," is to provide a history for desire: that what is lacking, or at least vastly diminished in the waste land of the modern period, once flourished and inspired the greatest poets. Eliot was "manipulating a continuous parallel between contemporaneity" and the late Renaissance, as "a way of controlling, of ordering, of giving a shape and significance to the immense panorama of futility and anarchy that is contemporary history." I have never thought that his famous description of Joyce's mythic method really fits *Ulysses*, because Joyce did not share Eliot's bleak assessment of the present; but it does describe perfectly well what Eliot was doing in *The Waste Land* in general and in "The Fire Sermon" in particular. Our world is made to look degenerate and fallen in comparison to a happier world where eros was celebrated without shame or anxiety.

The story of Philomel, "so rudely forced," is alluded to right after this section, importing from "A Game of Chess" the threat of sexual violence beneath the surface veneer of civilized human existence. That story can function as a reminder that eros has other possibilities than the innocent celebration for the Renaissance. In fact the sexual violence of "A Game of Chess" is largely depicted through allusion to Elizabethan and Jacobean plays, so even Renaissance England is no prelapsarian paradise of erotic joy and innocence. Eliot did not want to sentimentalize eros but to provide its history. Philomel's silence—her inability to name her rapist—also provides the opposite image of the beatific silence in "The Burial of the Dead."

After the long description of the mechanical sexual encounter of the typist with the young man carbuncular, a description that clinches the point about the degenerate present, Eliot uses a line from *The Tempest*—"'This music crept by me upon the waters'"—to introduce a brief passage in which a speaker walks through the city and hears some sounds that indicate something positive still in the city: "O City city, I can sometimes hear / Besides a public bar in Lower Thames Street, / The pleasant whining of a mandoline / And a clatter and a chatter from within / Where fishmen lounge at noon: where the walls / Of Magnus Martyr hold / Inexplicable splendour of Ionian white and gold." This is an extraordinary passage, as it is one of the few places in this poem where any positive associations can be made with the present world. It is worth noting that, at first at least, sounds give the speaker some hope. The sounds of the mandoline and the chatter of workingmen can be signs in the present of the permanence of some past glory. These are sounds that allow the poet to feel as if the legacy of Renaissance England is not all faded into vulgarity but has left some audible traces. And as the passage moves abruptly to an appreciation of the walls of one of Christopher Wren's great churches, we move from the auditory to the visionary: Magnus Martyr is a visible and tactile reminder of the past, a past that still lingers into the present.

From these traces in the present we can be sent imaginatively back to Elizabethan England, where the peal of church bells accompanies the queen and her consort the Earl of Leicester. This sound is a sign of celebration on the part of her subjects, a spontaneous celebration of the procession of their beloved queen, and a celebration of eros itself. The boat is described in such a way as to evoke Botticelli's Venus as she comes to shore on her gilded shell, and so we hear and see signs of a happier age where people can enjoy their queen's sexuality without squeamishness or hypocrisy. The letter that Eliot cited in his notes on the poem states that the queen and Lord Robert were talking nonsense, and the nonsense quality of the scene is advanced by the sound of the bells, "Weialala leia Wallala leilala." We will jump from one of the Thames daughters' song (which doubles as a presentation of Eliot himself at Margate unable to connect fragments back together) back through centuries to Augustine and Buddha with nothing more than the nonsense transition, "la la"—an echo of these celebratory bells, perhaps; or just pure sound with no meaning or associations. However we see it, we have moved from Renaissance England back to Augustine and Buddha, propelled by the nonsense of "la la." Close to silence, nonsense has the power in this poem to propel us toward prayer.

For "The Fire Sermon" ends with prayer. This middle section of *The Waste Land* is about desire, and as Eliot tells us in his notes, "The collocation of these representatives of eastern and western asceticism, as the culmination of this part of the poem, is not an accident." We must be careful not to understand Augustine or Buddha and their asceticism as rejections or denials of desire. Focusing on Augustine, we can be sure that desire for him is not something to be overcome but redirected, away from the things of the world and toward the divine. In his *Confessions* he enacted a serious and sustained meditation on the nature of human desire, noting especially and emphatically how the world is filled with beautiful things and creatures that we long to possess and enjoy. But Augustine also noted, with sadness and frustration, that every attempt to enjoy the beautiful things of the world ends in failure, and he blamed the flesh for being too sluggish and too slow, always unable to catch and hold onto the thing of beauty it has perceived and desired. Desire is swift, our bodies slow, and as the attempts to satisfy the itch of desire continue and intensify, the more it seems like a disease. Augustine came to a profound question: why would God create us in such a way that we desire the things of beauty in the world but are unable to enjoy them? Why make beauty? Why make us able to apprehend beauty we cannot enjoy? Why would he make our desire something that cannot be satisfied but instead makes us feverish and ill? Augustine concludes that it is to force us to move away from the things of the world and toward the unseen God, whom alone can satisfy our desire. The inadequacy of human love as depicted in this poem now makes more sense, as we are meant to move away from the one and toward the other. On fire for the things of the world, the ascetic turns to God in prayer: "O Lord thou pluckest me out." We have traveled back in time,

"In the fullness of time"   169

from the present, through Renaissance England, back to Augustine and Buddha, simply to be able to pray again. And a broken prayer at that.

A long way for so little, some might be tempted to say. But it is part of Eliot's religious sensibility that genuine prayer is a difficult sound to utter. If we want to invent a "plot" of sorts for *The Waste Land*, we can say we have moved from the silence at the center of "The Burial of the Dead," through a cacophony of sounds and some exquisite nonsense, to this moment where we can discern a turn toward God in this broken prayer.

And the prayer is to be plucked out of the fire of desire for things of this world. Water puts out fire, so we embark on a sea voyage, which will either kill us or allow us to be renewed. Madame Sosostris told us to fear death by water, and now we must move through a section with that title, as we must take that very risk, facing the thing we fear so much and hoping that we can come ashore again.

Silence, nonsense, prayer, and now God's voice: "What the Thunder Said" brings us back even further, back to primordial times where we might be able to hear God speaking moral commands that can inform human life. The poem has wrought a series of mediations on language that have brought us near the possibility of hearing a divine language. In the final section, Eliot continued to develop what we may call a "poetics of nonsense," as the poem brings us to the borders where logic and illogic meet, where rational language reaches its limit and we enter beyond sense, beyond rationality. The Enlightenment faith in reason is not rejected out of hand but critiqued as limited and too narrow for us to hear God, for language to bring us back to a place/time where we may hear sounds that are God's voice. Like the other writers in this study, Eliot was eager to demonstrate the limits of reason and the need for something to supplement it, some agency of the human mind that reaches beyond reason to something more permanent and satisfying. God speaks nonsense in *The Waste Land*.

Of course this moving beyond sense and beyond logic entails a great risk: any move beyond the rational may be into the irrational; any move beyond logic may bring us to madness. And so this final section teeters on the verge of delusion and psychosis. After an eerie scene comprising images reminiscent of Christ's Passion—a sweaty crowd with torches, gardens where prayers are met with frosty silence, an agony, shouting and crying in prison and palace—after this Passion scene that is notably missing any hint of resurrection ("He who was living is now dead"), we pass to an equally weird evocation of the journey to Emmaus. It is in his handling of this scene that Eliot introduced the possibility of madness. Eliot's notes inform us that he was inspired for this scene by an account of Shackleton's expedition where the utter whiteness of the landscape caused the optical illusion that there was always one more person traveling with them than there in fact was. Might not the vision of the post-Resurrection Jesus by two of his disciples on the road to Emmaus merely be the product of extreme wishful thinking, of a delusion—an optical illusion—brought on by pain and despair? Is not our hope for resurrection irrational, or at least nonrational? Is it not nonsense? Is it not merely our wistful hope brought on by our painful and fearful apprehension of our mortality?

The Waste Land is at best a hopeful poem, one that has brought us back before logic and reason and maybe to a moment just before language itself, where the thunder roars and the noise becomes—perhaps—articulate sound. This reaction against reason and logic is Eliot's critique of the Enlightenment, at least as far as faith in the divine may be concerned. It requires a profound sense of nonsense to be able to pray: recall that we moved from Margate to Carthage through the nonsense of "lala"; and now we will hear God's voice in the nonsense of "DA." Faith, or at least hope, is something beyond logic and beyond reason, and we must return to the very origins of language to hear the noise that may be God's voice.

Eliot famously uses "DA" as the sound of the thunder, and it is a remarkable coincidence that his Hindu source could allow him a sound that in 1922 would surely and immediately have called to mind the avant-garde intellectual and artistic movement called Dada. Eliot wants his thunder's speech to be associated with Dada in its antirationalist assault on the values and ideals of modern culture, its assault on the faith in reason and logic to bring humanity to ever higher levels of civilized life. Tristan Tzara wrote in his 1918 "Dada Manifesto": "Logic is a complication. Logic is always false. It draws the superficial threads of concepts and words towards illusory conclusions and centres. Its chains kill, an enormous myriapod that asphyxiates independence" (279). Kurt Schwitters wrote in "Merz" (1921): "I play off sense against nonsense. I prefer nonsense, but that is a purely personal matter. I pity nonsense, because until now it has been so neglected in the making of art, and that's why I love it" (282). Eliot had different ends in mind than Tzara and Schwitters, but he had the same fundamental affinity for nonsense and its powers as these founders of Dada express.

DA is a perfect nonsense sound, meaning nothing in itself yet having reference to a movement that advocated "non-sense." Eliot was working hard as a poet to make poetic language, to make language at its purest and most powerful, capable of bearing the "non-sense" of God's voice. DA brings us to a moment of pure origin, before language itself, perhaps even to the moment that inaugurates language and meaning and thus humanity, where we first hear God's speech and begin the process of interpretation, which for Eliot in this poem at least meant making God's noise articulate sound. We interpret DA as *datta, dayadhvam,* and *damyata,* which are then translatable as "give," "sympathize," and "control." This is nonsense; why should the sound of thunder be the voice of God? Is it once again a symptom of our desperate need that we take this noise and transform it into God's voice uttering three primal commands around which we can renew the project of civilization? Is it delusion, or has the poem brought us to a moment where we can at least approach the possibility of hearing eternal truths entering the human world through language? *The Waste Land* is a poem of hope, perhaps slender hope bordering on delusion and hallucination, but nevertheless pointing at the possibility of our discovering a point of intersection of the timeless with time, a moment when we can encounter the divine.

Eliot's Christian Humanism

The Waste Land is a major poetic statement of modernism in its attempt to push language toward its very limits, where an encounter with the divine may occur. It is a poem that explores the need for an experience beyond the merely human, a love that is larger and higher than merely human love. As Eliot said most forcefully in his essay on Baudelaire, published in 1930, "In much of romantic poetry the sadness is due to the exploitation of the fact that no human relations are adequate to human desires, but also to the disbelief in any further object for human desires than that which, being human, fails to satisfy them" (*Selected Essays*, 379). That statement helps us understand the almost ruthless depiction of the inadequacy of human relations in the poem, and it also explains the movement of the poem toward a burning desire for a "further object" that may indeed be satisfying as we strain to hear God's voice and feel God's love.

It may be strange to say that *The Waste Land*, with its negative depiction of humanity and human love, constitutes the beginning of Eliot's exploration of humanism, but such is my thesis. Eliot's 'humanism" is distinctly Christian, and it is something he was rather explicitly developing in his prose toward the end of the 1920s, when he was preparing for his conversion to the Anglican Church, especially in his essays on Irving Babbitt's humanism. His main point of contention with his much-respected former teacher was that Babbitt's humanism is a humanism without religion and as such is doomed to failure. His humanism is a version of Enlightenment or rationalist humanism.

In "The Humanism of Irving Babbitt," it is clear that for Eliot the humanism Babbitt advocated is an "*alternative* to religion" designed for those who, as Babbitt admitted of himself, are unable to take the religious view. But for Eliot any assessment of the human that does not "take the religious view" into account cannot succeed in elevating humanity. Babbitt engaged in a critique of humanitarianism, which he saw as a concealed form of naturalism, but Eliot thought that the same critique could be applied to Babbitt's humanism. According to

Eliot, Babbitt's "humanist has suppressed the divine, and is left with a human element which may descend again to the animal from which he sought to raise it" (*Selected Essays*, 420–21). Without religion, humanism cannot succeed in elevating humanity to something higher than the animal: "Humanism is either an alternative to religion, or ancillary to it. To my mind, it always flourishes most when religion has been strong; and if you find examples of humanism which are antireligious, or at least in opposition to the religious faith of the place and the time, then humanism is purely destructive, for it has never found anything to replace what it destroyed" (423). This point is crucial to Eliot's position and to the overarching concern of this book as a whole: a concern about the lack of anything to be constructed or to be placed at the center of a culture after a thoroughgoing skepticism has demolished the corrupt and degenerated values that have been occupying place of privilege. Is there any center, or telos, or ideal that can survive vigorous demystification? Eliot's disapproval of Babbitt's humanism is that it provides no upward goal for human desire, nothing higher for Babbitt's famed "higher will" to aim at. Eliot anticipated this problem in "The Fire Sermon," where the human subject, now on fire with desire again, turns finally to God, using desire as the motive force to turn to something higher. Now Eliot was ready to conclude that, because religion provides that upward object for the will to aim at, "the humanistic point of view is auxiliary to and dependent upon the religious point of view. For us, religion is Christianity; and Christianity implies, I think, the conception of the Church" (427).

While Eliot saw "the weaknesses" of humanism, there was much for him to admire, especially in Babbitt's depiction of the inner check as the way an individual can assume self-control and discipline. Babbitt's notion of the self capable of such will is perhaps the cornerstone of humanism, and Eliot's quarrel was rather with rationalist humanism's failure to provide that "further object" for desire, that something higher for the human will to aim at. A year after his Babbitt essay, Eliot wrote "Second Thoughts about Humanism," an essay that does not withdraw his critique but rather refines and expands it. At the beginning of these "second thoughts" he reiterated that he had begun as a "disciple of Mr. Babbitt" and that he later "rejected nothing that seems positive in his teaching" (429). Again what disturbed Eliot is humanism's failure to take into account anything higher: "Man is man because he can recognize supernatural realities, not because he can invent them. Either everything in man can be traced as a development from below, or something must come from above. There is no avoiding the dilemma: you must be either a naturalist or a supernaturalist. If you remove from the word 'human' all that the belief in the supernatural has given to man, you can view him finally as no more than an extremely clever, adaptable, mischievous little animal" (431). Here Eliot managed to say, with a clarity and a finality that are almost alarming, what he was struggling to record in *The Waste Land*. From the perspective of this critique of Babbitt's humanism, *The Waste Land* stands as a poem that struggles its tortuous way to this dilemma, whether to adopt the position of the naturalist or the supernaturalist, to decide whether or not humanity has the capacity to raise itself toward the divine. Do we peer into a heart of darkness or a heart of light?

In the essays he wrote just before, during, and after his conversion, Eliot frequently returned to a concept that had become crucial to his understanding of human being: an unbridgeable gap exists between the divine and the human, but nonetheless only by trying to rise upward toward the divine can we truly be said to be human and not animals. One cannot look at only one side of this problem if we are to appreciate the central tension of Eliot's poems. To believe that human beings can rise up and attain the divine is a loose and sentimental romanticism that Eliot abhorred, but with this gap there is the certainty of painful frustration of our deepest or highest longings. While we must accept the fact that this gap between the human and the divine is not one we can erase in this life, we must also understand that we are most human when we nonetheless persist in that desire for the movement upward.

Eliot concluded his 1930 Baudelaire essay by evaluating the modern poet's understanding of humanity in light of Dante's. By assessing the limitations of Baudelaire, one is ready to appreciate Dante's fuller and happier resolution of the relation of the human and the divine. About Baudelaire, Eliot wrote that "there is for him a gap between human love and divine love" (381). Because of this gap, Baudelaire developed a misogyny: "The complement, and the correction to the *Journaux Intimes,* so far as they deal with the relations of man and woman, is the *Vita Nuova* and the *Divine Comedy.*" Eliot presented Baudelaire as a representative of the modern poet who bravely seeks to find things out for himself and in so seeking finds out quite a bit about the inadequacy of human love; but the modern poets—and this includes Eliot as well as Baudelaire—are not capable of learning on their own what Dante knew: "in the adjustment of the natural to the spiritual, of the bestial to the human and the human to the supernatural, Baudelaire was a bungler compared to Dante" (379).

There is a clear and vital distinction to be made between what the medieval poet was able to discover and what the modern poet, in a very different culture, can find out. In the year before the Baudelaire essay, Eliot published his "Dante" essay, in which he developed an argument against what we may properly call a "psychological" interpretation of certain aspects of human experience that is characteristic of the modern age. Discussing the "Divine Pageant" that concludes the *Purgatorio,* Eliot seems almost defensive about how a modern audience may respond to such an event and to such poetry: "It belongs to the world of the *high dream,* and the modern world seems capable only of the *low dream"* (223). Thanks to a cynical turn of mind that is distinctly modern, we are ready to interpret our dreams when they can be found to come from some "lower" source but not when they are about higher things. Eliot was ready to launch into a more sustained argument against Freud and the kind of reductive interpretation of human existence he made popular; he did so when he described the *Vita Nuova,* which, interestingly enough, he saved for the end of his Dante essay, as if this earlier and minor work were the culmination of Dante's career. It is instead the culmination of Eliot's argument against modernity.

That a child of nine could have the experience that Dante describes in *Vita Nuova* troubled Eliot, and he claimed to have consulted a psychologist for reassurance that not only is such an experience possible at that age, it most likely would have occurred earlier, at age five or six. It is part of Eliot's sly manner of argumentation to show respect for the profession and the position he was about to challenge and reject. "The same experience, described in Freudian terms, would be instantly accepted as fact by the modern public. It is merely that Dante, quite reasonably, drew other conclusions and used another mode of expression, which arouses incredulity" (234). Dante's method of drawing conclusions is not unreasonable; it is just so alien to the modern mind trained by "Freud" to look for "lower" motivations that it seems incredible. Eliot identified clearly the difference between Dante's method of interpretation and what he called the "Freudian": "The attitude of Dante to the fundamental experience of the *Vita Nuova* can only be understood by accustoming ourselves to find meaning in *final causes* rather than in origins. It is not, I believe, meant as a description of what he *consciously* felt on his meeting Beatrice, but rather a description of what that meant on mature reflection upon it. The final cause is attraction to God" (234). We are so accustomed to searching for origins as a cause that it takes a bit of reorientation to think of ends as causes. Once we make this shift, we have exchanged a modern and psychological process of interpretation for a medieval and theological one. We may consider that a desire for God may indeed lead to an interpretation of events quite distinct from the psychological, and just as valid. Rather than reduce the sensation to its lowest possible terms, which "would be instantly accepted by the modern public," this mode of interpretation allows us to consider "higher" meanings. Dante provided an alternative to Freud in understanding human erotic attraction: "the love of man and woman (or for that matter man for man) is only explained and made reasonable by the higher love, or else is simply the coupling of animals" (234–35). Eliot insisted that Dante's method of interpretation as every bit as reasonable as Freud's, just as valid but much more satisfying: "His account is then just as reasonable as our own; and he is simply prolonging the experience in a different direction from what we, with different habits and prejudices, are likely to take." Eliot went so far as to call *Vita Nuova* "a very sound psychological treatise on something related to what is now called 'sublimation'" (234). Modern psychology has invented a term that designates the "higher things" we turn our desire toward as mere substitutes for something more genuine and more primal, whereas Dante's "psychology" treats these higher things as equally real but much fuller in satisfaction and meaning. The main difference between Dante's mode of interpretation and Freud's is the direction in which we seek for explanation and meaning. Dante prolongs the experience (that's what poetry can do, as the formalists understood it, prolong our perception of human experience) in a different direction from the one we are accustomed to, and that direction is upward toward divine things. Dante taught Eliot a psychology that is also a theology, a psychology that seeks meaning in final causes rather than in primal origins, in higher rather than lower things, in attraction upward toward God rather than downward toward the bestial.

Eliot's humanism is based on this mode of interpreting the human, as something to be understood from the higher, religious perspective. We are human when we reach upward, and the modern psychological perspective advanced by Freud actually denies our humanity by interpreting the human from lower causes rather than from final ends.

But Eliot's respect for Dante is not based on some loose sentimental appreciation of a lost sensibility. Eliot ended his "Second Thoughts on Humanism" with a quotation from T. E. Hulme on the difference between the humanist conception of life, which is inadequate, and the religious one: "I hold the religious conception of ultimate values to be right, the humanist wrong. . . . I have none of the feelings of *nostalgia,* the reverence for tradition, the desire to recapture the sentiment of Fra Angelico, which seem to animate most modern defenders of religion. All that seems to me bosh. What is important, is what nobody seems to realize—the dogmas like that of Original Sin, which are the closest expression of the religious attitude. That man is in no way perfect, but a wretched creature, who can yet apprehend perfection" (438). Eliot had obviously found in Hulme a thinker who, like himself, felt that man is a severely limited creature whose greatness is his ability to apprehend divine things. Hulme was a kindred spirit who insisted on both the radical gap between the human and the divine and the necessity for us to be able to apprehend divine things if we are to fulfill our higher nature. But Eliot was also announcing, through Hulme, that his "religious" attitude is not based on the loose emotion of a romantic nostalgia but on something more rational and more intellectual, on dogma.

Turning back to Eliot's distinction between a religious poet, who at best can only be a minor poet, and the major poet who deals with the whole range of human experience in a religious spirit, one might be led into thinking that with this focus on dogma Eliot was narrowing his range. But Eliot used Hulme to advance and defend an attitude toward humanity at its fullest that is best expressed in certain dogmas and that are called religious. While Hulme used the dogma of original sin to illustrate his point, the dogma at the heart of Eliot's religious attitude toward humanity and at the heart of his poetry from this point on is the dogma of the Incarnation. It is a dogma that leads to an intense focus on the complex relation of the human and the divine, which will become for Eliot the subject for his greatest poetry.

As he was in the process of making his conversion, Eliot was reading, among other things, the sermons of Lancelot Andrewes. In an essay by that name, published in 1926, the year before his conversion, he recommended as his readers' introduction to Andrewes his *Seventeen Sermons on the Nativity,* "all on the same subject, the Incarnation; they are the Christmas Day sermons preached before King James between 1605 and 1624" (*Selected Essays,* 304). "Bishop Andrewes, as was hinted above, tried to confine himself in his sermons to the elucidation of what he considered essential in dogma; he said himself that in sixteen years he had never alluded to the question of predestination, to which the Puritans, following their Continental brethren, attached so much importance. The Incarnation was to him an essential dogma, and we are able to compare seventeen developments of the same idea" (304). Eliot shared with Hulme a strong conviction that "the religious conception of life" is not based on loose or sentimental feelings of nostalgia but on an intellectual consideration of essential dogma. Both in his life and in his poetry, the essential dogma is Incarnation, which allowed him to formulate an understanding of human being as capable of glimpsing higher things, a conception of humanity and humanism in which the human can indeed be joined with the divine. As he wrote in his essay on Blaise Pascal in 1931, the Christian thinker "finds himself inexorably committed to the dogma of the Incarnation" (360)—so does the Christian poet.

Eliot wrote a series of what he called *Ariel* poems—"single poems published as illustrated pamphlets for Christmas" (Ackroyd, 164). Critics have long noted that the first poem begins with an abbreviated quotation from one of Andrewes's sermons, and the connections between Eliot's reading of Andrewes, this poem, and his conversion are quite intricate. "The Journey of the Magi"—a poem Ackroyd has called "the poem of a convert"—might be the most important of the series, because it was written shortly after Eliot's conversion and dramatizes the effect of the Incarnation on someone unprepared for this experience and incapable of understanding it. The poem is a dramatic monologue in which one of the magi recalls the experience of having witnessed the Incarnation. The greatness of the poem lies partly in the vivid re-creation in memory of this unexpected and life-changing experience through the accumulation of the homely details leading up to the event; but also in the complication rendered by the speaker's last lines, in which he registers his confusion about what the experience meant. (Eliot wrote later, in *The Dry Salvages* that "we had the experience but missed the meaning.") In British understatement the speaker of "The Journey of the Magi" does tell us that the experience "was (you may say) satisfactory," and he is certain he would do the whole thing over again if he could. But he is not sure how to interpret the experience, other than telling us that "this Birth was / Hard and bitter agony for us, like Death, our death." It was like a death, we may presume, because he was "no longer at ease here, in the old dispensation, / With an alien people clutching their gods." His own people now seem alien to him; he is no longer at home in his own culture; he has been shaken out of the old ways of living. The poem may be taken as a measure of Eliot's "progress" as a recent convert, having turned from "the old dispensation" because of the powerful effects of the Incarnation but still unsure of what it signifies.

The experience is emotional or spiritual, and it smacks of the nostalgia for religious feeling that Eliot used Hulme to critique; but while the experience is emotional, it must be understood by the intellect; it must be interpreted by the active intelligence. This will be crucial to *Four Quartets*.

"A Song for Simeon" is the other Ariel poem that has as its explicit theme the Incarnation, as the old man from Luke's Gospel expresses his satisfaction at having witnessed the infant Jesus, "the still unspeaking and unspoken Word." Simeon is content with the experience, and does not need nor want the fuller experience: "Not for me the martyrdom, the ecstasy of thought and prayer, / Not for me the ultimate vision." There is something sufficient for the old men in these poems (Eliot himself was just turning forty) at merely having arrived at the mystery of the Incarnation, as if this experience is the "turning point" in their lives but they do not know what it means or what it demands next. Eliot arrived at the mystery of the Incarnation in and through his poetry, and like Pascal he quieted his skepticism by drawing near this central mystery of the Christian faith. These poems may indeed be, as Ronald Bush has suggested, dramatizations of "'what it feels like' to hold Christian belief in an age of skepticism" (112–13), but a problem remains: what to do after this experience as we continue to move forward in time.

Facile Claims of Transcendence in *Burnt Norton:* "That was one way of putting it—not very satisfactory"

In 1935 Eliot wrote a poem that tackles the problem of time head on, and for a while it may have seemed to achieve a solution that satisfied. But a few years later, in 1940—after the start of World War II and the 1938 commitment of his wife, Vivienne, to a mental hospital—the poem must have seemed inadequate to stand on its own and required three additional poems, three additional "quartets." *Burnt Norton* offers a facile depiction of transcendence, one that is open to the critiques against modernism that recent critics have advanced.

As in my discussion of Pound, Roger Griffin's distinction between programmatic modernism and epiphanic modernism is useful to my analysis of the problems in *Burnt Norton*. Programmatic modernism is categorized by its desire "to change society, to inaugurate a new epoch, to start time anew," while epiphanic modernism focuses on "the cultivation of special moments," "a purely inner, spiritual kind with no revolutionary, epoch-making designs" (62). *Burnt Norton* is almost the epitome of epiphanic modernism. Griffin seems to have been thinking precisely of *Four Quartets,* and we can use Griffin's critique to underscore the facile nature of *Burnt Norton*. Eliot must have recognized this, and when he returned to the same issues in 1940 with the other three quartets, he developed his project and his understanding of time in a way that makes Griffin's critique seem shortsighted and facile.

Burnt Norton begins by announcing that time is a problem. The main point of the opening lines—with their various and contrary attitudes toward time—is, first and foremost and among other things, to make the problem of time seem, if not overwhelming to the human intellect, at least formidable and daunting. What jump-starts the lyric consideration of "special moments" in the poem is the proposition about time that also ends the first section, "What might have been and what has been / Point to one end, which is always present." These lines may be paying homage to Emily Hale, with whom Eliot took many happy walks through the gardens at Burnt Norton: "what might have been" his life if he had married her instead of Vivienne? That is an expression of profound longing and wistful nostalgia, personal to Eliot but common to all in one way or another. But the "what might have been" is more than impotent expression of frustration; it leads to a depiction of a moment of heightened intensity that becomes, for this poem, the standard against which all other such moments are to be measured and with which all other such moments come to take on meaning.

The "what might have been" awakens footfalls that "echo in the memory / Down the passage we did not take / Towards the door we never opened / Into the rose-garden. My words echo / Thus, in your mind." The poet has confidence that his words can activate in our minds a memory of something we never experienced, the opening of the door in our "first world." The rose garden is a wonderful conflation of the garden where he and Emily walked, the Garden of Eden, perhaps the garden where Saint Augustine had his conversion experience,[6] and most especially the rose garden from *Alice in Wonderland*. The base moment of

Four Quartets is a "nonsense" moment of childish innocence, epitomized by the image of children "hidden excitedly, containing laughter." The "what might have been" is Eliot's poetic allusion to a state of innocence: while we may never have actually experienced innocence, we do indeed feel as if we know what it "might have been" like. Not actual and only imaginary, it is nonetheless real for us in our memories. It is fundamental to Eliot that what is purely or only imaginary may indeed be as real, and more important than, what we normally refer to as reality. The nonsense verse opens "the first gate, / Into our first world" of innocence.

Beginning with this imaginary and real moment we all share, *Burnt Norton* suggests that this moment in the rose garden is also our way to beatitude. As in *The Waste Land,* which also turned upon nonsense, in *Burnt Norton* there is a second reference to the "heart of light," bringing that ineffable experience from "The Burial of the Dead" into this later poem as its point of inception. Here we are asked to look down into a drained pool, and we watch as "the pool was filled with water out of sunlight." This line may be read simply and literally and so nonsensically: the sunlight fills the pool with water. As in the upper reaches of Dante's *Paradiso* and in the late cantos of Pound, there is flowing light. We have entered the nonsense world of innocence and beatitude.

Eliot linked the *Alice* books with Dante. In discussing the necessity to immerse oneself in the study of other medieval poets in order to understand *Vita Nuova,* he also said that "such study is vain unless we have made the conscious attempt, as difficult and hard as rebirth, to pass through the looking-glass into a world which is just as reasonable as our own" (236). Study is vain unless we have made the effort in our personal lives to pass through the looking glass of nonsense; only then may we are to enter the world of Dante. The nonsense of *Alice* is connected to something as life-changing as conversion; for Eliot nonsense is the beginning of the process. We make the conscious effort to "turn and become like children" in order to enter this "first world." This moment of innocence is the base moment of the entire *Four Quartets*.

Written well before Eliot saw the need for the elaboration of three other poems, *Burnt Norton* was meant to stand on its own as a complete and satisfactory handling of the problem of our lives in time. As such it has a certain coherence that allows us to see how this moment is then made central to the theme of time. But, while this poem does seek to be an expression of the religious attitude, what it lacks is the full development of the poetic possibilities of the dogma of Incarnation.

Burnt Norton works to develop a religious understanding of the place of such a moment in our lives, in our experience of temporality. In part 2, usually a section of philosophical reflection in *Four Quartets,* this moment is described as "at the still point of the turning world," that point at the center that is made perfectly still by the even and regular turning of the world. He claims for this moment that it grants "the inner freedom from practical desire," bringing us away from the world of desire and toward a world of grace, "a white light still and moving"; that is something both in and out of time. The poet also claims that this moment can give us a heightened consciousness and that this consciousness can help us conquer time:

> To be conscious is not to be in time
> But only in time can the moment in the rose-garden,
> The moment in the arbour where the rain beat
> The moment in the draughty church at smokefall
> Be remembered; involved with past and future,
> Only through time time is conquered.

This moment in the garden is "not in time" and is already being used as the standard by which other similar moments—moments that may have occurred in the personal life of the poet, but that is just conjecture. These moments are intended to represent purely personal moments of heightened consciousness that just happen randomly to an individual and that seem wholly different from ordinary experience. All such moments, which are here and throughout the poem always to be measured against the standard of the base moment in the rose garden, are accumulated and remembered in time and used in time to conquer time. If that seems a bit facile and vague, Eliot, on review of the poem five years later, may have felt the same way. Indeed, when he reviewed his life's accomplishment, it was *The Waste Land* and the last three quartets that "had been worth writing" (Ackroyd, 329).

The purpose of *Burnt Norton*—the purpose of each quartet—is to interpret these moments. They make the rest of our lives—"Time before and time after" such moments of consciousness—seem a "place of disaffection" and the world "a twittering world." The phrase "time before and time after" makes these moments, as brief and infrequent as they may be when judged by ordinary standards, seem central to our lives, literally the center of our existence in time. He repeats his conviction that these moments can free us from the metaled ways of appetency, but it seems quite odd how a handful of moments can accomplish so much while doing so little to redeem the rest of time. It is too easy a solution to the problem of time, as if these moments, without any further reflection, can redeem time and conquer time. In 1935 Eliot had not yet understood the immense difficulty of conquering time, the intense agony required for conversion and salvation, and the need for committed temporal action even in the moment of transcendence.

This facile solution also brings us to the problem Griffin identified in "epiphanic modernism": this easy escape from time and the material world into a timeless realm allows the world of material reality to seem unimportant and hardly worth any effort of engagement. The radical indifference to human life is an escapist aspect of modernism that may indeed allow for others to run things, for others to take control.

Eliot made one gesture toward what became the main line of poetic argument in the last three quartets when he introduced Christ in the last section of *Burnt Norton,* as he thinks about the nature of words and music as they struggle to reach the stillness:

> Words strain,
> Crack and sometimes break, under the burden,
> Under the tension, slip, slide, perish,
> Decay with imprecision, will not stay in place
> Will not stay still. Shrieking voices
> Scolding, mocking, or merely chattering,
> Always assail them. The Word in the desert
> Is most attacked by voices of temptation.

This introduction of Christ as the Word does not seem integrated into the rest of the poem; in fact it is sudden and unexpected. It seems as if his meditation on the temporality of poetry and music—arts that move in time, that keep time, and that take time to unfold—leads the poet to think of the Word as some stable and permanent feature of language that mere words can only struggle to point to but never attain. "The Word in the desert" alludes to the temptations that Christ had to overcome to begin his ministry, and worldly temptations might indeed be the obstacles to our ability to fasten on the special moments, to make them the center of our lives, and so to "conquer time"; but it still appears that this allusion to Christ was not prepared for by what preceded it nor in any meaningful way integrated into the poem. Indeed *Burnt Norton* ends with a last look at that moment in the rose garden that seems to have nothing to do with Christ:

> Sudden in a shaft of sunlight
> Even while the dust moves
> There rises the hidden laughter
> Of children in the foliage
> Quick, now, here, now, always—
> Ridiculous the waste sad time
> Stretching before and after.

The special moments of heightened consciousness—for that is as far as this poem has advanced them in meaning and significance—come suddenly upon us in the here and now but somehow also partake of some timeless realm of "always." Yet their achievement seems mainly negative: they make the rest of our lives seem "waste sad time." From the perspective of these moments, our lives are made to look ridiculous. Time is not redeemed if all we can say about most of our lives is that they are twittering, sad, waste, and ridiculous. These moments have not been integrated into the rest of our lives in time, as the Christ event has not been integrated into the poem.

"The point of intersection of the timeless with time": Redeeming Time in the Incarnation

East Coker enacts a descent to darkness in which the speaker tells his reader to abandon hope (as Dante is told as he enters hell) and love, but not faith: "I said to my soul, be still, and wait without hope / For hope would be hope for the wrong thing; wait without love / For love would be love of the wrong thing; there is yet faith." While these lines can be read as if the poet is recalling that there is yet one more thing, faith, to be abandoned, the more obvious reading is that faith is the one thing that he holds onto in this descent to darkness. This reading underscores that for Eliot the intellect that wills to believe is foundational to the feelings of religiosity, that dogma still trumps emotion and sentiment, that dogma (as Eliot used Hulme to say) "is the closest expression of the religious attitude." When everything else is to be doubted and perhaps even denied, the one thing left is faith in the dogma that Eliot said "the Christian thinker is inexorably committed to," the Incarnation.

This "essential dogma" allowed Eliot to resolve one of the most profound and persistent problems in human experience, our lives in time. *Four Quartets* is not (to use Eliot's distinction) a religious poem and so only minor poetry, but a great and major poem that deals with an important aspect of human experience in the religious spirit. No matter how the poem was conceived in Eliot's mind, the manner of its presentation suggests the problem of time comes first, the poetic handling of lyric moments second, and only finally a move toward "dogma" as the resolution. Indeed *Burnt Norton* was hardly able to refer to the Christ event and did not work at all to integrate it into the poem. The remaining three quartets make the dogma of Incarnation the base of Eliot's poetic solution to time; the next three poems are grounded in personal human experience, and the poet "discovers" the dogma of Incarnation as he meditates on the poetic fragments of our lives. He begins as a lyric modernist poet and becomes a thinker "inexorably committed to the dogma of the Incarnation."

East Coker begins the process of restatement, complication, and extension of *Burnt Norton*, which now must be read as the first poem in a series of four. Read in this new way, *Burnt Norton* can be seen as proposing a major human problem and an initial solution to that problem that now require responses and restatements. *East Coker* challenges the first quartet by emphasizing that our lives in time end in "dung and death," and there is nothing that "special moments" can do to alter our destiny. Our lives in time end in decay and death, and nothing stops that process, not even these moments. If the hope in the first quartet was that we could order these moments into a pattern that reaches the stillness, in this poem even that hope is challenged:

> There is, to seems to us,
> At best, only a limited value
> In the knowledge derived from experience.
> The knowledge imposes a pattern, and falsifies,
> For the pattern is new in every moment
> And every moment is a new and shocking
> Valuation of all we have been.

Time is relentless in its linear movement toward "dung and death," and the new "moments" we experience along that linear path only falsify the pattern we thought we had achieved. The additional "moments" that will occur in our lives bring us "new and shocking valuations" of our entire lives, so there is no longer even the comfort of having attained some self-knowledge that is lasting and true. As such, these moments cease to inspire us but instead become painful. The opening of *East Coker* is a bit of poetic naturalism that challenges and denies the now facile comforts of *Burnt Norton*. This second quartet is blunt in presenting the case against the facile transcendence of *Burnt Norton:* human beings can never escape from time to some timeless realm. When time is viewed in this fashion, we are no better than the beasts born merely to decay and die.

The greatness of the second quartet lies in Eliot's ability to turn from naturalism back to supernaturalism at the very point that might seem the strength and foundation of naturalism. For it is in the painful reminder of our mortality that Eliot begins to make the Christ event central to the poem's meaning:

> I said to my soul, be still, and wait without hope
> For hope would be hope for the wrong thing; wait without love
> For love would be love of the wrong thing; there is yet faith
> But the faith and love and hope are all in the waiting.
> Wait without thought, for you are not ready for thought:
> So the darkness shall be the light, and the stillness the dancing.

> Whisper of running streams, and winter lightning,
> The wild thyme unseen and the wild strawberry,
> The laughter in the garden, echoed ecstasy
> Not lost, but requiring, pointing to the agony
> Of death and birth.

As we abandon all things in the descent to darkness, we might be able to keep faith. By reaching this darkness of the negative way, we achieve light; in the stillness of no motion comes perfect motion of the dance. Something quite important has been suggested here, that by the negative way we achieve something positive. This happy formulation of the negative way leads first to another series of "moments"—some new ones, alongside the base moment in the rose garden of course—and next a new interpretation of those moments. If before they were moments of consciousness, here they are moments of "echoed ecstasy / Not lost, but requiring, pointing to the agony / Of death and birth." They are *echoed* ecstasy because in memory they are only echoes—faint and less powerful—of the original moments we experienced earlier in time. They are painful in that their memory might only make us feel wistful nostalgia as we continue to decay but can recall better days: the special moments now only mark our being farther and farther away from happiness and closer and closer to "dung and death." These moments no longer seem to form a pattern that can reach the stillness and thus liberate us from time; instead they require agony and point to agony. They require our agony of being in time and moving toward our death, and they point to another's agony in a garden. Our holding onto such moments, which in *Burnt Norton* was a religious act but not in any precise or meaningful way Christian, now in *East Coker* brings us into some clear and definite association with Christ, who also partook of a life in time and agonized over an impending death. As we continue to meditate on such moments and their place in our lives, we as it were stumble upon the Christ event; as Dante discovers as he pursues his itinerary in the *Divine Comedy*, we are learning that our lives may indeed follow the same pattern as Christ's. This is one of the cardinal insights of Singleton and Freccero in their groundbreaking studies of Dante's allegory, that Dante is actively discovering the conjunction of the pattern of his own life with the Christ event. This may be Eliot's deepest insight into Dante and his most successful imitation of his poem.

This began Eliot's most sustained and focused attempt to write his "Christian humanism," his version of "a modernist humanism." In this emerging and ever developing but never fully achieved union of our ordinary lives in time with the Christ event, we are learning how to find that "point of intersection of the timeless / With time" and to elevate our human status toward its highest possible level, occupying a space that is both human and divine in a way analogous to Christ in the Incarnation. Eliot found a way—the same way Dante discovered—to bridge the gap between the human and the divine, the natural and the supernatural. In "Second Thoughts on Humanism," Eliot stated, "Man is man because he can recognize supernatural realities, not because he can invent them" (*Selected Essays*, 433). In the last three quartets, we have more than glimpses of the supernatural: we are learning how we may occupy that "point of intersection." In this "Christian humanism," Eliot followed a path that allows for the elevation of the human toward a nobility and a divinity that it may actually attain in the way Christ attained it. Eliot was resolving many of the issues that had plagued him: the problem of time and mortality; the elevation of the human from the bestial and toward the supernatural; the role of the poet, whose lyric sensibility has turned to the presentation of isolated images or fragments defying meaning and unity; and the relation of dogma or belief to poetry.

In *East Coker* Eliot did not in any way give up on a meditation of these special moments—now called moments of "echoed ecstasy," growing in poignancy and meaning and now pointing to Christ; they no longer, however, offer us comfort or solace, as the now facile first quartet promised, but instead bring us to our own passion, modeled on Christ's Passion. In retrospect *Burnt Norton* was naive enough to suggest that just holding onto such moments in memory can "conquer time," as if we can rise above the temporal flow and simply look down on the rest of our lives as ridiculous. That's hardly a satisfying way to look at the vast bulk of our lives, as "waste sad time." It is noteworthy that Eliot himself saw what was wrong with his first attempt to resolve time, as if anticipating the critique of "epiphanic modernism" as escapist fantasy failing to engage with the somber and recalcitrant realities of the temporal order. *East Coker*, realistically and even naturalistically, insists on our always being within time, even in these moments, and that such acute awareness of this limit of our humanity is an agony to us. Eliot's great achievement, in correcting the flaws of "epiphanic modernism," was to use the Christ event as the base of his more complex and satisfying solution to the problem of time. We are indeed becoming aware of our imitation of Christ here: always within time we have in these moments glimpses of an atemporal order.

To underscore our conjunction with Christ in his Passion, the lyric fourth section of *East Coker* presents a vision of humanity as diseased because of "Adam's curse" and requiring the compassion of the "wounded surgeon" if we are to recover. We are all dying, this quartet constantly reminds us, and we turn to Christ and his Passion as our hope for a cure. The fourth section ends with a clear reference to the Eucharist and to Good Friday, bringing Christ's Passion loudly into the poem. This quartet ends with a romantic depiction of humanity as "old men" who remain committed to being "explorers," who remain committed to moving forward in time seeking ever "a further union, a deeper communion." No longer claiming to have transcended time, we accept that we must move forward in time but now with the hope of finding meaning in our union with Christ and our communion with other explorers.

The Dry Salvages continues the analogy of the sea voyage, as we move out of the river of our youth (for Eliot, the Mississippi) into the open sea (for Eliot, the Atlantic off the Massachusetts coast). We move from one consideration of time, as the river that is always flowing and (Heraclitus tells us) we can never enter twice, to another, as the vastness of the ocean whose motion is almost undetectable. "The tolling bell" off the coast of Cape Ann "measures time not our time, rung by the unhurried / Ground swell, a time / Older than the time of chronometers, older / Than time counted by anxious worried women." The image of the vastness of space indicates the vastness of time when counted not by chronometers or anxious humans but by archaeology and geology. The time of the geologists is the closest we as humans have achieved in thinking eternity; we are led onto the ocean of eternity, there to face our fate as measured by a different sense of time than *East Coker* presented as its challenge. And on this ocean of vast time, we are "In a drifting boat with a slow leakage," an image that suggests that, while we may have slowed down our conception of time and so feel less hurried, less pressured by its movement toward dung and death, we are still slowly sinking down toward our inevitable demise. We are told, "We have to think of them as forever bailing, / Setting and hauling," forever making the effort to stay afloat, though the effort is clearly doomed. We are also told, "There is no end" to the wailing that the seamen might be making, no end to "The bone's prayer to Death its God" except "the hardly, barely prayable / Prayer of the one Annunciation." The only "end" of this doomed effort to stay afloat is a prayer.

We are back to *The Waste Land,* more specifically to "The Fire Sermon," where the entire movement is to bring us back to a condition from which we can once again utter a prayer to God: "O Lord thou pluckest me out." The capital letter—"Annunciation"—indicates that this is not a metaphor for or an analogy to that event but an attempt to bring the "prayer of the one Annunciation" into the poem, as we utter the angel's words to Mary when she is asked to become the mother of God's son. In *The Dry Salvages,* as we try to keep our boats afloat, we pray what we have come to call the "Hail Mary," the prayer of the one Annunciation, asking her to "pray for us sinners, now and at the hour of our death." As we look at the vastness of the sea and recognize the inevitability of our fate, we make this prayer and so once again join in the pattern of the Christ event.

It is a deeply felt conviction on Eliot's part that genuine prayer is a significant achievement, and in *The Dry Salvages* he seems prepared to suggest that he has achieved the capacity for such speech to God. This prayer, that we might indeed be part of the Christ event from its inception, immediately precedes one of the most important passages in Eliot's entire oeuvre:

> It seems, as one becomes older,
> That the past has another pattern, and ceases to be mere sequence—
> Or even development: the latter a partial fallacy
> Encouraged by superficial notions of evolution,
> Which becomes, in the popular mind, a means of disowning the past.
> The moments of happiness—not the sense of well-being,
> Fruition, fulfillment, security or affection,
> Or even a very good dinner, but the sudden illumination—
> We had the experience but missed the meaning,
> And approach to the meaning restores the experience
> In a different form, beyond any meaning
> We can assign to happiness.

As we persist in "bailing, / Setting and hauling," we continue to think about the moments we can retain in memory and the pattern they form. Here we deny any "linear" meaning these moments may take on, as development (as from seed to fruit) or as evolution (from lower to higher forms). As we look back on these moments in memory, they form "another pattern" and so are transformed from "moments of happiness" to moments of "sudden illumination." "Illumination" is a word that suggests the light of the divine, and it is "sudden" because in memory, as we continue to think about such moments, they suddenly seem to shine with the light of the holy. The "plot" of *Four Quartets*—up to this point and right through to its end—is to develop the "meaning" of these moments more and more fully: from moments of consciousness, to moments of echoed ecstasy pointing to agony, and now moments of sudden illumination. They have grown in meaning as we continue to dwell on them in memory, and they continue to grow in significance as the poem continues.

Memory is a transformative power, an agency of the human mind capable of developing these moments toward their ever-growing theological significance.[7] "We had the experience but missed the meaning, / And approach to the meaning restores the experience / In a different form": as we approach the meaning of these moments, they are restored in new forms, closer and closer to their fullest revelation of meaning in our lives. Soon, in this third quartet, they become signs of the Incarnation.

There is a complication that needs to be addressed. In the passage just quoted, the moments of happiness become the sudden illumination whose meaning is "beyond any meaning / We can assign to happiness." Eliot is very careful about claiming happiness for himself in this process, but seems more comfortable with what he calls in just a few line later "the moments of agony." These are, he now tells us, "permanent / With such permanence as time has." "People change, and smile: but the agony abides." These moments are always an agony to us, even as they are elevated by higher meaning into happier experiences, or, to use Eliot's distinctions more precisely, into experiences beyond mere happiness. Eliot was always interested in understanding human suffering and never eager to find ways to cast it off or ignore it. Our participation in the Christ event is not one that ever erases the required agony in the garden even as the moments of agony become more meaningful, more consoling, and more uplifting.

The last section of *The Dry Salvages* begins with Eliot's condescension toward fortune-tellers and all those whose fear and anxiety lead them to seek to see into the future. It is worth noting how *The Waste Land* established certain themes—time, prayer, fortune-telling, quests, God's presence—that *Four Quartets* picks up and resolves. Eliot had advanced his critique of fortune-telling since his mockery of Madame Sosostris in "The Burial of the Dead" twenty years earlier. Now such behavior is a sign of a very dangerous attitude toward time:

> Men's curiosity searches past and future
> And clings to that dimension. But to apprehend
> The point of intersection of the timeless
> With time, is an occupation for a saint.

When we seek out fortune-tellers and the like, it is evidence that we are "clinging" to the dimension of time, putting all our hopes in events that will occur in the future and so occur only within time. Though there is no escape from time possible for human being, it is still a mistake to cling to the dimension of time. Rather we are to try to apprehend this point of intersection of two dimensions, the temporal and the timeless. We are not to flee from the one and enter the other: that is an impossible task for human beings, at least from Eliot's perspective. Again Eliot anticipated Griffin's critique of "epiphanic modernism" and rejected this facile resolution. Like his friend Hulme, Eliot rejected such sloppy romantic bosh and insisted on limits. Time is a limit for humanity beyond which we, as humans, cannot pass. But we can try to find within time a special place where we can apprehend the timeless. "Apprehend" is a nicely chosen word, for it implies not only understanding something with the intellect and perceiving it with the senses, but also arresting, stopping, and holding onto that something. Eliot did not make this seem easy or even likely for anyone but the saint, and he was careful not to count himself among their number:

> For most of us, there is only the unattended
> Moment, the moment in and out of time,
> The distractions fit, lost in a shaft of sunlight,
> The wild thyme unseen, or the winter lightning
> Or the waterfall, or music heard so deeply
> That it is not heard at all, but you are the music
> While the music lasts. These are only hints and guesses,
> Hints followed but guesses; and the rest
> Is prayer, observance, discipline, thought and action.
> The hint half guessed, the gift half understood, is Incarnation.

Most of us cannot "apprehend" that point of intersection and are left only with the moments "in and out of time" that we have been accumulating in experience and retaining in memory. They are hints at whose significance we guess, and they are gifts because God gave Jesus, his only begotten Son, as a gift to humanity. We have steadily advanced our understanding of the nature of these moments; they are now indications of Incarnation, that most essential dogma of Christianity.

This is a tour de force. Eliot was able to make the poet's talent, the ability to experience and record such moments, the basis of a major poem expressing the religious sensibility of a modern Christian, as these lyric moments that happen to us all can become the bearers of such divine grace. He was able to make the modernist poet's experiments in fragments and images into the basis of a profound refection on life from a Christian perspective. These poetic moments are our way of approaching that point of intersection of the timeless with time, as they now are moments both in and out of time. We all experience these moments, and for the Christian poet they lead inexorably to the dogma of the Incarnation.

The Incarnation in History: "Upon this rock I will build my church"

In some ways this is the climax of *Four Quartets*. It certainly is a climactic moment for the Christ event to be so plainly named and made the central point of the poem. But the Christian life based on the Christ event does not end with Christ; after his Ascension, there is the life of the church.

Little Gidding develops the implications of these moments and the meditative practice that has made them so deeply meaningful. In the final quartet, once again, Eliot insisted that such moments of Incarnation do not bring us out of the temporal order into the safety of the timeless realm. Like Christ, we are always within time even as we experience the timeless. The contribution of *Little Gidding* to *Four Quartets* is to bring the dangers of war into the poem, as if to subject these moments to a last challenge, of being in *historical* time, within a most pressing and urgent kind of time. Far from being naively "epiphanic" and seeking to escape from history, this last poem forces us to reckon with war and war's alarms. Though *East Coker* has already made the point that time is relentless in its movement toward death, *Little Gidding* makes the point that living in time can be in special ways and at special times more broadly deadly and more generally dangerous. What happens to these moments when we are living through a most anxious and even desperate set of temporal circumstances? In Eliot's hands they become ablaze with Pentecostal fire.

According to Ackroyd, Eliot had long wanted to write a poem organized around the four natural elements; and clearly *Little Gidding* is a poem about fire. The opening lines presents a flash of "midwinter spring," with a "glow more intense than blaze of branch, or brazier, [that] / Stirs the dumb spirit: no wind, but Pentecostal fire / In the dark time of the year." We return to one of Eliot's most persistent themes, the difficulty of praying, which is why we come to Little Gidding in the first place: "You are here to kneel / Where prayer has been valid." As the fire of Pentecost stirred the early Christians into articulate and inspired speech, so here we are spurred to a kind of speech that is beyond ordinary communication: "the communication / Of the dead is tongued with fire beyond the language of the living." These moments enkindle a Pentecostal fire that inspires us to speak a new language, and this new language allows us to commune with the dead, to participate in a timeless conversation in the communion of saints. Pentecost marks the beginning of the church, which is commissioned by Christ to continue the Gospel in time into the future.

We were promised at the end of *East Coker* a movement "Into another intensity / For a further union, a deeper communion," and it is fitting that we go to Little Gidding for this communion of saints in an imagined church. For Little Gidding, which Eliot visited in May 1936, was established by Nicholas Ferrars during the English civil war as an Anglican religious community. To its chapel we come to pray to God and communicate with the church, whose members, both alive and dead, are the body of Christ. The moments, now moments of Pentecostal fire, enable us to make this communion.

The church had for quite some time been an important idea for Eliot, and he was happy to have been commissioned in the early 1930s to write "The Rock." Ackroyd describes Eliot's developing devotion to the church, his role as warden of the church starting in 1934, his pleasure in writing these verses for the pageant designed to raise money for the building of new churches in the north London suburbs, his delight in their popular reception, and even Eliot's satisfaction at the negative reaction of some of his friends at his abandoning poetry for practical verse more akin to preaching (209–14). Ackroyd defends "The Rock" as good poetry, and these verses do provide context for *Little Gidding*. In retrospect the "ragged rock" of *The Dry Salvages* may indeed be an image of the ideal church that Eliot wanted us to imagine:

> And the ragged rock in the restless waters,
> Waves wash over it, fogs conceal it;
> On a halcyon day it is merely a monument,
> In navigable weather it is always a seamark
> To lay a course by; but in the somber season
> Or the sudden fury, is what it always was.

The special moments—that in this section of *The Dry Salvages* had become "the sudden illumination"—are a rock to steer by, and the rock may already be an image of the church. It certainly looks forward nicely to *Little Gidding*, both the poem and the place that gave the poem its title, for Eliot brings his reader in this final quartet, which is also his last significant poem, to a consideration of our communion with the saints and a participation in an ideal and invisible church. It is upon this rock that Eliot built his church.

The second section of *Little Gidding* presents an encounter the poet had in the middle of the night, after an air raid, with one of the dead, "a familiar compound ghost." While the most obvious candidate for this shadowy figure is Dante (because the section is Eliot's attempt to write terza rima), it is literally a *compound* ghost, one made up of many different figures perhaps, drawn from literary history but also perhaps from other arts and disciplines as well. It is a voice of the tradition that Eliot had so long advocated and cherished, a voice representing the dead who can still communicate to us in the special language of poetry. The scene is Dantesque, with echoes of Dante's encounter with his beloved teacher Brunetto Latini in the fifteenth canto of *Inferno*, but the more pertinent Dantesque analogue is from canto 26 of *Purgatorio*, where Guido Guinicelli points out to Dante "il miglior fabbro," the better craftsman, Arnaut Daniel. As Dante is finishing his ascent up Mount Purgatory, he meets poets (first Sordello and Statius, then Bonagiunta and finally Guinicelli) and engages in conversation with them about poetry. It is an important fact about *Purgatorio* that it is where Dante places most of his poetic forebears (at least those who were not pagan and so unable to get beyond Limbo). The point is that poetry for Dante is purgatorial, bringing us through desire near to Edenic perfection; and Eliot's encounter with his ghost ends with words that echo the end canto 26: "From wrong to wrong the exasperated spirit / Proceeds, unless restored by that refining fire / Where you must move in measure, like a dancer."[8] The fire of

Pentecost becomes the fire of Dante's purgatory. The wisdom of the dead is that we must accept the fire of purgatory as a way to purify and restore us, bringing us nearer a final blessedness.

This transformation of Pentecost into purgatory occurs again in the short fourth section of *Little Gidding*, where "the dark dove with flickering tongue" descends:

> The dove descending breaks the air
> With flame of incandescent terror
> Of which the tongues declare
> The one discharge from sin and error.
> The only hope, or else despair
>   Lies in the choice of pyre or pyre—
>   To be redeemed from fire by fire.

This "dark dove" is an image of a German dive bomber, the Stuka, descending on London—it often had flames painted on its front that gave it a ghastly and sinister smile of fire. Even if this dive bomber was not used in the blitzkrieg, it presents a powerful image of the war for the poem. What brings us "Pentecost" is history, seen here at its most dangerous and most violent. Eliot's insight here is that we have a choice in how we regard the fire that one way or another comes our way as beings in history: we can see it as a fire of despair or as a fire of hope, the fire of hell or the fire of purgatory. We are to continue our meditation on the special moments even as "history" unfolds around us and challenges our peace. They are moments now of Pentecost and purgatory.

The third section of *Little Gidding* includes lines about the nature of memory that might be considered the clearest statement of what the entire *Four Quartets* is all about; it is noteworthy that we have to wait until the poem is nearly over to read this clear statement of thesis, as if Eliot had only after much effort finally arrived at its articulation:

>   This is the use of memory:
> For liberation—not less of love but expanding
> Of love beyond desire, and so liberation
> From the future as well as the past. Thus, love of a country
> Begins as attachment to our own field of action
> And comes to find that action of little importance
> Though never indifferent. History may be servitude.
> History may be freedom.

Memory is for liberation: that is a clear and important statement, as didactic as can be, in the middle of the final quartet, as if Eliot has finally and fully understood something that he has been working on and approaching. We do not use memory to flee from the world and so feel indifferent to it, but to love it; and love is freedom. The memory of these special moments, associated in various ways with the Christ event, allows us to transform the desire that is attachment to "self and to things and to persons" into a love that is detachment, a love that is freedom. This section ends with yet another aspect of the Christ event to which these moments point us: "See, now, they vanish, / The faces and places, with the self which, as it could, loved them, / To become renewed, transfigured, in another pattern." We are transfigured, as was Christ, by the meditative practice of this poem. The self is transfigured, made brighter and more resplendent by the proper use of memory. This renewed and transfigured self is the basis of Eliot's Christian humanism, the ordinary self made higher and holier.

But these moments have always been fraught with pain and suffering, and that remains central as we approach the climax of their possibility. The meditative practice is never one of easy consolation or escape. It requires agony, requires what is called "torment" in the lyric fourth section of this final quartet:

>Who then devised the torment? Love.
>Love is the unfamiliar Name
>Behind the hands that wove
>The intolerable shirt of flame
>Which human power cannot remove.
>　We only live, only suspire,
>　Consumed by either fire or fire.

Once again we must note how we do not leave the body in Eliot's achievement of transcendence. Love, which is God's "unfamiliar Name," has devised the torment of our 'being-in-the-flesh." This is similar to Augustine's central problem in the *Confessions:* why would a loving God create a being whose desire impels him outward toward the beautiful things of Creation but whose flesh is too sluggish to ever possess and enjoy them? In Augustine's language the itch of desire only increases until our flesh festers and becomes diseased. In Eliot's terms the torment of this "intolerable shirt of flame" forces us to make a choice between the fire of hell and the fire of Pentecost/purgation. Living in the flesh brings on desire; desire is a fire that consumes us. Over that we have no control; over that we can assert no agency. But we can assert our will and choose to regard this "burning, burning, burning" as the fire of purgation. When we choose purgation, we are committed to a process in which desire can become love, a process that brings us closer to the God who devised this torment.

Little Gidding bears deep similarity to Dante's *Purgatorio,* and like that poem, *Little Gidding* can be called a love poem, in the sense that it expounds an understanding of love. We have already seen how Eliot used Dante's understanding of the purgative process as a foundational insight for *Little Gidding;* but he followed Dante's example more profoundly in coming to a similar understanding of love as the outcome of the purgative process. In the exact middle of *Purgatorio,* and so in the precise middle of the *Comedia,* Virgil explains to Dante that purgatory is organized according to love or, more precisely, according to how love was not properly developed. Love is perverted when what we love is the harm of another, and on the first three terraces are purged the sins of pride, envy, and anger. Love is defective when the love that impels us outward toward the world is sluggish, and on the fourth terrace sloth is purged. Love is excessive when it is not properly controlled and directed toward the things we desire, and on the last three terraces avarice, gluttony, and lust are purged. Dante's fundamental insight in *Purgatorio* is that desire must be purified, controlled, and directed if we are ever to be able to ascend to the blessed spheres, and this insight controls Eliot's understanding of the purgative process in *Little Gidding.* For both Eliot and Joyce, who follow Augustine and Dante, one does not seek to be without the body and so without desire, but to perfect desire so that it can lead us upward, still in the body, toward blessedness. The special moments of *Four Quartets* are in the last poem on fire with Pentecostal flame that becomes purgative fire. We can use these moments of hopeful suffering to reach beatitude.

The last lines of *Little Gidding* weave many threads into a final climactic statement:

> We shall not cease from exploration
> And the end of all our exploring
> Will be to arrive where we started
> And know the place for the first time.
> Through the unknown, remembered gate
> When the last of earth left to discover
> Is that which was the beginning;
> At the source of the longest river
> The voice of the hidden waterfall
> And the children in the apple-tree
> Not known, because not looked for
> But heard, half-heard, in the stillness
> Between two waves of the sea.
> Quick now, here, now, always—
> A condition of complete simplicity
> (Costing not less than everything)
> And all shall be well and
> All manner of thing shall be well

> When the tongues of flame are in-folded
> Into the crowned knot of fire
> And the fire and the rose are one.

The commitment to explore that ends *The Dry Salvages* opens this climactic passage, as the poet reiterates that the exploration of these moments is part of a process that must continue as long as we live; but there is an "end" to the exploration, a goal or a telos for the exploration: that we return to "where we started and know the place for the first time." Knowing casts us out of Eden; knowing brings us back. We had the experience but missed the meaning; we were in the rose garden at the start but we did not know it, did not know what it meant; we did not experience the moment with knowledge of its significance. The practice of exploring these moments has yielded, finally, some knowledge.

The passage continues by returning us to that moment in the rose garden where the children were hiding, this time in an apple tree, bringing in with that detail the popular image of Eden and the fruit of the fall from innocence. We pass through an "unknown, remembered gate" on the way back, again pointing to the paradox that we remember something that never really happened, our first world of innocence. The ending of *Little Gidding* brings us around and back to the opening moment of *Burnt Norton*—after all, in my end is my beginning, and in my beginning is my end. M. H. Abrams admired this circular return, comparing it to the "plot" of the Bible, as we return to a higher innocence at the end of the age with Christ's Second Coming, a higher Eden if you will. Abrams in fact included a chapter on *Four Quartets* in *Natural Supernaturalism,* his masterful survey of Romanticism and the Romantic paradigm. The enormous complexity of our lives in time is made into a "condition of complete simplicity," as we have given up on everything but these moments and the often painful itinerary they entail. The fire of Pentecost and purgation returns as we come to the very end of the poem, as "tongues of flame" that are "in-folded" form a "crowned knot of fire." Eliot took this image from Dante, from the twenty-third canto of *Paradiso,* where we see the "coronate fiama," the crowned flame (line 119). It accompanies a description of Gabriel as he flies toward Mary to perform the Annunciation. It is fitting that Eliot could find a Dantesque analogue for his ultimate image, flames folding in upon themselves to form a pattern that first looks like a crown and then takes the form of a rose: "And the fire and the rose are one." When made into the perfect pattern, the special moments, which have been explored and deepened and developed into our communion with Christ and then with the church, become a fiery rose. This is Eliot's version of Dante's celestial rose, which is the pattern formed by all the angels and saints in the heavenly city at the very end of *Paradiso*. Innocence and beatitude are joined here, as the initial image of *Four Quartets* is set aflame and becomes the rose.

What Eliot accomplished in this poem is a resolution of the various issues that haunted him and his work from its beginning in the Christian dogma of Incarnation. In particular he had been obsessed with the problem of our mortality, of suffering, and of our living within a temporal order that brings us through suffering toward our death. The dogma of the Incarnation allows for some resolution here, as Eliot discovered in his poetry and as a poet a way for our human life in time to join in the pattern of the Christ event. The special moments of heightened consciousness are worked upon in and by memory until they become light-filled signs of the Christ event: Annunciation, Passion, Incarnation, Transfiguration, and Pentecost. The meditative practice that brings us into conformity with the Christ event never brings us out of time or provides ease and comfort. The pain of our temporal lives is always on display in Eliot's verse, and these moments become at their highest development Pentecostal and purgative fire. The modernist poet famous for radical experimentation discovered a way to use the fragmented moments of our lives as the basis of a poem rivaling Dante's for sublimity, a poem that achieves a religious expression of our lives in time.

Conclusion

Modernist Humanism—A Love Story

Concluding his *Sources of the Self,* Charles Taylor made the case for a theistic humanism as the only sure base for defending "the ethic of benevolence." Taylor considers Nietzsche the thinker who made the most powerful challenge to this kind of humanism and to this kind of ethic, saying poignantly, "Only if there is such a thing as *agape,* or one of the secular claimants to its succession, is Nietzsche wrong" (516).

The postmodern critique of ideals and values, which can indeed be traced back to Nietzsche, has similarly challenged the concept of humanism in the twentieth and twenty-first centuries. Certain writers of the modernist period, those we have long called the high modernists, both anticipated this critique and saw beyond it. We may turn to these modernist writers as the last, or at least the most recent, literary artists to engage their culture with the aim of establishing a base for a successful and sustainable humanism. My methodology has been to provide new readings of these highly canonical texts as a way of following their responses to cultural conditions, a formalism with historical aim. Beginning as iconoclasts who sought to blast away the detritus of a decadent and corrupt culture, the Men of 1914 incorporated into their writing a scathing critique of values similar to postmodern skepticism, but they also went beyond that critique to lay a new foundation for a new humanism, one based on love—or rather a renewed foundation for a renewed humanism.

For modernist humanism has more in common with the Christian humanism of the early modern period than it does with the more rationalist humanism developed by Enlightenment thinkers. Perhaps the first step in revitalizing the possibility of humanism for us today is to distinguish, as Taylor does, between theistic humanism on the one hand and rationalist or naturalist Enlightenment humanism on the other. Eliot perhaps stands out from the others in this regard, for in his prose especially, he was clearly rejecting the humanism based on rationality advocated by his teacher Irving Babbitt and was calling for a humanism based on our ability to apprehend the supernatural.

The four Men of 1914 all began their careers as literary radicals and experimenters who sought forms and themes capable of breaking up the conventions and clichés of a culture they regarded as in serious decline and in much need of renewal and reform. They saw themselves as "English Rebel Artists," and Lewis used the two issues of his little magazine *Blast* (1914–15) to introduce this group to the literary world as a set of young iconoclasts at war with the mainstream culture. This antagonistic and radically skeptical attitude toward modernity is their opening gambit and one that they retained as part of their modernist projects. But each of them—beginning with Joyce in *Ulysses* and with the other three over the next two turbulent decades—moved beyond mere critique and sought something on the other side of nihilism and skepticism. Each in his own way discovered love, or agape, as the permanent and constant ideal capable of grounding a sense of human being and of value. This "theistic humanism" allows for confidence in the reality of an ideal with which to anchor civilized life and value while not becoming rigid and mechanistic and perhaps even totalitarian as Enlightenment humanism tends to become in its demand for universal values. Avoiding the nihilism of naturalism and the coerciveness of rationalist humanism, a theistic humanism can ground culture in the transcendent ideal of love without demanding total conformity and rigid compliance. Its politics would be open not totalitarian, benevolent not coercive.

That Joyce discovers this principle before the others, during the Great War as he wrote *Ulysses* in relative isolation from any literary or cultural center, may indicate his deeper insight into culture and its modern problems, his fuller commitment to a study of a philosophical, religious, and literary heritage that has, in different ways, been grappling with these issues perhaps for centuries. It took the turbulence of the 1930s to move Lewis toward these insights. It took the failure of Italian Fascism and his own dire predicament to move Pound. Eliot is a bit more difficult to figure, for he was always a religious-minded poet seeking transcendence from history, but even with him it seems to have taken the onset of World War II to force him to bring his longing for transcendence back into the political and historical circumstances of England in 1940. Each of the Men of 1914 developed his own version of modernist humanism as a response to powerful circumstances that demanded something stable and permanent to ground civilization. Modernist humanism includes what we have come to call a postmodern skepticism that clears away fraudulent constructions and then, as a necessary second movement, seeks the renewal of traditional truths and values, retrieved from a humanist past also based on the Christian values of love and mercy.

For that is what the Men of 1914 discovered, each in his own way and each with his own difference: that love is an ideal that transcends time and place and can function as a stable anchor for a renewed humanism. Stephen Dedalus seeks to learn "the word known to all men," which is clearly love. That this word is "known to all" makes it a primary human category of experience, an ideal made real for Stephen in the spontaneous and unexpected actions of Leopold Bloom. That this "love" is to be regarded as Christian agape is certainly at least a strong possibility when Joyce has Stephen see in Bloom "the traditional figure of hypostasis," which clearly and baldly refers to Christ in the Incarnation. In fact to argue that Joyce's climax is wholly secular seems a much more strained position than mine. When we watch Bloom continue to act after Stephen's departure, when we watch him return to the violated bed and maintain a loving relation with Molly, we are watching a human enactment of mercy and forgiveness analogous to God's mercy upon an adulterous race.

Lewis was the most unlikely of these four to have ever developed a humanist position. Like *Ulysses*, *The Revenge for Love* enacts a scathing critique of the false positions and false ideals that were animating the politics of the 1930s, but, in a manner that most critics have noted and seemed surprised by, this most skeptical and suspicious novel reaches a climax that appreciates and even elevates the love of one character for another. Percy Hardcaster's claim of friendship for Victor and his sympathy for the lovers' sad fate are a throwback to a traditional novel's valorization of bourgeois love. Yet in Lewis's hands this love is tested and found genuine, and it moves beyond mere human love toward something higher and more divine.

Pound's case is perhaps the most instructive, in that he was forced to reevaluate his project once he was incarcerated for treason and sent back to the United States, where he remained captive until the late 1950s. The cantos he wrote in captivity differ radically from the ones written before. There is a break in *The Cantos* and in the kind of humanism the poem seeks to form. Pound was forced to reevaluate his commitment to rationality as the principle capable of correcting his culture's errors; his own suffering had a purgative effect, and the arrogance that dominated the first section of *The Cantos* is softened as a more humble and chastened poet emerges. Perhaps the most telling moment for the poem, and for this study as a whole, is when he rewrote the cogito: no longer a rationalist humanism based on "cogito ergo sum," *The Cantos* begins to enact a modernist humanism based on "amo ergo sum, and in just that proportion."

Pound indicates the supernatural nature of this love in his sudden and repeated allusions to Dante's *Paradiso* in the late cantos. Eliot, as the only avowed Christian in this study, was the most direct in indicating the way in which certain Christian truths, most notably the Incarnation, figure in his poetry. He clearly and directly used some of the central mysteries of Christian dogma—the Annunciation, the Incarnation, the Transfiguration, the Passion, and the Pentecost—as pivots of what a poetic mediation on lyric moments of human experience can come to signify. He was the most explicit in wanting a modernist humanism to be grounded in Christianity, a renewal of early modern humanism fit for the twentieth century.

The mystery of the Incarnation is central to this study, even if only Eliot and Joyce made explicit use of it as a grounding principle for their texts. For in this central mystery of Christianity the human and the divine are joined in the person of Jesus Christ, and we are invited to understand the possibility of reconciling of our lives within material history with our equally real participation in a timeless spiritual order. This mystery holds together at once our commitment to history and our ability to transcend it, our urgent need to value our life in space and time as well as our ability to reach a timeless perspective from which to understand that life and to assign it permanent and universal value. Dante's *Commedia* is based on just this principle of apprehending "the point of intersection of the timeless with time," and all four Men of 1914 were students of Dante. (We may tend to forget how deeply indebted to Dante is Lewis's *The Human Age*.) Perhaps Dante is the mediator these writers needed in order to understand how the Incarnation could be the foundation for their literary projects and for a modernist humanism.

Can these modernists provide us with a humanism adequate to our own placement in an even more violent and complex historical context? While present conditions obviously differ from theirs, we can still learn from the most recent effort to establish humanism because we are still in a "postmodern" moment, still in an intellectual climate of skepticism and doubt that needs something positive to build on. There are still conventional and clichéd expressions of value that are easily shown to be hollow and fraudulent, and we still lack an intellectual culture encouraging the search for permanent, not to say, transcendent values to anchor a civilization aspiring to be humane and decent. While their humanism is based on a Christian mystery and is in some ways a renewal of early modern Christian humanism, it is not at all necessary that a twenty-first century humanism be Christian, but it does need to be a theistic humanism, one grounded in the supernatural. These modernist writers maintained the healthy skepticism necessary to sweep away the fraudulent and the corrupt while not succumbing to a cynicism unable to find something to believe in, something to ground our claims for value and ideals.

NOTES

Preface

1. Peter Nicholls's book *Modernisms* is a particularly important resource in helping to expand the range of possible configurations of modernist writers, as is Bonnie Kime Scott's *Reconfiguring Modernism,* in which she works to establish a feminist alternative in her "Women of 1928" (Rebecca West, Virginia Woolf, and Djuna Barnes) to the masculine modernism of the Men of 1914. While these are welcome expansions of an old definition of modernism, we can still benefit by learning to reread and reevaluate those we may still consider the high modernists: Joyce, Lewis, Pound, and Eliot.

2. In an essay on Lewis in the collection *Volcanic Heaven,* Giovanni Cianci has described the militant attitude of the Men of 1914, who openly used the metaphor of war (even before the open hostilities of the Great War) to describe their attitude toward their culture. Cianci calls the prewar years "the heroic, exuberant years of the avant-garde's utopian phase" (14) and warns us not to confuse their later developments with this early martial phase. That is precisely my point: the Men of 1914 always remained in combat attitude toward modernity as they developed something positive on the other side of their blasting, something of universal and transcendent value.

Introduction

1. I do not think this linkage is either new or far-fetched, and it seems a much more plausible case to argue for the complicity of the modern sciences of the human with the death camps than of the modernist literature so glibly linked in some recent studies. Indeed I cannot help but think of Hannah Arendt's indictment of the bureaucratic institutions and her famous diagnosis of the banality of evil in *Eichmann in Jerusalem* as a relevant analysis of the human nightmare facing the writers in this study.

2. It is part of poststructural or postmodern theory to insist that the term "alienation" is outdated: "We can no longer conceive of the individual as alienated in the classical Marxist sense, because to be alienated presupposes a coherent rather than a fragmented sense of self from which to be alienated" (Harvey, 53). It is the "nineteenth-century error" that Louis Althusser identifies, claiming alienation as a humanist critique against oppressive social customs and practices because an alienated self

implies a true self. The modernist humanism I champion does not despair of a "true self" and so is fundamentally humanist in this most Althusserian way.

3. This whole section of my argument can be referred to the powerful critiques of systems enacted by Michel Foucault. No other thinker has made the case more urgently for the need to find a way to intervene in a culture that has become oppressive and cruel, and no thinker has been more aware of the difficulty of locating the space for meaningful engagement. The systems and institutions Foucault studied all had their (human) origin in the eighteenth century, but they have become so massive and so entrenched that they seem natural and permanent.

4. At this point I would like to point to the monumental work of Gilles Deleuze and Felix Guattari in their *Anti-Oedipus: Capitalism and Schizophrenia*. Especially in part 3 of their book, "Savages, Barbarians, Civilized Men," they have argued against the universality of Oedipus as a source of guilt and located it as a function of a westernized way of thinking brought to extremity in modern capitalism. They went so far as to say that "the commentators most favorable to the universality of Oedipus recognize nonetheless that one does not encounter in primitive societies any of the mechanisms or any of the attitudes that make it a reality in our society. No superego, no guilt" (143). They make this statement in a section called "The Inscribing Socius." These authors would agree with Kafka that modern Western society writes guilt into our very bodies, and they refer twice explicitly to "In the Penal Colony" and the machine that writes guilt.

5. Jean-François Lyotard concluded his seminal "What is Postmodernism?" with these words: "We have paid a high enough price for the nostalgia of the whole and the one" (*The Postmodern Condition*, 81). This is only the best-known instance of the postmodern critique of nostalgia, and part of my intention is to rescue modernism in literature from the negative charges attendant to this term. Nostalgia in the hands of the modernist humanist may well indeed be made a fruitful and happy attitude.

6. The work of Walter J. Ong details the changes in European culture that came as a result of the advent of print. In *Orality and Literacy*, he has advanced the argument that the technology of the printing press "embedded the word itself deeply in the manufacturing process and made it into a kind of commodity. . . . Despite the assumptions of many semiotic structuralists, it was print, not writing, that effectively reified the word" (118–19). Ong cites Elizabeth Eisenstein's *The Printing Press as a Agent of Change* as the seminal text documenting the effects of the printing press on European culture at the time of the early modern humanists: "how print made the Italian Renaissance a permanent European Renaissance, how it implemented the protestant Reformation and reoriented Catholic religious practice, how it affected the development of modern capitalism, implemented western European exploration of the globe, changed family life and politics, changed family life and politics, diffused knowledge as never before, made universal literacy a serious objective, made possible the rise of modern sciences, and otherwise altered social and intellectual life" (Ong, 117–18). Marshall McLuhan's *The Gutenberg Galaxy* and George Steiner's *Language and*

Silence call attention to the way in which print affected consciousness. Their work established the intellectual and cultural background I assume as I sketch the work of the early modern humanists.

7. More's sense of what the genuine Christian project entails reminds me strongly of Dante's critique of Epicureanism in the tenth canto of *Inferno*. One of the men in the sixth circle of hell—the place assigned to heretics—is Farinata, a great statesman of northern Italian politics in Dante's time, who made the tragic error of not believing in the immortality of the soul. That is Dante's objection to Epicurus and to his followers, such as Farinata: not that he advocates the reduction of pain and the modest pursuit of pleasure (that is what good politics aims at, after all, and Dante respects Farinata as a politician), but that he makes the soul die with the body. It is belief in the Resurrection—for Dante as for More—that is the most important part of Christianity, and it is the most nonrational feature as well. Much of what can be said about both early modern humanism and a modernist humanism can be traced back to Dante, and Dante's sense of the human potential helps make him the important precursor he is for the modernists in this study.

8. William Lynch's *Christ and Apollo* is a classic study of the issue of time and literature. For Lynch, Apollo stands for an attitude toward time that sees time as an enemy to be escaped by flight to a timeless realm, whereas Christ stands for an attitude toward time that does not deny the possibility of transcendence but insists on the temporal as a inescapable aspect of human existence. Lynch's work stands behind much of what I assume on the Incarnation.

Chapter 1. Bloom and the Vulgar Body

1. "By reading these books of the Platonists I had been prompted to look for truth as something incorporeal" (book 7, section 20). Augustine was clear that he learned much from the Platonists and that he owed them a great deal for setting him on the road to truth, but he was also quite determined to show, as this quotation makes clear, that the Platonists did not respect the claims of the body and that the Christian faith does.

2. In the Resurrection narratives of Luke's and John's Gospels, the point is emphatically made that the risen Christ has a material body that still eats and drinks. In Luke, Jesus explicitly says as much: "'Look at my hands and my feet, that it is I myself. Touch me and see; for a ghost does not have flesh and bones as you can see I have.' . . . And while they were still incredulous for joy and were amazed, he asked them, 'Have you anything here to eat?' They gave him a piece of broiled fish; he took it and ate it in front of them" (Luke 24: 39–43).

3. "Then he said to Thomas, 'Put your finger here, and see my hands; and put out your hand, and place it in my side; do not be faithless, but believing'" (John 20: 27). Jesus also eats in John's Resurrection stories. In one of John's letters, John clearly takes aim at anyone who doubts the Incarnation: "For many deceivers have gone out into the world, men who will not acknowledge the coming of Jesus Christ in the

flesh; such a one is a deceiver and the antichrist" (2 John 7). One can also connect this back to the *Odyssey,* where Odysseus's old nurse recognizes him through his scar. But Christ is the more important and relevant reference.

4. When he has Guinicelli call Daniel the better craftsman, Dante indicates at one stroke Daniel's greatness and his own (Dante's) superiority to the Provençal poet; for Dante surpasses him and goes into Paradise, where he is the only poet among the blessed. Eliot used this phrase from *Purgatorio* both to compliment Pound and indicate his own ambition to be the poet who reaches highest. It is worth noting how these three writers—Joyce, Eliot, and Pound—competed with each other to be the "true Dantescan voice" and how this competition may have fueled some of their most ambitious projects and experiments with language and style.

5. In *Madness and Civilization,* Foucault enacted a powerful set of descriptions of the anxious care with which various institutions—the legal, the political, and the medical—went about confronting nonreason, defining it and delimiting it. The Age of Reason was an age almost desperate to make reason a normal and essential state above and controlling feeling.

6. This is the title of Karen Lawrence's very fine 1983 study of *Ulysses,* and it is "postmodern" in spirit because it denies any telos for Joyce's stylistic innovations and extravagances. In true postmodern spirit, we are to enjoy the pure play of the text and not insist on purpose for the styles. This attitude toward *Ulysses* has been dominant since then, and any effort to see a purpose or a goal is suspect. I argue that those who see the postmodern turn of mind in *Ulysses* are correct but shortsighted.

7. Joyce's awareness of the problem of anti-Semitism and his anticipation of its nightmarish future marks him as someone to be careful with when trying to tie modernist literature to fascist political tendencies. Critics have used the cultural views of Eliot and Pound to argue for some form of complicity between modernist art and fascist ideology, and Joyce has always been exempted from this argument. Critics such as Roger Griffin want to tie claims of transcendence to fascist ideology, and so the one half of "Nestor," where Blake wants to flee the temporal for the timeless realm, is open to that critique. But it is Mr. Deasy, who is deeply tied to the temporal and committed to history and its processes, who is explicit and shameless anti-Semite in the episode. One might want to argue that both extremes lead one to a mistaken view of the temporal, and the Christian tradition of Incarnation allows for a successful solution to these problems.

8. Sinfield's "Cultural Materialism, *Othello,* and the Politics of Plausibility" makes the case that the culture determines the conditions of plausibility for its stories and that we can contest our culture at a deep level by exposing these conditions, resisting them, and perhaps even laying out alternatives derived from a different subgroup within the larger culture. Literary artists, then, may be seen as a subgroup giving us new conditions for plausibility and new stories for us to consider.

9. "The last two episodes, 'Ithaca' and 'Penelope,' supply missing facts for so many suspended patterns, momentous and trivial, that a reader who should work

carefully through them sentence by sentence, equipped with perfect knowledge of the rest of the book, would experience bewilderment from the very profusion of small elements dropping into place" (Kenner, *Ulysses*, 79). Hugh Kenner believes that this "aesthetic of delay" has the effect of rendering Bloom and his past "substantial."

10. Brook Thomas's book on *Ulysses* is another of the very fine studies in the last twenty years that are "postmodern" in spirit, denying the place of anything stable or fixed governing the meaning of Joyce's text. Thomas wants us to laugh at "mistaken identities," and I presume he would join with Mulligan in mocking any pretension to the ideal or to my identification of Bloom with Christ. I value such studies because they bring to light Joyce's powerful "postmodern" critiques, but they miss the larger and ultimate goal, the elevation of Bloom to an ideal figure.

Chapter 2. A Most Unlikely Humanist

1. I sketched my sense of the development of the novel in the second half of the nineteenth century in my earlier book on Joyce, and I shall reiterate some of that thinking in this chapter. I would like to point to George Levine's *Darwin and the Novelists* and Gillian Beer's *Darwin's Plots* as reliable accounts of the ways in which Darwin's sense of humanity struggling within a violent natural world affected the novel and its sense of what was possible for human beings to accomplish. Darwin's thinking is largely responsible for the narrowing of the range of human action and the reduction of any conviction about human agency.

2. Tess is another character who cannot escape her fate. She is doomed to die her tragic death because she is "of the D'Urbevilles," and the novel is loaded, especially its ending, with images of Britain's prehistoric landscape, as if one's destiny is as old as the hills.

3. Kermode's *The Sense of an Ending* is an important set of lectures on the philosophical implications raised by the formal demands of the novel, especially how the demand for a cohesive and unifying plot may affect the illusion of freedom and autonomy the characters may be able to assert. The need for closure in plot may limit the range of possibilities and discourage the introduction of accident into the events of the novel. The need for design may work against the characters' ability to act freely. Not only Darwin, but the very form of the novel may have worked to narrow the range of movement and possibility for the characters depicted in this genre, which so strongly features plotting and design.

4. One of the cardinal insights in Benjamin's classic essay is that the mechanical reproduction threatens the notion of authenticity, and "the instant the criterion of authenticity ceases to be applicable to artistic production, the total function of art is reversed. Instead of being based on ritual, it begins to be based on another practice—politics" (224). Lewis was obsessed with the problem of forgery and counterfeits, largely because he wanted to bring to the forefront of his novel the problematic relation of art to politics. He seems to have been anxious indeed that painting (which

Benjamin gives particular attention to as the one art most historically tied to the notion of "the original" and "the authentic") has become overcome by the political and now serves it.

5. Peppis argues that *Tarr* was Lewis's deliberate and pointed response to the great modernist bildungsroman *A Portrait of the Artist as a Young Man* (135–39). That *The Revenge for Love* is a bildungsroman is another instance of how Lewis is doing something radically different and radically new in this novel.

Chapter 3. Conflicting Humanisms

1. In his preface to *The Order of Things*, Foucault suggested that "there is a worse kind of disorder than that of the *incongruous*, the linking together of things that are inappropriate; I mean the disorder in which fragments of a large number of possible orders glitter separately in the dimension, without law or geometry, of the *heteroclite;* and that word should be taken in its most literal, etymological sense: in such a state, things are 'laid,' 'placed,' 'arranged' in sites so very different from one another that it is impossible to find a place of residence for them, to define a *common locus* beneath them all" (xvii–xviii). In a late interview, Pound used the word in a way that indicates his growing anxiety that his project could not succeed: "A epic poem is a poem containing history. The modern mind contains heteroclite elements. The past epos have succeeded when all or a great many of the answers were assumed. . . . The attempt in an experimental age is therefore rash" (Hall, 57).

2. John Freccero has offered a most subtle and poignant reading of the Ugolino story in an essay from his *Dante: The Poetics of Conversion*. When Ugolino's children offer themselves for their father to eat, he should be able to hear in their voices the voice of Christ who gave his flesh for the life of the world; he should have been open to this invitation to the Eucharist, not to eat them literally (which he does, after they die), but to repent of his own sin and to ask for forgiveness; in short, he failed to hear an invitation for conversion. Pound may indeed have wondered if he was open to change and conversion.

Chapter 4. "In the fullness of time"

1. The lines on the "hyacinth girl" are exactly dead center of "The Burial of the Dead," occupying lines 35 through 41 of a 76-line section. Such line counting proves little on its own of course, but it is too neat to be coincidental if this is indeed the "central voice" of the poem.

2. This name also provides us with a clue about how to read the poem, or rather how *not* to read it: "Equitone" suggests that we can read the poem all in the same voice, in one equal tone, but that would be as disastrous as following Madame Sosostris's fortune-telling. We need to hear distinct voices and make judgments about not only what they mean but how they sound.

3. Eliot called Baudelaire "a fragmentary Dante" (*Selected Essays,* 372) and claimed that "Baudelaire is essentially Christian." "Genuine blasphemy, genuine in spirit and

not purely verbal, is the product of partial belief, and is as impossible to the complete atheist as to the perfect Christian. It is a way of affirming belief. . . . He is discovering Christianity for himself; he is not assuming it as a fashion or weighing social or political reasons, or any other accidents. He is beginning, in a way, at the beginning; and being a discoverer, is not altogether certain what he is exploring and to what it leads" (*Selected Essays*, 373).

4. This is one of Lyndall Gordon's main points in her critical biography *Eliot's Early Years*. In a chapter titled "Eliot's Ordeals," she has documented his unhappy erotic life, both before and after meeting Vivienne, and has made the case that his turn to religion was a turn away from sexuality, that the failure of the one fueled the movement toward the other. Clearly *The Waste Land* depicts eros as incapable of meeting our deepest needs.

5. Donald Childs quoted approvingly this observation of Manganiello: "The protagonist's eyes fail as he gazes into the heart of light, or heavenly city, just as Dante's eyes fail when he encounters Beatrice in the earthly paradise, or when he gazes at the beatific vision" (quoted in Childs, *From Philosophy to Poetry*, 109). To see the hyacinth girl as Beatrice seems strained on several levels: tonally the hyacinth girl seems silly; dramatically the two do not connect; symbolically the man is not seeking guidance from her in any way I can see. But I still appreciate the efforts of Childs and Manganiello, because in another way we share a similar goal for our reading of the poem. They want there to be something akin to Dantesque transcendence and so do I.

6. Eliot used Augustine, briefly but profoundly, in "The Fire Sermon" as a way to indicate his own understanding of desire, and that understanding was later developed in *Four Quartets*, especially *Little Gidding*. But if *Four Quartets* as a whole is about conversion, then Augustine's story in *Confessions* becomes a relevant and meaningful base. Augustine's long and painful process of conversion culminated in a friend's garden, where he heard children playing a game in which they chanted, "Take up and read." Augustine was prepared to hear in that childish sound God's voice speaking to him, a precious bit of nonsense from the most important church father.

7. In an essay I wrote almost twenty years ago, I argued how Eliot is enacting in *Four Quartets* a medieval "art of memory" in which memory is not merely a storehouse of images (as it was in the classical age) but also a more active agency of the human mind capable of transforming images into signs of God's light, signs of God's presence. The classic text describing the development of the understanding of memory from the classical to the medieval period is Frances Yates's *The Art of Memory*.

8. The last line of this canto from Dante's *Purgatorio* is translated by Sinclair as "Then he hid himself in the fire that refines." Eliot quoted this line in the original as one of the fragments shored against the ruins at the close of *The Waste Land*. He also quoted these lines in his 1930 essay "Dante," where he noted that the "souls in Purgatory suffer because they *wish to suffer,* for purgation. And observe that they suffer more actively and more keenly, being souls preparing for blessedness, than Virgil suffers in limbo. In their suffering is hope" (*Selected Essays*, 217).

REFERENCES

Abrams, M. H. *Natural Supernaturalism*. New York: Norton, 1971.
Ackroyd, Peter. *T. S. Eliot: A Life*. New York: Simon & Schuster, 1984.
Adams, James Luther, and Wilson Yates, eds. *The Grotesque in Art and Literature: Theological Reflections*. Grand Rapids, Mich.: Eerdmans, 1997.
Althusser, Louis. "Ideology and Ideological State Apparatuses." In *Literary Theory: An Anthology*, 2nd ed., edited by Julie Rivkin and Michael Ryan, 294–304. Malden, Mass.: Blackwell, 2004.
Altieri, Charles. *Canons and Consequences*. Evanston, Ill.: Northwestern University Press, 1990.
———. *Postmodernism Now: Essays on Contemporaneity in the Arts*. University Park: Pennsylvania State University Press, 1998.
Arendt, Hannah. *Eichmann in Jerusalem: A Report on the Banality of Evil*. New York: Viking, 1963.
———. *The Origins of Totalitarianism*. New York: Harcourt Brace Jovanovich, 1973.
Augustine. *Confessions*. Translated by R. S. Pine-Coffin. New York: Penguin, 1986.
Bakhtin, Mikhail. *Rabelais and His World*. Bloomington: Indiana University Press, 1984.
Barkan, Leonard. *The Gods Made Flesh: Metamorphosis and the Pursuit of Paganism*. New Haven: Yale University Press, 1986.
———. *Nature's Work of Art: The Human Body as Image of the World*. New Haven: Yale University Press, 1975.
Barthes, Roland. *The Pleasure of the Text*. Translated by Richard Howard. New York: Hill & Wang, 1975.
Beer, Gillian. *Darwin's Plots: Evolutionary Narrative in Darwin, Eliot, and Nineteenth-Century Fiction*. London & Boston: Routledge & Kegan Paul, 1983.
Bell, Robert. *Jocoserious Joyce: The Fate of Folly in Ulysses*. Ithaca, N.Y.: Cornell University Press, 1991.
Benjamin, Walter. *Illuminations: Essays and Reflections*. New York: Schocken, 1968.
Boldrini, Lucia. *Joyce, Dante, and the Poetics of Literary Relations*. Cambridge & New York: Cambridge University Press, 2001.
Booker, Keith. *Joyce, Bakhtin, and the Literary Tradition: Toward a Comparative Cultural Poetics*. Ann Arbor: University of Michigan Press, 1995.
Borges, Jorge Luis. *Ficciones*. New York: Grove, 1962.

Boyle, Frank. *Swift as Nemesis: Modernity and Its Satirist*. Stanford: Stanford University Press, 2000.

Boyle, Robert. *James Joyce's Pauline Vision*. Carbondale: Southern Illinois University Press, 1978.

Brown, Dennis. *The Modernist Self in Twentieth-Century English Literature: A Study in Self-Fragmentation*. New York: St. Martin's, 1989.

Bush, Ronald. *T.S. Eliot: A Study in Character and Style*. New York: Oxford University Press, 1983.

Casillo, Robert. *The Genealogy of Demons: Anti-Semitism, Fascism, and the Myths of Ezra Pound*. Evanston, Ill.: Northwestern University Press, 1988.

Chapman, Robert. *Wyndham Lewis: Fictions and Satires*. New York: Barnes & Noble, 1973.

Childs, Donald. *From Philosophy to Poetry: T. S. Eliot's Study of Knowledge and Experience*. New York: Palgrave, 2001.

———. *T. S. Eliot: Mystic, Son, and Lover*. London: Athlone, 1997.

Cianci, Giovanni. "A Man at War: Lewis's Vital Geometrics." In *Volcanic Heaven: Essays on Wyndham Lewis's Painting and Writing*, edited by Paul Edwards, 11–24. Santa Rosa, Calif.: Black Sparrow Press, 1996.

Conrad, Joseph. *Lord Jim*. New York: Penguin, 1989.

Corbet, David Peters. "History, Art and Theory in *Time and Western Man*." In *Volcanic Heaven: Essays on Wyndham Lewis's Painting and Writing*, edited by Paul Edwards, 103–22. Santa Rosa, Calif.: Black Sparrow Press, 1996.

Coyle, Michael. *Ezra Pound, Popular Genres, and the Discourse of Culture*. University Park: Pennsylvania State University Press, 1995.

Dante. *Inferno*. Translated by John Sinclair. New York: Oxford University Press, 1948.

———. *Paradiso*. Translated by John Sinclair. New York: Oxford University Press, 1948.

———. *Purgatorio*. Translated by John Sinclair. New York: Oxford University Press, 1948.

Deleuze, Gilles, and Felix Guattari. *Anti-Oedipus: Capitalism and Schizophrenia*. Minneapolis: University of Minnesota Press, 1983.

Descartes, René. *Meditations, Objections, and Replies*. Edited and translated by Roger Ariew and Donald Cress. Indianapolis & Cambridge, U.K.: Hackett, 2006.

Edwards, Paul. *Wyndham Lewis, Painter and Writer*. New Haven: Yale University Press, 2000.

———, ed. *Volcanic Heaven: Essays on Wyndham Lewis's Painting and Writing*. Santa Rosa, Calif.: Black Sparrow Press, 1996.

Eisenstein, Elizabeth. *The Printing Press as an Agent of Change: Communications and Cultural Transformations in Early Modern Europe*. Cambridge & New York: Cambridge University Press, 1979.

Eliot, T. S. *Collected Poems, 1909–1962*. New York: Harcourt, Brace & World, 1963.

———. *Selected Essays*. New York: Harcourt, Brace & World, 1964.

———. *Selected Prose*. Edited by Frank Kermode. New York: Harcourt Brace Jovanovich, 1975.

Ellmann, Richard. Preface to *Ulysses*. Edited by Hans Gabler. New York: Random House, 1986.

Erasmus, Desiderius. *The Praise of Folly and Other Writings*. Edited and translated by Robert M. Adams. New York: Norton, 1989.

Etlin, Richard. *In Defense of Humanism: Value in the Arts and Letters*. New York: Cambridge University Press, 1996.

Fiske, John. "Culture, Ideology, Interpellation." In *Literary Theory: An Anthology*, 2nd ed., edited by Julie Rivkin and Michael Ryan, 305–11. Malden, Mass.: Blackwell, 2004.

Forster, E. M. *Howards End*. New York: Bantam, 1985.

Foucault, Michel. *The Archaeology of Knowledge*. Translated by A. M. Sheridan Smith. New York: Pantheon, 1972.

———. *Madness and Civilization: A History of Insanity in the Age of Reason*. Translated by Richard Howard. New York: Vintage, 1973.

———. "Nietzsche, Genealogy, History." In *Language, Counter-Memory, Practice: Selected Essays and Interviews*, edited by Donald F. Bouchard and translated by Bouchard and Sherry Simon, 139–64. Ithaca, N.Y.: Cornell University Press, 1977.

———. *The Order of Things: An Archaeology of the Human Sciences*. New York: Vintage, 1973.

Freccero, John. *Dante: The Poetics of Conversion*. Edited by Rachel Jacoff. Cambridge, Mass.: Harvard University Press, 1986.

Furia, Philip. *Pound's Cantos Declassified*. University Park: Pennsylvania State University Press, 1984.

Gordon, Lyndall. *Eliot's Early Years*. New York: Oxford University Press, 1977.

Griffin, Roger. *Modernism and Fascism: The Sense of a Beginning under Mussolini and Hitler*. Basingstoke, U.K.: Palgrave Macmillan, 2007.

Groden, Michael. *Ulysses in Progress*. Princeton: Princeton University Press, 1977.

Habermas, Jürgen. "Modernity: An Incomplete Project." In *Postmodernism: A Reader*, edited by Thomas Docherty, 98–109. New York: Columbia University Press, 1993.

Hall, Donald. "Fragments of Ezra Pound." In *Remembering Poets*, 111–99. New York: Harper & Row, 1978.

Hardy, Thomas. *The Mayor of Casterbridge*. New York: Oxford University Press, 2008.

Harvey, David. *The Condition of Post-Modernity*. Cambridge, Mass.: Blackwell, 1990.

Hofstadter, Richard. *The Age of Reform: From Bryan to F.D.R.* New York: Vintage, 1955.

Huyssen, Andreas. *After the Great Divide: Modernism, Mass Culture, Postmodernism*. Bloomington: Indiana University Press, 1986.

Jameson, Frederic. *Fables of Aggression: Wyndham Lewis, the Modernist as Fascist*. Berkeley: University of California Press, 1979.

Joyce, James. *Dubliners*. New York: Penguin, 1992.

———. *Letters of James Joyce*. Vol. 1. Edited by Stuart Gilbert. New York: Viking, 1966.

———. *A Portrait of the Artist as a Young Man*. New York: Penguin, 1992.

———. *Ulysses*. Edited by Hans Gabler. New York: Random House, 1986.

Kafka, Franz. *The Metamorphosis, the Penal Colony, and Other Stories*. New York: Schocken, 1988.

Kayser, Wolfgang. *The Grotesque in Art and Literature*. Bloomington: Indiana University Press, 1963.

Kenner, Hugh. *The Pound Era*. Berkeley: University of California Press, 1971.

———. *Ulysses*. Rev. ed. Baltimore: John Hopkins University Press, 1987.

———. *Wyndham Lewis*. Norfolk, Conn.: New Directions, 1954.

Kermode, Frank. *The Sense of an Ending: Studies in the Theory of Fiction*. New York: Oxford University Press, 1966.

Kinney, Arthur. *Continental Humanist Poetics: Studies in Erasmus, Castiglione, Marguerite de Navarre, and Rabelais*. Amherst: University of Massachusetts Press, 1989.

Kolocotroni, Vassiliki, Jane Goldman, and Olga Taxidou, eds. *Modernism: An Anthology of Sources and Documents*. Chicago: University of Chicago Press, 1998.

Lawrence, Karen. *The Odyssey of Styles in Ulysses*. Princeton: Princeton University Press, 1981.

Lethen, Helmut. "Modernism Cut in Half: The Exclusion of the Avant-Garde and the Debate on Postmodernism." In *Approaching Postmodernism*, edited by Douwe Fokkema and Hans Bertens, 233–38. Amsterdam: John Benjamins, 1986.

Levenson, Michael. *A Genealogy of Modernism: A Study of English Literary Doctrine, 1908–1922*. Cambridge & New York: Cambridge University Press, 1984.

———. *Modernism and the Fate of Individuality: Character and Novelistic Form from Conrad to Woolf*. Cambridge & New York: Cambridge University Press, 1991.

Levine, George. *Darwin and the Novelists: Patterns of Science in Victorian Fiction*. Cambridge, Mass.: Harvard University Press, 1988.

Lewis, Wyndham. *Blasting and Bombardiering*. Berkeley: University of California Press, 1967.

———. *Men without Art*. New York: Russell & Russell, 1964.

———. *The Revenge for Love*. Santa Rosa, Calif.: Black Sparrow, 1991.

———. *Time and Western Man*. Boston: Beacon, 1957.

Lock, Graham. "Subject, Interpretation, and Ideology." In *Post-modern Materialism and the Future of Marxist Theory*, edited by Antonio Callari and David F. Ruccio, 169–90. Hanover & London: Wesleyan University Press, 1996.

Longenbach, James. *Wallace Stevens: The Plain Sense of Things*. New York: Oxford University Press, 1991.

Lynch, William. *Christ and Apollo: The Dimensions of the Literary Imagination*. New York: Sheed & Ward, 1960.

Lyotard, Jean-François. *The Postmodern Condition: A Report on Knowledge*. Translated by Geoff Bennington and Brian Massumi. Minneapolis: University of Minnesota Press, 1984.

Manganiello, Dominic. *T. S. Eliot and Dante*. New York: St. Martin's, 1989.

Marsh, Alec. *Money and Modernity: Pound, Williams, and the Spirit of Jefferson*. Tuscaloosa: University of Alabama Press, 1998.

Materer, Timothy. *Wyndham Lewis the Novelist*. Detroit: Wayne State University Press, 1976.

Mazzotta, Giuseppe. "Inferno: The Language of Fraud in Lower Hell." In *Patterns in Dante: Nine Literary Essays,* edited by Cormac O'Cuilleanain and Jennifer Petrie, 169–88. Dublin: Four Courts Press for the Foundation for Italian Studies, UCD, National University of Ireland, 2005.

McLuhan, Marshall. *The Gutenberg Galaxy: The Making of Typographic Man*. Toronto: University of Toronto Press, 1962.

Meisel, Perry. *The Myth of the Modern: A Study in British Literature and Criticism after 1850*. New Haven: Yale University Press, 1987.

More, Sir Thomas. *Utopia*. 2nd ed. New York: Norton, 1992.

Morrison, Paul. *The Poetics of Fascism: Ezra Pound, T. S. Eliot, and Paul de Man*. New York: Oxford University Press, 1996.

Nadel, Ira. *Ezra Pound: A Literary Life*. New York: Palgrave Macmillan, 2004.

———. *Joyce and the Jews: Culture and Texts*. Iowa City: University of Iowa Press, 1989.

Nicholls, Peter. *Modernisms: A Literary Guide*. Berkeley: University of California Press, 1995.

North, Michael. *Reading 1922: A Return to the Scene of the Modern*. New York: Oxford University Press, 1999.

Ong, Walter J. *Orality and Literacy: The Technologizing of the Word*. London & New York: Methuen, 1982.

Otto, Rudolf. *The Idea of the Holy*. Translated by John W. Harvey. London: Oxford University Press, 1923.

Peppis, Paul. *Literature, Politics, and the English Avant-Garde: Nation and Empire*. Cambridge: Cambridge University Press, 2000.

Perloff, Marjorie. *21st-Century Modernism: The "New" Poetics*. Malden, Mass.: Blackwell, 2002.

Plato. *Five Dialogues*. Translated by G. M. A. Grube. Indianapolis: Hackett, 1981.

Pound, Ezra. *The Cantos of Ezra Pound*. New York: New Directions, 1986.

———. *Guide to Kulchur*. New York: New Directions, 1970.

———. *Jefferson and/or Mussolini*. New York: Liveright, 1935.

———. *Selected Prose*. Edited by William Cookson. New York: New Directions, 1973.

Rabelais, François. *The Histories of Gargantua and Pantagruel*. Translated by J. M. Cohen. Harmondsworth, U.K.: Penguin, 1955.

Rainey, Lawrence. *Ezra Pound and the Monument to Culture: Text, History, and the Malatesta Cantos*. Chicago: University of Chicago Press, 1991.

———, ed. *A Poem Containing History: Textual Studies in the Cantos*. Ann Arbor: University of Michigan Press, 1997.

Redman, Tim. *Ezra Pound and Italian Fascism*. Cambridge & New York: Cambridge University Press, 1991.

Schenker, Daniel. *Wyndham Lewis, Religion, and Modernism*. Tuscaloosa: University of Alabama Press, 1992.

Schlossman, Beryl. *Joyce's Catholic Comedy of Language*. Madison: University of Wisconsin Press, 1985.

Schwartz, Sanford. "The Postmodernity of Modernism." In *The Future of Modernism*, edited by Hugh Witemeyer, 9–32. Ann Arbor: University of Michigan Press, 1997.

Schwitters, Kurt. "Merz." In *Modernism: An Anthology of Sources and Documents*, edited by Vassiliki Kolocotroni, Jane Goldman, and Olga Taxidou, 281–84. Chicago: University of Chicago Press, 1998.

Scott, Bonnie Kime. *Refiguring Modernism*. Bloomington: Indiana University Press, 1995.

Sheehan, Paul. *Modernism, Narrative, and Humanism*. Cambridge & New York: Cambridge University Press, 2002.

Sherry, Vincent. *The Great War and the Language of Modernism*. New York: Oxford University Press, 2003.

Sicari, Stephen. "In Dante's Wake: T. S. Eliot's 'Art of Memory.'" *CrossCurrents* 38 (1988): 413–34.

———. *Joyce's Modernist Allegory: Ulysses and the History of the Novel*. Columbia: University of South Carolina Press, 2001.

———. *Pound's Epic Ambition: Dante and the Modern World*. Albany: SUNY Press, 1991.

Siebers, Tobin. *Cold War Criticism and the Politics of Skepticism*. New York: Oxford University Press, 1993.

Sinfield, Alan. "Cultural Materialism, *Othello*, and the Politics of Plausibility." In *Literary Theory: An Anthology*, 2nd ed., edited by Julie Rivkin and Michael Ryan, 804–26. Malden, Mass.: Blackwell, 2004.

———. "Reinventing Modernism." In *Literature, Politics, and Culture in Post-War Britain*, 182–202. Berkeley: University of California Press, 1989.

Singleton, Charles. "Allegory." In *Essays on Dante*, edited by Mark Musa, 45–78. Bloomington: Indiana University Press, 1964.

Smith, Steven B. *Reading Althusser: An Essay on Structural Marxism*. Ithaca, N.Y.: Cornell University Press, 1984.

Spanos, William. *The End of Education: Toward Posthumanism*. Minneapolis: University of Minnesota Press, 1993.

Steiner, George. *Language and Silence: Essays of Language, Literature, and the Human*. New York: Atheneum, 1982.

Stirner, Max. *The Ego and Its Own*. Edited by David Leopold. Cambridge & New York: Cambridge University Press, 1995.

Surette, Leon. *Pound in Purgatory: From Economic Radicalism to Anti-Semitism*. Urbana & Chicago: University of Illinois Press, 1999.

Swift, Jonathan. *Gulliver's Travels*. New York: Penguin, 1985.

Taylor, Charles. *Sources of the Self: The Making of Modern Identity*. Cambridge, Mass.: Harvard University Press, 1989.

Thomas, Brook. *James Joyce's Ulysses: A Book of Many Happy Returns*. Baton Rouge: Louisiana State University Press, 1982.

Todd, Dennis. *Imagining Monsters: Miscreations of the Self in Eighteenth-Century England.* Chicago: University of Chicago Press, 1995.

Toulmin, Stephen. *Cosmopolis: The Hidden Agenda of Modernity.* New York: Free Press, 1990.

Tratner, Michael. *Modernism and Mass Politics: Joyce, Woolf, Eliot, Yeats.* Stanford, Calif.: Stanford University Press, 1995.

Tzara, Tristan. "Dada Manifesto." In *Modernism: An Anthology of Sources and Documents,* edited by Vassiliki Kolocotroni, Jane Goldman, and Olga Taxidou, 276–80. Chicago: University of Chicago Press, 1998.

Vendler, Helen. *On Extended Wings: Wallace Stevens' Longer Poems.* Cambridge, Mass.: Harvard University Press, 1969.

Witemeyer, Hugh, ed. *The Future of Modernism.* Ann Arbor: University of Michigan Press, 1997.

Wordsworth, William. *Selected Poems and Prefaces.* Edited by Jack Stillinger. Boston: Houghton Mifflin, 1965.

Yates, Frances. *The Art of Memory.* Chicago: University of Chicago Press, 1966.

Yeats, William Butler. *The Collected Poems of W. B. Yeats.* Rev. 2nd ed. New York: Simon & Schuster, 1996.

INDEX

ABC of Economics (Pound), 132–33
Abrams, M. H., *Natural Supernaturalism*, 195
Ackroyd, Peter, 190–91
Adams, John, 128, 131–32
Adams, John Quincy, 131
Adorno, Theodor, 8, 10
alienation, 1, 4–7, 201n1
Althusser, Louis, 25–26, 28–29, 31, 80, 93, 118; "Ideology and Ideological State Apparatus," 92; and subjectivity, 92, 139, 201n2
Altieri, Charles, xi; *Canons and Consequences*, xii
American Revolution, 24
Andrewes, Lancelot, *Seventeen Sermons on the Nativity*, 176
Anglican Church, 171
Annunciation, 186, 196, 199
antihumanism, 25, 92–94, 111, 121. *See also* Althusser, Louis
anti-individualism, 99, 121
anti-Semitism, 2, 68, 129, 131, 137–38, 147, 160, 204n7
"Araby" (Joyce), 96
Arendt, Hannah, *Eichmann in Jerusalem*, 201n1
Ariel (Eliot), 176–77. *See also* "Journey of the Magi, The"; "Song for Simeon, A"
Aristotle, 145–46
art and aesthetics: and alienation, 4; as counterfeit, 112; and history, 140; and independent value, 112; and politics, 110–11, 205n4
Ascension, 76, 85–86, 189
asceticism, 168

Augustine, Saint, 30, 35, 37–41, 54, 65, 88, 164, 169, 178; *Confessions*, 39, 41, 44, 47, 168, 193, 207n6; and Dante, 50, 51, 53, 168–69, 194; and Platonists, 77, 203n, 206n2
Auschwitz, 8, 124
Austen, Jane, *Sense and Sensibility*, 108–9
authority, 12–14, 22, 28, 51
avant-garde, x

Babbitt, Irving, 32, 171–73, 197
Bakhtin, Mikhail, 49, 73; *Rabelais and His World*, 50–52, 54–55
Barkan, Leonard, 51
Baudelaire, Charles, 164, 171; *Journaux Intimes*, 173, 206n3; and misogyny, 173
Baudrillard, Jean, 8
Bayle, Pierre, 128
Beer, Gillian, *Darwin's Plots*, 205n1
Bell, Robert, *Jocoserious Joyce*, 76, 83
Beltramelli, Antonio, 147; *The Temple of Love*, 129
Benjamin, Walter, 111, 205n4
Bergson, Henri, 162
Bible, 53, 88, 146–48. *See also* Gospels; Hebrew scriptures
bildungsroman, 120
Blake, William, 68, 77, 83
Blasting and Bombardiering (Lewis), ix–x, xiii, 91–95, 98–123
Boldrini, Lucia, 165
body, human, 30, 34–42, 46–47, 50–54, 59, 63, 66, 68, 74, 76–77, 86, 88, 193–94, 203nn1–2; as enemy, 36–37; and humanism, 58; as machine, 71, 73;

body, human (*continued*)
  and ugliness, 60–61; vulgar, 38–39, 48, 57, 65, 72, 75
Booker, Keith, 51, 72, 86, 88–89
Borah, William, 135
Borges, Jorge, 1–2, 22, 25; "Pierre Menard, Author of *Don Quixote*," 3–5; "Tlön, Uqbar, Orbis Tertius," 3
Botticelli, 146–47; *Venus*, 158, 168
bourgeois novel. *See* novel, traditional
Boyle, Frank, 64
Boyle, Robert, 66
Bryan, William Jennings, 133, 136
Buddha, 168–69
Budgen, Frank, 81, 85–86
Burckhardt, Jacob, 129, 147
bureaucracy, 5–7, 23–25, 201n2
Burnt Norton (Eliot), 161, 177–85, 195
Bush, Ronald, 177

Cantos, The (Pound), 32, 124–28, 131–32, 140–42, 147, 149, 152, 156, 157, 161, 199
—Canto XXII, 141
—Canto XXXVI, 149
—Canto XXXVIII, 157
—Canto XLVI, 141
—Canto LXXIV, 144–45, 148
—Canto LXXX, 144, 149, 152
—Canto XC, 157
—Canto XCI, 155–56
—Canto XCII, 154–56, 158
—Canto XCIII, 156–58
—Canto XCV, 151–52
—Canto CXVI, 154
—Cantos XIV–XV (Hell Cantos), 131
—Cantos XXXI–XXXIII (Jefferson Cantos), 131
—Cantos XXXI–XLI (*Eleven New Cantos*), 124, 131–32, 139, 134, 157
—Cantos LXXIV–LXXXIV (*The Pisan Cantos*), 124, 141–42, 145, 149–50
—Cantos LXXXV–XCV (*Rock-Drill*), 124, 150–51
—Cantos XCVI–CIX (*Thrones*), 124, 150–51, 159
—Cantos CX–CXVII (*Drafts and Fragments*), 150, 153
capitalism, xii, 12, 102, 110–11, 202n2, 202n6
carnival, 52–53
Carroll, Lewis, *Alice in Wonderland*, 178–79
Cartesianism, 9, 11, 12, 21, 24, 34–36, 47, 58, 61–62, 64, 72, 75, 77, 89, 130, 133. *See also* Descartes, René
Casillo, Robert, 137; *Genealogy of Demons*, 129
Catholic Church, 66–67; mass, 144
Chapman, Robert, 94
Childs, Donald, 207n5
Christ and the Christ event, xiii, 15–20, 38–41, 44–45, 53, 64, 72, 88, 129, 163–64, 170, 181–83, 185, 187–90, 199, 203n2; and Bloom, 80, 83–87; historicity of Jesus, 67–68
Christian humanism. *See* humanism
Christian imagination, 41, 47, 50, 59, 64, 66, 88–89
Christianity and Christian faith, 15, 17–18, 20, 35–36, 38, 50, 52, 57, 65, 67, 140, 147, 163, 172, 177, 189, 200
Cianci, Giovanni, *Volcanic Heaven*, 201n2
Cicero, 37
city, ideal, 141, 143, 146–49, 154
City of God. *See* city, ideal
cold war, 8
Comedia (Dante), 39–47, 86, 128, 139, 142, 173, 184, 194, 200
—*Inferno*, 39–40, 42–43, 45, 56, 96, 143, 164, 191, 203n7; canto 1, 40; canto 2, 56; canto 3, 40, 44, 45; canto 5, 44–45; canto 26, 42–45; canto 33, 143; canto 34, 42
—*Paradiso*, 88, 153–59, 165, 179, 195, 199; canto 2, 42, 47; canto 20, 159; canto 24, 159; canto 33, 88, 165, 195, 199, 204n4
—*Purgatorio*, 40, 139, 143, 159, 173, 191, 193–94, 207n8; canto 3, 41, 57; canto 4, 46; canto 20, 46; canto 24, 42; canto 26, 45–47, 57, 139, 143; canto 27, 42
communism, 103–5, 108–9, 115

Conrad, Joseph, 96; *Heart of Darkness*, 167; *Lord Jim*, 96–98
conspiracy, 131–32, 137
Convivio (Dante), 44, 173
Copernican revolution, 12, 48
counterfeiting; 205n4; in literary art, 118–19; in painterly art, 110–13. *See also* false bottoms
Coyle, Michael, 124, 126

Dada, 170
Dante, 19, 27, 32, 35, 40, 48, 53, 65, 87, 144, 165, 196, 206n3; and psychology, 174–75. *See individual works under title*
Day, John, *Parliament of Bees*, 166
Darwin, Charles, 24, 72, 76, 83, 89, 92, 96, 99, 105, 205n1; and the human, 75, 106
Deleuze, Gilles, 8, 202n4
Derrida, Jacques, 92, 136; and language theory, 104
Descartes, René, 10, 11, 12, 19, 20, 23, 27, 30, 35, 58, 64; and cogito, 23, 24, 150; "cogito ergo sum," 149–50, 199
desire, 38, 41–42, 47, 106–7, 110, 172, 180, 193; in the novel, 119; sexual, 52, 108–9, 142
Dickens, Charles, 116
Douglas, C. H., 141
Dry Salvages, The (Eliot), 177, 186–88, 191, 193, 195
Dubliners (Joyce), 74–75, 95, 96. *See also* "Araby"
Dujardin, Edouard, *The Source of the Christian Tradition*, 67
Durkheim, Emile, 24

early modernist humanism. *See* humanism, early modernist
East Coker (Eliot), 182–86, 190
economics, 31, 130–32, 136–38, 142, 149; crisis, 134; monetary reform, 145; usury, 135, 141–42, 157; "volitionist economics," 133. *See also* money
education, 126, 130
Edwards, Paul, 100, 115–16; *Wyndham Lewis*, 91

eighteenth-century humanism. *See* humanism
Eisenstein, Elizabeth, *The Printing Press as an Agent of Change*, 202n6
Eliot, T. S., ix, xi, xiv, 1, 3, 19, 20, 22, 27, 32, 94, 149, 161–96; and Christianity, 168–72, 175; and dogma, 182, 189; and silence, 162, 165–66. *See individual works under title*
Ellmann, Richard, 35, 69
English civil war, 190
English novel. *See* novel, traditional
Enlightenment, 1, 8–11, 21, 25, 27, 29, 32, 35, 62, 128, 132, 134–35, 139, 169–70
Enlightenment hero. *See* hero and heroism
Enlightenment humanism. *See* humanism, Enlightenment
Enlightenment project, 9, 10, 31, 33, 126, 130, 136, 137, 142, 150, 154, 157
Enlightenment rationality. *See* rationality
epic, 41, 124, 141, 148
epic hero. *See* hero and heroism
Erasmus, Desiderius, 11–12, 14, 16; *The Praise of Folly*, 15, 17–18, 20, 22–23, 52, 53, 58
Etlin, Richard, 21, 139; *In Defense of Humanism*, 104
Eucharist, 44, 76, 185

Falstaff, 105–6
false bottoms, 31, 99–100, 102, 105, 113, 116–17, 121–22
fascism, xiii, 124, 128–29, 132–33, 135, 149, 198; fall of, 140, 148
Ferrars, Nicholas, 190
Fiske, John, 93
folly, 14–15, 17, 23
formalism, 19, 197
Forster, E. M., *Howards End*, 108
Foucault, Michel, 8, 25, 59, 104, 150; *The Archaeology of Knowledge*, 151, 202n3, 206n1; historiography versus genealogy, 25, 128; *Madness and Civilization*, 204n5; *The Order of Things*, 5, 104, 127
Four Quartets, The (Eliot), 20, 24–25, 27, 30, 32, 161–62, 177–95, 200, 207n6. *See*

Four Quartets (continued)
  also *Burnt Norton*; *Dry Salvages, The*; *East Coker*; *Little Gidding*
Freccero, John, 39–40, 47, 184; *Dante*, 206n2
French Revolution, 10, 18–19, 24
Freud, Sigmund, 24, 26, 80, 89, 96; and Dante, 156, 174–75
Furia, Philip, *Pound's Cantos Declassified*, 126, 131

Galileo, 10, 12, 20, 24
Ginsburg, Allen, 138
God, 18, 20, 35, 38, 40, 42, 53, 83, 85, 168–69, 174; of Israel, 146–47
Goethe, Johann Wolfgang von, 119; *The Art of Being Loved*, 94
Gogh, Vincent van, 112–13
"Gold and Work" (Pound), 138
Gordon, Lyndall, *Eliot's Early Years*, 207n4
Gospels, xiii, 18, 36, 40, 47, 56–57, 88, 177, 203n2
Griffin, Roger; 204n7; epiphanic and programmatic modernism, 134–35, 154, 178, 181, 188, 204n7
Groden, Michael, 75, 78
grotesque, the, 48–51, 61, 81; and Christian virtue, 54–55, 57
Guattari, Felix, 8, 202n4
Guide to Kulchur (Pound), 126, 132. See also "New Learning, The"

Habermas, Jurgen, 9, 10, 140
Hale, Emily, 178
Hamilton, Alexander, 131
Hardy, Thomas, *The Mayor of Casterbridge*, 95
Harvey, David, 9–10, 33, 201n7
Hebrew prophets, 145–48, 163
Hebrew scriptures, 146, 148
Hegel, Georg Wilhelm Friedrich, 83
hell, 143–44
hero and heroism, 34, 64, 104, 129–30, 139–41, 144, 149–50; Christian, 65, 70; Christian versus Enlightenment, 139; epic, 28, 87, 133–35; materiality of, 71; sentimental, 59

Hitler, Adolf, 143
Hiroshima, 8, 10
history, 68, 83, 106, 124, 125, 127–29, 131, 136, 140–41, 150–52, 192, 200; of the novel, 95
"History and Ignorance" (Pound), 128
"Hollow Men, The" (Eliot), 165–68
Homer, *The Odyssey*, 152, 153, 158, 159, 204n3
Horkheimer, Max, 10
Hugh Selwyn Mauberley (Pound), 140
Hulme, T. E., 175, 177, 188
human agency, xii–xiii, 3, 6, 26, 74, 92, 95, 98–99, 101, 169; and ideology, 80
humanism, ix–xiv, 3–4, 6, 8, 93, 111–12, 119–20, 122, 128, 172; Christian, ix, 18, 30, 35, 48, 64, 90, 128, 139, 171, 184–85, 197, 200; early modernist, 8, 11–19, 23, 28, 126–27, 135, 150; education into, 120; Enlightenment, 1, 8–11, 29, 32, 34–35, 47, 62, 64, 80, 90, 124, 126, 128, 130, 133, 139, 149, 171–72, 197–99; modernist, ix, xi, xii, xiv, 1, 8, 11–12, 18–19, 21, 25–26, 28–30, 32–33, 35–36, 52, 65, 89, 91–93, 99, 101, 110, 113, 116–17, 120–24, 126, 134–35, 139, 141, 149, 150, 153, 159–60, 184, 197–200; Renaissance, 10
"Humanism of Irving Babbitt, The" (Eliot), 171–73
humanitarianism, 102, 171
humans and humanity; 3, 7, 12, 14–15, 19, 50, 62–63, 94, 100, 164; as caricatures, 92, 94; in Darwin, 75, 106; divine versus human, 170, 171, 173, 176, 185; as machines, 94, 97–99; as puppets, 94, 99, 117–18
humility, 38–39, 42, 140–42, 147–49
Huyssen, Andreas, 69
hypostasis, traditional figure of, 82, 86, 88
Hythloday, Raphael, 15–18

ideal and idealism, x, 125, 131; Christian, 55, 89

ideology, 92–94, 99–104, 106–7, 118–20; agrarian, 136; as a false front, 101; genuine, 102
ignorance, 130–31, 136, 142
imperialism, 5, 108–9
Incarnation, 19–23, 30, 32, 35, 37–40, 42, 44, 47–48, 52–54, 57, 64, 66, 81–83, 87–88, 161–63, 177, 185, 199, 200; and Christian tradition, 64, 77, 162, 176, 179, 182, 200, 203n3, 204n7; as dogma, 176, 179, 182, 189, 196
individualism and the individual, 93, 99, 115, 122; "fate of the individual," 121
Inferno (Dante). See under *Comedia*
information, "Heteroclite" mass of, 127–28. *See also* knowledge
Irish civil war, x
Irish nationalism, 78
irony, 15, 138, 141–42

James, William, 9
Jameson, Frederic, 100, 117, 123
Jefferson, Thomas, 128, 131–34
Jefferson and/or Mussolini (Pound), 125, 133, 137
"Journey of the Magi, The" (Eliot), 176–77
Joyce, James, ix, 19, 34–90, 150, 161, 165, 167. *See individual works under title*
justice, 141, 146, 149, 153–54

Kafka, Franz, 1, 5; "In the Penal Colony," 6, 202n4; "The Metamorphosis," 20, 22, 25, 202n4; *The Trial*, 7, 23
Kant, Immanuel, 10, 19, 21, 23–24
Kayser, Wolfgang, *The Grotesque in Art and Literature*, 49
Kermode, Frank, 98; *The Sense of an Ending*, 120, 205n3
Kenner, Hugh, 69, 71, 116, 205n9; *Wyndham Lewis*, 100
Keynes, John Maynard, 141
Kinney, Arthur, 22
knowledge, 31, 126–28, 132; versus information, 127

language, 45, 78, 85, 92, 165–66; and the divine, 162, 169–71; as fraudulent, 39, 42–44, 65, 79, 117–18
Lawrence, D. H., 23
Lawrence, Karen, 204n6
Lethen, Helmut, 9, 21, 28
Levenson, Michael, *Genealogy of Modernism*, 121; *Modernism and the Fate of Individuality*, 120
Levine, George, *Darwin and the Novelists*, 205n1
Lewis, Wyndham, ix, 20, 29–30, 91–123, 150, 161, 162, 198, 205n4. *See individual works under title*
Little Gidding (Eliot), 189–95, 200, 207n6
Lock, Graham, 93
Locke, John, 19, 24
love and feeling, xiv, 14–15, 30–32, 43, 46–47, 58, 64, 79–80, 92, 100–101, 107, 113–17, 121–23, 140, 152, 157–59, 165, 168, 171, 173, 193–94, 197–98; *agape*, 115, 148, 197–99; as the "bottom," 112, 116, 122; bourgeois, 101, 121, 199; Christian, 67, 81, 86, 102, 115, 161; divine, 165, 171, 174; and freedom, 113, 193; and politics, 115; and self, 112, 149
"Love Song of J. Alfred Prufrock, The"(Eliot), 164–65
Lyotard, Jean-François; 8; "What is Postmodernism?," 202n5

Malatesta, Sigismundo, 129, 130, 135, 142, 147
Malinowski, Bronislaw, 25
Marsh, Alec, 133
Marx, Karl, and Marxism, 24, 83, 92, 111–12, 134, 136
Marvell, Andrew, "To His Coy Mistress," 166
Materer, Timothy, 100
Mauberley, Hugh Selwyn, 140
McKinley, William, 133
McLuhan, Marshall, *The Gutenberg Galaxy*, 202n6
memory, 74, 150, 184, 187, 192–93

"Men of 1914," ix, xi–xiv, 8, 11, 30, 91, 197–200, 201nn1–2
Men without Art (Lewis), 122
metaphysics, 36–37
Micah, 145–48. *See also* Hebrew prophets
Middle Ages, xi, 34; medieval theology, 14
misanthropy, 63–64
mockery, x–xii, 18–19, 21, 23, 34, 54, 76
modernism, ix, xiii, 4, 6, 8, 69, 96–99, 109, 171; early modernism, 126–27, 129, 130; "epiphanic," 134–35, 154, 178, 181, 185, 188; and the fate of individuality, 121; high modernism, 1, 91; and modernity, 1, 8–11, 64, 125, 134; and the novel, 98, 108; in painting, 109; as postmodern, 65; "programmatic," 134–35, 154, 178; and Romanticism, 91
modernist humanism. *See* humanism, modernist
modernity, xiv, 10–12, 33, 59, 64, 89, 125, 129, 134, 139, 160, 174, 198; Enlightenment, 75–76; history, 24; origins, 58
money, 17, 109, 136, 157
monstrous, the, 60–61, 81
Montaigne, Michel de, 12, 58, 127
More, Thomas, 11–12, 15–16, 203n7; *Utopia*, 17–18, 20, 22, 52, 53, 58, 138
Morrison, Paul, 125, 140
Mussolini, Benito, 31, 125, 128–39, 143, 147–49, 157, 160

Nadal, Ira, 67, 149
Nagasaki, 10
naturalism, 27, 34–36, 66, 71, 82–83, 95–96, 171, 198; and supernaturalism, 172–73, 183, 185
Nazism, 2
neopaganism, 142, 148, 158
"New Learning, The" (Pound), 31, 126–27
New Testament. *See* Bible
Newton, Isaac, 19, 24
Nicholls, Peter, *Modernisms*, 201n1
Nietzsche, Friedrich, 9, 24, 76, 129, 130, 140, 150, 197; and eternal return, 96; and nihilism, 115

North, Michael, 25–26
novel, traditional, 95, 100, 106–9, 119–21; history of (*see under* history); modernist, 98, 119; moral, 97; political, 100, 102–3, 106, 119–20; political versus personal focus, 105–7

Old Testament. *See* Bible
Ong, Walter J., *Orality and Literacy*, 202n6

paganism. *See* neopaganism
Paradiso (Dante). See under *Comedia*
paralysis, 96
Parker, Valerie, 100
Pascal, Blaise, 176–77
Passion of Christ, 169, 185, 196, 199
Paul, Saint, 55, 78, 114, 148, 158
pedagogy, 145
Pentecost and Pentecostal fire, 190, 192, 193–94, 196
Peppis, Paul, 99, 105, 121, 206n5
Perloff, Marjorie, *21st-Century Modernism*, xii
Peter, Saint, 158
Picasso, Pablo, 111–12
Plato and Platonism, 15–16, 20, 27, 30, 34–39, 40–42, 47, 50, 54, 58, 62, 65–68, 72, 77, 82, 125, 138, 153, 203n1
politics, xi, 4, 106–15, 130, 132, 134, 137; and art, 110–11, 140; and "interventionist poetics," 125; and love, 115, 117
polytheism, 146
Pope, Alexander, 63
populism, 133
Portrait of an Artist as a Young Man, A (Joyce), 34, 206n5
postmodern critique and skepticism, xiii, 4, 10, 20–21, 26, 28, 30, 55, 70, 76, 80, 89, 92, 102–4, 110, 125, 197; of art and aesthetics, 111–13; Marxist, 93; of received knowledge, 128. *See also* skepticism
postmodernism, xii–xiv, 8, 91
poststructuralism, xi–xii, 20–21, 136
Pound, Ezra, ix, xi, 1, 3, 18, 20, 22, 27, 31–32, 124–60, 161, 179, 206nn1–2; and "amo ergo sum," 150, 199; and fall

of fascism, 140–50; and history, 125–29, 131, 136; and Mussolini, 128–40. *See individual works under title*
printing press, 12–13, 48, 202n6
propaganda, 104
puppets and natures, 94, 98–99, 117, 119. *See also* Goethe, Johann Wolfgang von
Purgatorio (Dante). See under *Comedia*
purgatory and purgation, 128, 143–44, 154, 192–94

Rabelais, François, 11–13, 22, 35, 77, 79, 127–28; *Gargantua and Pantagruel*, 48, 50–56, 61, 72; and the vulgar body, 18, 20, 48
Radcliffe-Brown, A. R., 25
Rainey, Lawrence, 135, 147; *Ezra Pound and the Monument to Culture*, 129; *A Poem Containing History*, 129
rationality, 8–10, 14–15, 17, 126, 130, 149, 150, 169. *See also* humanism, Enlightenment
rationalist humanism. *See* humanism, Enlightenment
Redman, Tim, 130, 132–36, 142
Reformation, Protestant, 12, 48, 50, 202n6
religion, 17–18, 171–72
Renaissance, ix, 129; English, 167–69; Italian, 202n6; Irish, 66; renaissance man, 135
repetition, problem of, 95; and Conrad, 96–98; and Hardy, 95; and Joyce, 95–96
Resurrection, 18, 35, 38, 40–41, 53, 57, 169–70, 202n2, 203nn2–3, 203n7
Revenge for Love, The (Lewis), 91–92, 95, 99–123, 199, 200
Richard of St. Victor, 153, 157
Romanticism, 29, 140, 195
Roosevelt, Franklin D., 135
Ruskin, John, 118–19
Russell, George, 20, 67–68, 83

sacrifice, 44–45
satire, 60–61, 81, 100
Saussure, Ferdinand de, 23, 79
scatology, 51, 52

Schenker, Daniel, 94, 100
Schlossman, Beryl, 65–66, 86
Schwartz, Sanford, 8–9; *The Postmodernity of Modernism*, 28
Schwitters, Kurt, "Merz," 170
Scott, Bonnie Kime, *Reconfiguring Modernism*, 201n1
"Second Thoughts on Humanism" (Eliot), 175, 177, 185
self and selfhood, 21, 23, 25, 93–94, 128, 137, 150; communal versus individual, 121; construction of, 201n2; humanist, 115; rational, 128; transcendent, 23, 26–27, 92–94, 139. *See also* human agency
Seneca, 15
Shakespeare, William, 105, 118; *Hamlet*, 67–68; *The Tempest*, 50, 167
Sheehan, Paul, 6, 11, 25, 97–98, 119–20
Sherry, Vincent, 9; *The Great War and the Language of Modernism*, 20–21
Sicari, Stephen, xi; *Joyce's Modernist Allegory*, 28, 64; *Pound's Epic Ambition*, 124
Siebers, Tobin, xi, xii, 104; *Cold War Criticism and the Politics of Skepticism*, xi
Sinfield, Alan, 4, 111, 125, 134; "Cultural Modernism, *Othello*, and the Politics of Plausibility," 204n5; "Reinventing Modernism," 19–20, 69
Singleton, Charles, 39–40, 45, 184
skepticism and radical skepticism, xi, xii, 12, 21, 26, 101, 103, 113, 138, 172, 177, 198, 200
"Song for Simeon, A" (Eliot), 177
Spanish civil war, 91
Spanos, William, *The End of Education*, 26–27
Spenser, Edmund, "Prothalamion," 166
Spitzer, Leo, 51, 77
Steiner, George, 165; *Language and Silence*, 202n6
Stirner, Max, *Egoist*, 99, 121; *The Ego and His Own*, 121; *New Freewoman*, 121
subjectivity and the subject, 26, 27, 29, 92–94. *See also* Althusser, Louis

suffering, 142–43, 145, 148, 163
Surette, Leon, *Pound in Purgatory,* 129, 137, 204n7
Swift, Jonathan, 35, 48, 57–64, 77; *Gulliver's Travels,* 60; and the human body, 61; monsters, 63
Symonds, John Addington, 129

Tarr (Lewis), 99, 120, 206n5
Taylor, Charles, 27; *Sources of the Self,* 29, 30, 32, 58, 94, 98, 115, 197
theistic humanism. *See* humanism, modernist
Thirty Years' War, 11
Thomas, Brook, 86, 205n10
time and temporality, problem of, 32, 161–62, 171, 178–89, 196
Time and Western Man (Lewis), 94, 115, 122
Todd, Dennis, 60–61
totalitarianism, 2–3, 5, 8, 129
Toulmin, Stephen, 10–12, 20, 24, 29; "From Humanists to Rationalists," 58, 64
tragedy, 141, 148
transcendence, 23, 30, 91, 113, 115, 139, 153, 158–59, 162, 165, 180, 183, 193; of literature, 4; in Plato, 47, 54, 62, 66
transcendent human self. *See* self and selfhood, transcendent
Transfiguration, 196, 199
Tratner, Michael, 20–21
Trinity, 66
tyranny and the unconscious, 80–81, 98
Tzara, Tristan, "Dada Manifesto," 170. *See also* Dada

Ulysses (Joyce), 24–25, 28–29, 34–36, 72, 76, 88–89, 114, 140, 198, 200, 204nn6–7, 204n9, 205n10
—"Aeolus," 75
—and Bloom's ascension, 81–89
—"Calypso," 80
—"Circe," 81, 66

—"Cyclops," 70, 76–78, 85
—"Hades," 64, 86
—"Ithaca," 71, 81–82, 84–86
—"Lestrygonians," 74, 77, 80, 84, 85
—"Lotus Eaters," 20, 75
—"Nestor," 71, 83
—"Penelope," 35, 74, 81–82
—as Rabelaisian, 72, 86
—"Scylla & Charybdis," 20, 66–67, 77
—and style, 68, 75, 79
—"Telemachus," 60–70, 77–78, 85
usury. *See under* economics
Utopia, 16–18, 63, 138

Van Buren, Martin, 131
Venus. *See under* Botticelli
"Visiting Card, A" (Pound), 128
Vita Nuova (Dante), 44, 159, 173–75, 179

Wagner, Richard, *Tristan and Isolde,* 165
Waste Land, The (Eliot), 24–25, 162, 164–71, 173, 179, 180, 186, 188, 207n4, 207n8
—"The Burial of the Dead," 164–67, 169, 179, 188, 206n1
—"The Fire Sermon," 164–68, 172, 186, 207n6
—"A Game of Chess" 164–68
will, free, and freedom, xiv, 95, 97–99, 101, 106, 114–15, 130, 139–40; autonomous will, 137; "direction of the will" (Pound), 133. *See also* human agency
Woolf, Virginia, *Jacob's Room,* 24, 118, 210n1
World War I, ix, 1, 5, 9, 30, 34, 136, 166, 198
World War II, 5, 178, 181, 198

Yates, Frances, *The Art of Memory,* 207n7
Yeats, William Butler, 149; *Meditations in Time of Civil War,* x; *Nineteen Hundred and Nineteen,* x
Yriatre, Charles, 129